ML   18756
390
F 7   Foss, Hubert, James

      The Heritage of Music

DATE DUE			
MAY 26 72	MAY 1 3 2008		
OCT 25 72			
APR 18 1973			
NOV 14			
NOV 30			
JAN 0 2 1991			
JAN 0 2 1992			
OCT 2 1 1993			
MAY 1 7 2006			
APR 1 4 2008			

Waubonsee Community College

THE HERITAGE OF
MUSIC

The Heritage of
M U S I C

Essays by R. R. TERRY, W. G. WHITTAKER,
GUSTAV HOLST, THOMAS F. DUNHILL,
W. J. TURNER, DONALD FRANCIS TOVEY,
HERBERT THOMPSON, J. A. FULLER-
MAITLAND, CECIL GRAY, RICHARD CAPELL,
and M. D. CALVOCORESSI

Collected and Edited by

HUBERT JAMES FOSS

18756

Essay Index Reprint Series

 BOOKS FOR LIBRARIES PRESS
FREEPORT, NEW YORK

ML
390
F 7

First Published 1927
Reprinted 1969

STANDARD BOOK NUMBER:
8369-1292-6

LIBRARY OF CONGRESS CATALOG CARD NUMBER:
73-93338

PRINTED IN THE UNITED STATES OF AMERICA

THE HERITAGE OF MUSIC

CONTENTS

FOREWORD

Following the admirable model of Mr. R. W. Livingstone's Legacy of Greece and Mr. Cyril Bailey's Legacy of Rome, I have gathered under this one cover ten studies by musicians of ten of the great composers, and (to avoid controversy) two others of two prominent modern influences. The endeavour is made to present here studies of composers that will be useful and readable to a public unlearned in the mysteries but no less appreciative of the beauties of music—to those indeed who have received the legacies of Greece and Rome. A single writer attacking twelve so individual critical problems would link his book together by his personal opinions, perhaps also by some historical ligature. Here, where it has seemed better to me to have as many expert opinions as there are problems, it has been left to the subjects of the essays themselves to provide their own link, and perhaps the book is none the less a whole for that.

It is an incidental matter, but one, I think, of considerable interest and relevance, that the invitations to authors were all made in precisely the same words, which requested ' not a biography or a criticism but a summing-up of the place the composer holds in musical tradition and his present and past influence '.

The compilation of this book demanded that a selection be made from the vast quantity of material open for treatment, a point sufficiently obvious to need no demonstration, were it not that the keen critical eye often sees that which is not present more clearly than that which is. In order, therefore, to forestall mention of one—the least perhaps—of the failings of the book as a whole, I would remark that it is a fault easily remedied. For immediately upon the discovery that the essays are welcome to the public which they intend to serve, they can be followed by a second volume, the sole function of which will be to fill up some of the holes in a leaky can. If, on the other hand, they are not, then my excuse for their unremedied omissions is that a smaller failure is better than a greater.

My thanks are first due to Sir W. H. Hadow, whose advice at the inception of this book was most valuable ; secondly, to those whom I unnecessarily troubled with a request, when already they were so busy that they could not even accede to it ; finally, and most of all, to those who have so willingly contributed to—indeed, made— this volume, especially to those who by their very promptitude were made to suffer. Their patience throughout the untoward delays which are inevitable in the production of a collective book was (in addition to its sweet reasonableness) as valuable as their contributions themselves. For, without it, where had the book been ?

H. J. F.

GIOVANNI PIERLUIGI DA PALESTRINA
(1525—1594)
By R. R. TERRY

Iteration and reiteration have their uses in music. Palestrina has been consistently acclaimed a classic by each musical historian, so we to-day are spared the necessity of proving his claim to the title, as we have been obliged to do with his English contemporaries (William Byrd, for example).

But recognition of a composer as a classic does not necessarily mean that we know much of his music, or, understand in what way—if any—he influenced other composers, or furthered the development of his art. That is just what has happened to Palestrina. Modern appreciations (or depreciations) of him have invariably taken the line of contrasting—or paralleling him—with composers more modern than himself. The best informed critics have shown in what respects his music differs from that of later Masters. Some of them have done it quite admirably too. But it leaves us just where we were, since each and every critic treats Palestrinian music as a step (an important step certainly, but a ' step ' all the same) on the road from crudity towards perfection.

It is only since the war that we have begun to question the Victorian dogma of continual progress. We have begun to see the hollowness of the comfortable belief that the world was continuously growing better and better, like a Coué patient. We have begun to see that there is really no such tendency in human affairs, but musical history being the thing that it is, the flyblown dogma of ' continual progress ' still holds the field in musical circles.

We may smile now at the complacent Victorian attitude of superiority towards the past ; at the belief that the age which possessed the steam engine and the electric telegraph was superior to the age which did not ; that the age which produced the Albert Memorial and the Crystal Palace was superior to the ages which produced Westminster Abbey and Hampton Court. But in music we still cling to the old superstition. It is no exaggeration to say that even well-disposed critics consciously or unconsciously adopt an attitude of patronage towards Palestrina (who knew nothing of three-manual organs or full orchestras). Until musical criticism comes down from this silly little perch no understanding of Palestrina or his contemporaries is possible. Until we abandon the now exploded belief in ' continual progress ' in music in the same way that the war has forced us to abandon it in every other department of life, so long will musical history remain a thing out of touch with realities.

We must really scrap the commonly accepted belief (either expressed or implied) that we as human beings are in any way superior to our 16th century ancestors ; that our brains are any better than theirs. Our music is *different* from theirs, and that is all there is to say about it. The dogma of ' continual progress ' breaks down in the matter of European music as completely as it has broken down in international affairs. Human nature never alters ; mankind remains the same. The only thing that alters is the form in which the human being seeks self-expression. That is all that art means, self-expression, whether in terms of music, or pigments, or stone. The modes of expression vary with the ages, but that is all. Art, like human nature, is eternal ; it is only its idioms which alter with the centuries. If the artist expresses what he intended to express, his idiom is a matter of secondary importance. He has conveyed his message in the language of his day, and what more do we require ? The history of European music is neither more nor less than the history of any other art ; the artist employs one idiom until its resources are exhausted, and then seeks for other means of self-expression. The musical idiom of the 16th Century is so different from ours that it has become a commonplace of musical criticism to regard it as less perfect than our own. The mere notation of the 16th Century is so different from ours that it is all but unintelligible to the modern musical practitioner. Hence the habit of treating it as ' crude '. It was, however, anything but crude. It expressed more completely what the 16th Century composer wished to say than our modern notation can. The change is not from crudity to perfection. The *difference* is no doubt rather startling, but there has been no revolution ; the change has been gradual, and was—so to speak—organic.

The failure of modern criticism lies in its habit of assessing ancient music in the light of modern ; of comparing things that are not comparable. It is no more possible to listen to 16th Century music with the ears of the 20th Century than it is possible to judge 16th Century art through the eyes of modern taste.

It seems almost childish to labour an argument in this way, but it is necessary, since musical criticism (up to the present) either says or implies that the transition from Palestrina to Brahms is one of progress. It is true that Brahms was the inheritor of more varied musical resources than Palestrina, but that no more implies ' progress ' than to say that because the builders of the Birmingham Town Hall had greater mechanical resources than the builders of Westminster Hall, they were therefore the more perfect architects. We cannot ignore the fact that musical criticism has too readily assumed that a composer who used the major and minor keys was in possession of a greater measure of enlightenment than his 16th Century ancestors who wrote in the (miscalled) ecclesiastical modes. But, like most other comfortable theories, this particular one is daily being proved fallacious by the tendency of ultra-modern composers to hark back to modal idiom for more subtle effects than are possible in the major and minor keys.

The sympathetic inquirer of to-day will not make the mistake of approaching Palestrina's art in the light of the music which followed him. He will endeavour rather to arrive at an understanding of the music which obtained in Europe before Palestrina arrived.

Roughly speaking (very roughly, indeed), European music divides itself into three periods : the Plainsong period (culminating in the ninth century), when all vocal music was in unison, and conformed to one or other of the (so-called ecclesiastical) modes ; the Polyphonic period (culminating in the 16th century), in which the music was contrapuntal in character, but still conformed to the modes ; and the modern period, which may be said to have begun with the 18th century, in which the music was harmonic in character and conformed to the major and minor keys.

It will thus be seen that plainsong and polyphony have, in common, one difference from modern music. They belong to the period of modes ; it belongs to the period of keys. This difference in tonality is a wider one than has hitherto been recognised by musical writers. It has been too readily assumed that a modern anthem differs less from a motet by Palestrina than does a Palestrina motet from a piece of (unison) plainsong. Both anthem and motet have the usual number of vocal parts ; both are written on five-lined staves ; both employ the same notation (semibreves, minims, crotchets, etc.) ; while the plainsong is written on a four-lined stave, in a notation that is unintelligible to the modern eye, and has, moreover, melodic progressions that sound strange to the modern ear. But each of these likenesses and differences is more apparent than real. Between polyphony and modern music there is little affinity ; between plainsong and polyphony the affinity is close and real.

One would not labour this point either, were it not for the almost general assumption amongst musical text-books that plainsong was the first halting attempt at

musical speech in Europe, and that its insufficiency led
to the creation of part-music. This half-truth is as misleading as most half-truths are. Plainsong did not fall
into desuetude because it was found to be too crude a
medium. On the contrary, it developed until it reached
its zenith in the ninth century as a highly technical and
highly polished art. It bred a race of skilled singers and
learned technicians. To those who believe that vocal
virtuosity only came in with Italian opera and the coloratura singer, it may be something of a shock to learn that
every vocal trick of the coloratura singer was known *and
practised* in the plainsong period. Plainsong disappeared
only when its resources had been worked out to the point
of exhaustion. That is very different from the text-book
legend that its disappearance resulted from imperfection,
and not—as was the case—because it had reached a perfection so complete that further development of that
particular idiom was not possible. Another fact—the
significance of which will appear later—is that an interval
of seven centuries separated the culminating point
of plainsong and the culminating point of polyphony,
but a short interval of a hundred years from
Palestrina's century found modern European music in
full swing.

But the really vital point which has so far escaped the
notice of every writer is this : in the voluminous literature on the subject of the 16th century Renaissance one
feature stands out clearly, and that is that the Renaissance
marked a complete break-away from medievalism in
literature and art. So it did, *except in the art of music.*
Obliviousness of this fact is responsible for much critical
obliquity when Palestrina's music has been under discussion in the past.

Chronologically, Palestrina belonged to the Renaissance period ; artistically, he was in no sense its product
He was in it, but not of it.

The Renaissance, with its revival of learning, and its

devotion to the arts, marked the end of, and complete
breach with, medievalism. The sealed book of Greek
drama and Greek philosophy was opened again. Sculp-
tors and artists turned their eyes backward to the serene
beauty of their Greek prototypes. The stiff, angular
figures on niche and monument were supplanted by
others bearing more resemblance to the human form
divine. The result was too often voluptuous. Too often
its intimacy stood out in sharp contrast with the serene
aloofness of ancient Greek models. But that is neither
here nor there. The point is that it constituted a complete break with, and overthrow of, medieval ideals, and
that it *was* a definite attempt to get back to the art of
ancient Greece. Even the rococo architecture at which
we now smile was a further attempt in the same
direction.

Since the ' new learning ' captivated the Princes of the
Church, even the Church—that stronghold of medievalism—was invaded. The Latin Office-Hymns were
recast in more or less classical form, which stood out in
contrast with the strong and direct, if less flowing,
periods of St. Bernard and the older hymn-writers.
Rugged force was replaced by elegance of style. Greek
terminology replaced the medieval. Such phrases as
' scaling the heavens ' became ' scaling Olympus,' and so
on. The ' new learning ' remained pagan in spirit even
when enlisted in the service of the Church.

(Here it is necessary to say that although ' pagan ' and
' medieval ' are nowadays used colloquially as terms of
reproach, I use them in their literal and not their
derogatory sense.)

The strange fact now emerges that in music alone of
all the arts was there no break with medievalism ; no
harking back to Greek models. In the Renaissance
period—to which Palestrina belonged—polyphonic
music reached its meridian. In its technique it exhibited
all the Renaissance polish, but in its spirit it was nothing

less than a faithful and logical development of medieval ideals. I have always wondered how a fact so patent (I had almost said startling) should have escaped the notice of every writer on the Renaissance period. But there it is, staring us in the face, and we must find the explanation.

The earliest musical speech of Western Europe was modal and unisonous. It is too often overlooked that the plainsong of the Church, and the folksong of the people were one and the same idiom, the only difference being that the latter was free and spontaneous, and the former was reduced to order, symmetry, and system. The (miscalled) ecclesiastical modes were the creation of the Church only in the sense that they systematised a musical idiom (the modal) already in existence.

Like all other forms of art, this plainsong was developed until it reached its zenith, and its resources were worked out—in this case about the year 1000 A.D. For two centuries more it held the field as a fully developed art form ; but even during that period men were beginning to try and combine two or more melodies, thus laying the foundation of mensurable music and part-singing—the *ars nova* that was to bourgeon in the fourteenth and fifteenth centuries, and burst into full flower in the sixteenth. In place of the free rhythm of the ancient plainsong we now had a highly elaborated mensural system. In place of the unison singing we now had complex compositions in any number of parts—from two to eight, or even twelve. (Our English Tallis wrote a motet for forty different voices).

The contrast between the one-dimensional plainsong and the multi-dimensional polyphony of Palestrina is tremendous, and to the superficial observer the break between sixteenth-century polyphony and medieval plainsong would appear as great as between Renaissance and medieval painting or sculpture. But really this was not so. Both plainsong and polyphony were written in the medieval modes. Plainsong themes formed the *canti fermi* of Palestrina's Masses and Motets. In the growth of part-music out of the one-dimensional plainsong there was no analogy in the Greek ' magadising'. The elaborate structure of sixteenth-century polyphony was a Western product that had no counterpart in ancient Greece. It was modal in character, as was the medieval plainsong. Its spirit was medieval, as was that of the ancient plainsong. However startling the difference between plainsong and the art of Palestrina, the latter was really a slow but well-ordered development of the former. The changes were gradual and *organic* ; they held no element of revolution. The plainsong *canti fermi* in Palestrina's music bound the present to the past as with bonds of steel. Aloof, impersonal, disembodied—it had no part or lot with the rich sensuousness of Renaissance art. It spoke to its own age in familiar and comprehensible language, but it spoke, as it' were, from another plane. Understandable it certainly was, but its detachment was that of the medieval eremite ; its rapture that of the medieval mystic.

It was in Palestrina that medieval ideals found their complete musical fulfilment. It was reserved for later composers to discard medieval modes as their key-sense was gradually developed (our English composers had begun the process already), but Palestrina was content to work in the modes as his forefathers had done, and we see no signs of his attempting to break away from this medieval system of tonality. To the end his work shows no signs of empiricism. Unlike his English contemporaries, he tried no bold experiments in the direction of a newer tonality, and this contented habit of mind gives his music very frequently an uneventful character. But the note of mysticism was always present. Serene, aloof, and detached from mundane affairs, there is no note of materialism to be found in it. When he rises to his highest flights, they are flights of spiritual ecstasy, not those of declamation or pictorialism. Even the dramatic moments of Holy Week are treated with a spiritual poise and balance that other composers never seem to have reached. Poignant anguish there is, but it is the anguish of a soul that pain can no longer daunt.

A typical example of this is his setting of the words *Peccantem me quotidie, et non me penitentem*. Note the desolate effect he produces by two simple alto notes on the second and third syllable of *quotidie*.

And again, at the words *Timor mortis conturbat me*, the long-drawn chords in the lower register of the voices strike the note of solemn fear, but it is a holy fear that holds no human affright. It is the antithesis of the almost hysterical outburst of Mozart in the *offertorium* of his Requiem, when he too contemplates the terror of death.

This almost superhuman restraint is most in evidence on occasions when human expressions of emotion would be most pardonable. The passion of Jeremiah's Lamentations moves even the English Tallis to an outpouring of personal emotion that at times almost approaches word-painting. But Palestrina's treatment of the same text :—

> *Quomodo sedet sola civitas, plena populo ; facta est quasi vidua domina gentium ; princeps provinciarum facta est sub tributo ?*

is aloof and detached as the utterances of a Greek chorus. He never forgets that impassioned as the mere words may be, they nevertheless form part of the solemn corporate rite of Tenebræ, and it is to this rite that he addresses himself. He is possessed by its broad aspect, as one of ' the Watches of the Passion', and he fears to intrude on a corporate liturgical act with any expression of personal or individual emotion. There are those (the writer amongst the number) who, on a first glance at Palestrina's Lamentations, have experienced a sense of disappointment at the apparent absence of correspondence

between the impassioned text and the gravely
'uneventful' music. But a hearing of them in their
proper setting brings the conviction that the composer
has deliberately avoided the pictorial, and applied himself
to establishing the atmosphere of the rite as a whole, of
which his music should be merely the appropriate background.

It is this idea of corporate worship as distinct from
pious personal acts that marks the work of Palestrina,
and accounts for its detachment as opposed to the intimacy of later composers. The nature of the services for
which Bach wrote gave opportunity for the outpouring
of the individual soul ; the aria for the single voice had
no liturgical place in Palestrina's time. Bach was free to
select his own text ; Palestrina confined himself to the
existing text of the liturgy. He was more concerned with
stressing the nature and character of the rite as a whole
than with a descriptive and pictorial setting of any part
of it, however tempting that part might be to the
musician. He was first of all a liturgist ; his primary
object was the adornment and embellishment of the
liturgy ; all other objects were secondary.

This is nowhere more evident than in his *Improperia*
(the Reproaches) for Good Friday. A long interval has
to be filled up by music during the Adoration of the
Cross. True, there is in the verbal text a certain element
of declamation as the two responsive choirs ejaculate
(in Greek and Latin alternately) ' Oh holy God, Oh Holy
Strong One, Oh Holy and Immortal One have mercy
upon us', but ever and anon comes the repeated appeal
from the Cross :—

>Oh my people, what have I done to thee ?
>Or in what have I offended thee ?
>Make answer to me.

reiterated after each recital of benefits wrought for the
chosen people.

The solemnity of the whole rite precludes anything

so paltry as musical pictorialism. There is nothing in Palestrina's musical setting to distract the participants in that rite. The plain chords—without imitation or figuration—give an other-worldly atmosphere, and the cumulative effect of constant repetition is one of poignant intensity.

I have given the music in full (pp. 12 and 13) because the only English volume in which it is quoted is Wooldridge's in the *Oxford History of Music* where the author falls into a ludicrous error. He has obviously used Proske's edition, in which the music of the first and second choirs is printed on opposite pages. Lacking (apparently) a knowledge of how the liturgical text should read, he prints the musical sentences on page 1 consecutively, whereas each sentence should alternate with its answer, as given by Proske on page 2. Finally, the rubrics direct that both choirs shall sing *Miserere nobis* together. Palestrina, therefore, writes his music in eight parts. Wooldridge—not knowing this—prints only the (four part) music of the first choir, and omits the music of the second choir (on the opposite page of Proske's edition), which ought to be sung with it. The result is so pathetically banal that the writer has heard more than one musician express surprise at the encomiums passed on these *Improperia* by musical historians.

But moving as is the appeal of Palestrina's music on the occasion of such solemnities as those of Holy Week, he can bubble over with *joie de vivre* on such feasts as Easter and Christmas. Compare the Sequences for Easter and Whitsunday with the music he writes for Lent, Advent, and the Office of the Dead. We then see his genius for establishing in his music the mood of the feast he was celebrating. It is this sense of liturgical fitness, and this broad vision of the contrasting moods and varying needs of the liturgy that give him the unerring touch that proclaims the master, and justify his title of *Princeps Musicæ*.

In his person he summed up the spirit of medievalism. He was unaffected by the classical revival of his time. He summed up in whole what his medieval predecessors had each achieved in part. He set a standard of technique in the medieval modes which was to prove invaluable to his modern successors writing in keys. He was more concerned with objectivity in corporate worship than with subjectivity. Hence, his music stands for all time as the perfect example of what is most fitting for liturgical purposes. After the pagan levity of the eighteenth century and the sentimentalism of the nineteenth, it is to the ideals of Palestrina that our best twentieth-century church composers are beginning to return.

JOHANN SEBASTIAN BACH
(1685-1750)

By W. G. WHITTAKER

THE story of the neglect, discovery, and triumph of Bach's music is without parallel in the history of art. There are many examples of want of appreciation, and of amends made by posterity, but such progress from obscurity to a position of dazzling splendour is a phenomenon an equal of which has not been recorded. Famous Bach certainly was in his lifetime, but almost solely as a performer. His fame did not prevent his being treated with contempt by his superiors in the little world of Leipzig, his position as Cantor was rather an inferior one even among the poorly paid posts available for musicians in those days, the forces at his disposal were meagre and, according to his own description, inferior in quality. Of all the great mass of his church music the parts of only one cantata were printed in his lifetime, and those not because it was esteemed, but because it happened to be written for an annual Burgomeister election. References to him in contemporary and immediately subsequent musical literature are not merely scanty, but show practically no insight into the value of his compositions. For fifty years after his death his music was only known in a few small circles, many of his manuscripts were carelessly dispersed and lost, and the great stream of music flowed on almost entirely undisturbed by the mighty waters which had issued from his pen. We find no trace in Haydn ; Mozart was conversant with some of his instrumental works ; but of his church music it appears that he knew nothing until the famous episode during his visit to Leipzig, when he was profoundly impressed by the motet, ' Singet dem Herr'n '. Certain compositions of Mozart show an increased attention to contrapuntal writing as the result of contact with Bach, but it is more a question of the letter than the spirit. Beethoven as a boy was famed for his playing of the Wohltemperirte Klavier, but signs of Bach's influence in his music are astonishingly few, and he unreservedly placed Handel as ' the Master of us all.' It is a strange anomaly that the composer who first revealed the unknown treasures to the larger world, and who was a sincere worshipper, is fast losing his hold on the public of to-day in England because the sacred music of Bach has revealed higher ideals.

In the early part of the nineteenth century there had been a slowly growing interest in the works written so long before. This found its initial notable outward sign in the first performance of portions of the St. Matthew Passion in Berlin, under the direction of the twenty-year-old Mendelssohn, on the 11th of March, 1829, exactly a hundred years after its obscure production at Leipzig.

The St. John Passion was performed four years later. In 1828, the Credo from the B minor Mass was given in Frankfort. Other portions followed, but the first complete performance did not take place until long after. Slowly the influence of Bach extended, and it goes on advancing, with no sign that the flood has reached its height.

His position at the present day is certainly extraordinary. There never was a time at which there were so many diverse ideals and methods in music. There is a bewildering galaxy of clever composers, and an almost equally bewildering confusion of aims and styles. Yet practically the whole of the musical world acknowledges Bach as the supreme master. He is more performed now than at any previous time. Not many years ago he was said to be a musician for musicians only; he was thought too intimate and introspective for the general public. Now, a performance of the B minor Mass will fill any concert hall in the kingdom, the St. Matthew Passion is given annually in many centres, his cantatas, practically unknown a quarter of a century ago in this country, are being heard everywhere—in small towns, in competition festivals, in many churches. There are no more popular orchestral numbers than the Brandenburg concertos ; his piano works are coming to their own in a way that would not have been thought possible a few years back. It was then considered that only arrangements, such as those of Tausig, Liszt, and D'Albert, were suitable for recitals, and a well-known virtuoso declared that the ' 48 ' should be confined to the study ; now, audiences listen with the greatest delight to all sections of the clavier works, played without a single extraneous note. Harold Samuel can attract six large audiences in a single week to hear Bach pure and undefiled. Junior piano pupils revel in his fascinating minuets and gavottes, and elementary school children sing his easier arias with surprising understanding. The old idea that Bach was a pedant with an enormous brain but no heart is rapidly disappearing, and his music has penetrated every home where art is regarded seriously.

It may be asked why this misconception lasted so long, or even why it existed at all. There are many reasons. An examination of a few may help an understanding of the nature of his music.

The general public can rarely take to its heart more idols than one. Handel was already firmly planted there, at any rate in England ; there was not room for another composer of the same period, the same nationality, the same general character. His simple, massive style, his fine melodic outlines, his splendid rhythms, his direct utterances, appealed straight to the music lover. On the Continent the more facile music of Telemann, Hasse, and Graun among the Germans, and the still more suave writings of the numerous Italian composers appealed to an age which was content with elegance, clearness and ' good modulation.' Later, the cheerful, captivating art of Haydn, the limpid melodies and clear harmonies of Mozart appeared to be in the direct line of succession from the Saxon giant. Bach seemed crabbed, his counterpoint too intricate, his harmonies too recondite, especially with the music of Haydn and Mozart in the mind's ear. Difficult to play, difficult to sing, and difficult to interpret, Bach had apparently no right to compete with Handel for supremacy, and so these contemporary composers were looked upon as rivals ; allegiance to one meant indifference to the other.

Handel was rarely introspective ; most of his music was written with the public in view. He never lowered his ideals, but continual contact with performers and with the public, in Germany, Italy, and England, whetted the edge of his understanding of the relation between music and its hearers. He learned to curb his fancy, to restrict his demands upon his interpreters, to weigh in the balance every factor in the situation. His music was for immediate and practical use. Not only was Bach's nature very different fundamentally, but, generally speaking, considerations for his hearers entered but little into his thoughts. His instrumental music, except that for the organ, was mainly written for the select chamber of a music-loving and sympathetic prince, or for the player who, in the intimacies of his study, could enjoy the leisurely development of all the forms of the day, and devote his hours of solitude to a reverent adoration of the muse. He was unaccustomed to concert audiences, and had no dealings with the theatre. In church services the musician does not come into direct contact with his hearers ; he cannot immediately tell whether music has had an effect upon his congregation or no. In many cases he never knows, for the people drift away, and other things intervene before an exchange of opinions is possible. In a concert room the music is the main issue, all attention is concentrated on it ; in a church it is only part of a great scheme ; it does not exist for its own sake, it is there merely to fulfil a purpose, and he is a poor musician in whose thoughts the question of the immediate effect of liturgical music bulks largely. Like all great messages, it appeals only to the highest qualities of the listeners ; it can only accomplish its purpose slowly and in due course of time. And so Bach came to regard his hearers as himself. He did not lose sight of them collectively, but wrote for them as if they were replicas of his own personality. Thus it is that we find in his church music so little that is purely external in effect. Disgusted by his relations with his superiors, he ceased to care whether it pleased them or not, and wrote for his ideal congregation. When his hearers approach him in that spirit they find that his introspection is not baffling, but is the revelation of one of the greatest of all minds and one of the most human of all hearts, in terms which they, too, can understand and appreciate.

A further cause of the long delay in the appreciation of Bach was the slow rate of publication of his works, and the order in which they became known. At first, only the keyboard compositions were current, and of these mostly the preludes and fugues. A piano or organ is not the best medium to enable a hearer to follow the intricacies of contrapuntal writing. Bach was considered as a writer of involved fugues which, though interesting to play and clearly constructed, were difficult to follow. Nor was this illusion dispelled by the manner of performance. It was considered right and ' classical ' to play organ fugues with full power throughout, and even on the piano it was deemed irreverent to treat him otherwise than severely. The human and romantic qualities of Bach were therefore hidden. Moreover, his extraordinary technical skill was insisted upon, and this served to heighten the impression.

Schweitzer remarks that in comparison with the church cantatas everything else that Bach has done appears as hardly more than a supplement. Yet these were virtually unknown until the latter part of the nineteenth century. It is a question whether Beethove knew a single specimen. Even Mendelssohn produc

none. In 1821 the first cantata to be published (except
that referred to) was issued by Breitkopf, and for a
decade was a drug on the market. The Bachgesellschaft
was founded in 1850 ; four years afterwards its publication of all the known works began. This took forty-six
years,so that it was only within the last quarter of the nineteenth century that it became possible to judge him by
that side of his work which is most completely representative. It is this, together with his marvellous suggestion
of modernity, which makes Bach practically a composer
of to-day. It is this which has caused us to revise most
of the criticisms of his works on which the older generation of musicians of to-day were nurtured. Tradition
dies hard ; statements are copied and re-copied, even
when there is abundance of evidence to prove them false.

One idea which has militated against the popularity
of Bach is the statement made in historical books, and
copied *ad nauseum*, that he is an unvocal writer. It is
assumed that his fondness for the organ dominated
everything, and the grateful vocalism of Handel's airs
and choruses is held up in contrast. This is a
serious error. No one who has studied and performed
the church cantatas can find a shred of truth in it.
All the evidence of Bach's life is to the contrary. He
was a choir boy until his voice broke. His second wife
was an excellent singer ; except for his period at Cothen
he was employed every day with choirs. His choruses
are numbered by hundreds, and there are a thousand
arias and duets extant. How could it be possible that
the greatest musical mind of the century, dealing continually with choir boys and amateur singers, and
familiar with the opera houses of Hamburg and Dresden,
could misunderstand the human voice ? The opposite
is the truth ; he understood the voice so well that he was
able to demand from it the extreme limits of power, of
flexibility, of control, of expressiveness. In orchestral
writing, as we shall see later, he exploited every instru-

ment and every combination of instruments that lay to
hand. He did the same with voices. There are clear
evidences in his church music that at certain periods he
encountered exceptional voices. From these he extracted
the uttermost farthing ; he studied their every possibility, just as he experimented with every type of composition known at the day, save opera. The average
vocalist, accustomed to Handel, who always contrived
to exhibit the best features of his singers to their audiences, finds, when he first approaches Bach, a lack of
external effect, and many problems, both technical and
interpretative, which he had not previously encountered.
A few years ago, the ordinary singer was only too ready,
on account of these things, to dismiss Bach with a wave
of the hand, but the earnest student is now finding that
to master Bach is to increase his technique enormously,
and to place at his command emotional resources which
he had not previously summoned from the deep. One
of our distinguished English musicians said a while ago
that to sing Bach well one needed the lungs of a giant,
the heart of a poet, and the mind of a saint. The converse is true, that an intensive study of his arias leads the
singer far along these paths. True it is that there sometimes are found problems which seem almost impossible
of solution, but the explanation is undoubtedly that these
numbers were written for singers with some exceptional
capacity and that unless that calibre of voice is present
the aria cannot be made effective. We do not suspect
Mozart's ability to write for the voice because the average ballad-warbler cannot undertake the part of the
Queen of the Night in ' The Magic Flute'. Anyone who
has conducted choirs which sing Bach frequently knows
how easily amateur vocalists learn the idiom, and what
great delight they find in him. There is never any complaint of unvocal qualities in these quarters.

In Handel, by virtue of his Italian experiences and his
long career as operatic composer, manager, and producer,

dealing with professional singers, the voice is always
predominant, and the accompanying instruments support
discreetly. But this was rarely the custom with his
contemporary. His singers were amateurs, students
from the university, boys from the St. Thomas's School.
Voice and instrument were to him on an equality. Each
line was made as interesting as possible, each expressed
itself in the way he thought most suitable to its character ;
the singer has to learn that he or she is not autocratic but
a member of a republican community. At first it
sometimes appears as if all were struggling for supremacy,

Ex. 1.   From a Church Cantata.

but in reality each factor is developed in such a way that
not only is every line amazingly interesting in itself, but
is unreservedly working for the common good. The
meaning of the music is not grasped so soon, but once
it is understood the wealth of beauty and expression is
truly boundless ; every repetition reveals new features,
and one can never say that one has plumbed its
uttermost depths.

This passion for utilising the full capabilities of each individual line makes much of Bach's vocal music appear over-elaborate ; in fact, in some cases, as, for instance, in the Peasant Cantata, a greater simplicity would have been more effective, the profusion of detail obscures the beauty of the foundational ideas. In reality, however, such passages are seldom found. In working practically with the cantatas one finds that frequently a study of the scheme of dynamics will reveal a proportion which had not been realised before, and will make clear that which had previously sounded obscure.

Bach was prone, also, to develop his ideas most leisurely, particularly in his later years, when he drew more and more into himself, and when his increasing satisfaction in the solution of intellectual problems was less counter-balanced by the emotional intensity of his middle age. Many of his last arias are of great length, and his habit of writing *Da Capo* often causes him to test the patience of his hearers unwisely. It must not be forgotten, however, that the difference between concert room and church is so essential that what may be uninteresting in the one may be profoundly impressive in the other. The practical musician knows that external conditions play a great part in determining the impression which music makes. The masses of Palestrina and Byrd cannot convey their noble messages fully in the glare and fashion of a concert room, a Haydn or Mozart quartet has a different personality when transferred from a large hall to a gathering of friends in a comfortable room, many a song of Schubert or Wolf makes its strongest appeal in the home. Recitatives in a church cantata, for example, frequently sound perfunctory, or didactic, or insincere on a concert platform, but in a church they are essential parts of the scheme.

Bach's melodic outline is much more involved than that of his contemporary, and the strong contrast between the simplicity and directness of the vocal

melodies of Handel and the more involved speech of
Bach has been a serious stumbling block. It requires not
only familiarity with the idiom, but a stronger intellectual
conception, a capacity for thinking not always exerted by
the listener. Generally speaking, Bach has so much
wealth to reveal that an aphoristic conciseness is not

possible. The direct unadorned sentences of Hakluyt's
blunt mariners are as essential to their narratives as are
the rolling periods of Gibbon and Motley to the grand
canvases which they painted, and to the morals they wish
to underline.

Bach was also extremely fond of decorating his melodies
with an extraordinarily rich profusion of detail, and frequently where he wished to express his deepest feelings
he found it necessary to twine wonderful arabesques
which penetrate and inter-penetrate the furthermost
recesses of one's heart. Handel, on the other hand, was
generally most touching when most simple, and rarely

in his expressive melodies sought such involved figurations as did his great contemporary.

Handel's harmony, again, is generally blunt and plain. He knew the value of poignant dissonances and chromatic chords, but he reserved them for rare occasions. The magnificent effect of ' Surely He hath borne our griefs ' in ' The Messiah ' is largely due to prolonged, acute dissonances coming after pages of common chords. Bach used a richer harmonic scheme as a general basis. If a line of Handel's figured bass and a line of Bach's are worked out the fundamental difference is apparent. Then Bach's passion for individuality of line caused him to

produce combinations of sound which must have seemed extremely dissonant in his day, and which, at any rate until the end of the nineteenth century, anticipated almost every harmonic device subsequently attempted. His parts move so freely that they cannot but jostle against each other sharply ; the clash of sound, harsh in itself when taken point by point, produces a sense of indescribable harmonic richness. If one tries the experiment of beginning to play even his simpler compositions, such, for instance, as the three-part inventions, in the middle, one finds it difficult to commence with a smooth

c

consonance. Dissonance follows dissonance in such a
way as to carry the mind inevitably forward. To the

already glowing harmonic scheme and the superimposed
temporary dissonances as one melody strikes against

another, is added the vivid rhythmical impulse of each line.

A comparison of the examples IV and V (pp. 27 and 28) in which chromatic harmonies are employed will illustrate this point. The sign × placed above the line shows the consonances, the sign + below calls attention to acute combinations of sounds.

It will be noticed that there are ten distinct and independent lines. The eleventh, the continuo (organ), merely punctuates with sustained chords. The basic harmony for each bar is a single common chord, yet only at the moments of the beginning of the third and fifth quaver of the first bar, and the first and third of the second, are the chords found in their pure condition. At all other points extraneous notes jostle against the fundamentals. On the fourth quaver of the first bar, for instance, six different notes are heard. This may seem an unnecessarily minute analysis of certain technical matters, but it illustrates the complexity of Bach's writing as compared with that of his contemporaries and immediate successors. Yet the ' Qui Tollis ' is one of the most touching and apparently simple numbers of the Mass, and makes an immediate and profound impression on every hearer.

Where moments of intense emotional expression are demanded, his already rich harmonic schemes give place to even richer. One has only to recall the *Crucifixus* in the B minor Mass, and the slow section which separates the long, severe first portion and the exultant close of the *Confiteor*.

His rhythmic schemes also are complicated. Every device of extension and contraction of sentence is employed to prevent that nakedness of square four-bar rhythm which became such an obsession of later writers. The hearer accustomed to the clear and simple outline of subsequent composers sometimes finds it difficult to grasp the endless chain of interdependent sentences ; the

mind is not lulled into an unthinking state by an unfailing
regularity of cadence.

This short consideration of technicalities shows partially why Bach was so long misunderstood. One device
might have been exploited without puzzling the listener,
but when each factor of the technical side of composition
is developed at one and the same time, the mind of the
novice is puzzled. But once the idiom is familiar, even
without being fully understood, it becomes an unfailing
joy, and the most uneducated audiences appreciate Bach
with surprising ease.

The fact that most of Bach's music was composed for
the church has been a hindrance to its popularity. Apart
from the fact that any music written for devotional
offices cannot be transferred to a concert room without
sacrifice, the peculiar trend of religious thought in the
Lutheran Church of the period prevents that measure of
universal sympathy towards many of his texts which is
extended towards Biblical words or the great hymns of
the Latin Church. Except in a few isolated verses, the
Jesu-lieder of those days, born of years of suffering,
famine, and depopulation, the fierce denunciatory lines
natural to a people decimated and torn by inhuman
wars, religious and dynastic, surrounded by countries
whose faith they regarded as anti-Christ, and the
crude literalism of Biblical interpretation, do not
strike a congenial note in the hearts of listeners
of to-day, especially if the verse is from the pen
of a poetaster, translated indifferently into English.
Moreover, a church cantata has no plot such as is
found in an oratorio, and the listener cannot always
grasp readily the subtle changes of thought which would
be comprehensible to people nurtured in that way of
thinking. The Passions appeal more directly, because
the Bible narrative is familiar, down to the smallest
detail, from childhood, but even there the reflective
numbers are sometimes as little in touch with the

nineteenth and twentieth centuries as are the meta-
physical poems of Donne.

Bach's whole life centred round the festivals and doctrines of his church, his music, and his family. His little
library of books was mostly theological ; his hymns and
his Bible he knew through and through ; he was ever
ready with a quotation or a comparison to heighten the
meaning of recitative, aria, and chorus. He wrote
libretti himself, and at other times planned out schemes
for his hack writers, frequently altering their texts to
meet his needs. It has been very truly pointed out that
Bach's picture of Christ is unique ; no Italian painting
is more distinctive. Nay, Bach's picture is by far the
most original, because he limns it from the experiences
of his own heart and faith, whereas a painter always has
the suggestion of human features on which to build.
The personality of the Christ of Bach is the most beautiful
and convincing in the whole history of music.

His attitude towards death is consistent : there is no
austerity, there is no morbidity ; it is solemn and impressive, but joy and anticipation are always there. His
disdain of the things of this world is not assumed ; it is
that of a man who has found real satisfaction in his
achievements, but who firmly believes that the joys of
the future and the welcome of his Saviour will outweigh
all the ills of this state of existence. He firmly upholds
doctrine. Over and over again he adopts a stern, un-
bending manner when a didactic text has to be set. The
political history of his time and the sufferings of generations before him, the tales of which would be handed
from father to son in those troublous centuries, explain
his grim dogmatism. His religion was a human one, a
comfort to him in the many difficulties of his family and
public life, and the source of inspiration of most of the
greatest music he wrote.

The foundation of a great part of his church music is
to be seen in the German chorale. For many years

before his time his fellow-countrymen had been gradually building up their church music upon these hymns of the people, which were the bedrock of the Lutheran Church, familiar to all, sung everywhere in the vernacular, several, indeed, associated with the great reformer. They formed the link between the popular music and larger art-forms. Much of the service music was restricted to choir and orchestra, but the chorales were everyman's inheritance. It was here that he revealed himself as a truly ' popular ' composer, for in almost every cantata, in Passion, motet, Magnificat, oratorio, and in his organ music, he gave his congregation the melodies they loved, which were sung on every occasion, public and private, in which the church ministered and in family devotions, and which called up to their minds familiar verses.

It is characteristic of Bach's work that he exercised as much care over harmonising these tunes as over any other part of his compositions. It is probable that his congregation would only sing in unison, and this enabled him to be freer in the addition of the lower parts, which, obtaining independence of movement and providing harmonic distinction, produce an amazingly rich effect. The 300 odd chorales collected by his second son, Carl Philip Emmanuel, are a never-failing source of joy ; they interpret intimately not only the general spirit of the hymn verse—every arresting harmonic progression has its origin in the poem—but at times the character of individual lines or words. Their extraordinary modernity never seems to grow less striking. Some of them, however, become so elaborate that the material is stretched beyond the limits of a simple hymn tune. The complaints of the church authorities during his first organ appointment, that he bewildered his congregation by his extempore harmonies, were, without doubt, well merited. Some of the free traditional plain-chant melodies are bound into a

Procrustean bed in such a way as to suggest that, widely as he cast his net (for he studied ceaselessly, copying examples by all composers from whom he could learn), there were some features of musical thought which did not appeal to him at all.

From these tunes sprang the organ prelude on the chorale, which, in the leisurely religious services of those days, served to introduce the melody to the congregation, or even to usurp the function of hymn-singing. Here Bach gave full rein to his exuberant fancy, and in the large number (well over a hundred) found in his organ volumes are most wonderful fantasies expressing the inner meaning of his favourite hymns. Sometimes we are given a general expression of a mood of verse or hymn, the melody becomes the material for a glorious arabesque, harmonies of wonderful richness and free counterpoints are added below until the simple plain tune is transfigured.

Ex. XI   First line of Chorale, "Allein Gott."

Version in an organ chorale prelude.

At other times he will take each separate line and amplify the meaning of the corresponding portion of the text by means of derived or independent ideas which serve to introduce and accompany the line of the tune, and to bring it to a conclusion. At others, again, he will construct a kind of scena, using the hymn verse as a foundation ; sometimes he will build a fantasia on melodic fragments. For many years these organ choral preludes were little understood, especially in this country, but thanks to recent critical writing and better opportunities of becoming acquainted with literal translations of the original texts, this once-neglected portion of his organ works is now being recognised as one of the finest of all, and worth the close study of every earnest student of music, whether organist or not.

The cantatas form by far the greatest mass of his church music. These were written mostly for the five hours' services customary on Sundays and Saints' Days in St. Thomas's Church, Leipzig and in the other three town churches, the music of which he superintended. A small choir and orchestra were available except during Lent and Advent. At all other ordinary services and on Feast Days a cantata was essential. Its extent is from 12 to about 40 minutes. The text is generally one especially written, though in a few cases it is made up of hymn verses. Biblical excerpts are frequently incorporated. There is no story or plot, but there is always some underlying current of thought which binds the various numbers together. The text is generally suggested by the scripture lesson for the day. Libretti, being in continual demand, vary considerably in quality ; some have excellent qualities, others are mundane and prosaic, others, again, show bad taste. Though schemes vary in detail, in the larger examples there is generally an opening and a closing chorus, the latter almost always a chorale in a comparatively simple congregational form. The first chorus is almost invariably extended ; sometimes it is an expansion of a chorale on the lines of an organ chorale prelude. The rest of the work usually consists of recitatives and arias ; occasionally duets, trios, or purely instrumental movements are included. Chorales often appear in these, vocally or instrumentally. About one-third of the cantatas have no important work for chorus, and these contain sometimes a simple chorale, sometimes nothing for concerted voices. These would be written when his choir was in a poor condition, or when he had at his disposal solo singers of exceptional merit. An orchestra is almost invariably employed.

The church cycle of five years needed 295 cantatas in order to complete it without repetitions. It was a common thing for composers of those days to undertake this great task. Some, indeed, covered the ground more than once. Bach is known to have composed the entire cycle, sometimes writing at the prodigious rate of one complete work every two or three weeks. During the first 21 years of his Cantorship he produced 265 church cantatas, practically one a month on an average. Ninety-three have been lost, three are incomplete, one-hundred-and-ninety-nine still remain, and form the richest and most varied collection of church music in existence. It is only to be expected that here and there, particularly in the earliest works, are to be found numbers which do not attract us, or numbers in which the fount of inspiration has run dry, in which haste is apparent, in which an indifferent text or an unsympathetic subject has failed to rouse him, in which experiments which are not successful, but as we read through volume after volume we are amazed to find how few pages there are in which his spirit does not soar. Here we find his conception of Jesus, presented from every aspect, his treatment of the subject of death, occurring not once but a hundred times, his reverence for dogma, his detestation of the infidel and the unbeliever ; we see the heart of a great man and a profound believer revealed in a way unlike anything else in the history of religious art.

There is music of all moods except that of utter despair ; there are choruses of the utmost sublimity, of praise, of mourning, of peace, of strife, of defiance ; there are arias tender and bold, of denunciation and of ecstatic bliss, which face death benignantly, which express all the experiences in the life of a Christian ; there are even dances in profusion, for Bach's happiness in his religion was so great that he turned naturally to the gavotte, the bourrée, the siciliano, the gigue, to express his joy. An extraordinary thing about these dance movements is that in the solemn aisles of a cathedral they sound perfectly fitting, they never jar on our sensibilities, they are always in perfect keeping with the rest of the work. To understand Bach fully we must know his cantatas and know them well ; they afford an endless field for exploration ; one never feels that one has touched more than the fringe of their possibilities. Unfortunately, the average music-lover in this country only hears one or two occasionally, and has little opportunity of judging them as a whole. The questions of translations, band parts, etc., are factors which create real difficulties ; as yet the subject has not been seriously grappled with so far as the English-speaking world is concerned.

Of less importance in the service was the motet, the direction of which Bach seems to have left generally to a student. Occasionally, however, he was apparently moved to take an interest in it (although the known occasions productive of his motets are all funerary), and there remain six motets, one an early and dull composition, but the others representing him at his best. The stupendous movement and vigour of the monumental eight-part motet, ' Singet dem Herr'n', is one of the greatest experiences in music, while the tenderness and haunting beauty of the lesser-known five-part ' Jesu, meine Freude' appeal to one in a different but no less real manner.

In Holy Week, it had been the custom in the Roman Church, to recite to plain chant the story of the Passion. Different portions of the narrative were assigned to different priests, the utterances of the crowd were eventually confided to the choir. In time this form was expanded in the Lutheran Church, and at suitable points reflective arias or chorales were introduced. The bare recitation of the Bible story became eventually a long and varied series of meditations on the incidents of Christ's sufferings and death, connected by the

Scripture narrative. The German form of the Passion was established by the beginning of the eighteenth century, Keiser, the Hamburg opera writer, having written some notable examples. Bach, in completing his cycle of church music, produced four or five, of which two remain in their original form. The St. John Passion, the earlier of these, is, as a whole, concise and dramatic, though the cries of the crowd are expanded into long and powerful choruses. The St. Matthew Passion is richer in incident, but there is more concentration on Christ and His sufferings, and the other factors do not deflect attention from the main issue. Here devotion, humility, and adoration reach their highest intensity in music. It is the most intensely personal document in the whole range of musical art; it stands above creeds and beliefs, and speaks from heart to heart in the most miraculous manner. Although it is cast in a colossal mould, lasting over three hours when performed fully, demanding double orchestra and double choir, with even, in one number, a ninth voice added, one forgets the elaborate means employed, and the story passes along in the simplest manner, viewed by a mind full of reverence, sympathy and faith.

To turn from the Passion according to St. Matthew to the Mass in B minor is to step from the intimacies of personal faith and adoration into some great structure erected to the Glory of God, where man is a mere infinitesimal unit. Few of the solos have any touch of deep emotion, but chorus after chorus of the most immense magnitude, and demanding enormous powers of endurance, roll along until one is lost in amazement at the power of the human mind which could conceive and carry out such a stupendous plan. Some choruses are intensely introspective; no one can ever forget the tender poignancy of the *Qui tollis* and the *Et incarnatus* and the suffering of the *Crucifixus*, with

its wonderful modulation at the end. Human joy seems
to have reached its limits in the *Gloria*, the *Cum sancto
spiritu*, and the *Resurrexit*. The first part of the Sanctus
is the noblest piece of music ever conceived, its strength
is amazing, it moves along with overpowering
majesty, and all the visions of glory of the Old Testa-
ment prophets are brought before our eyes ; here,
indeed, Bach seemed to have stepped from the finite into
the infinite.

Of purely instrumental music there is an immense
quantity, volume after volume of organ, harpsichord,
string, chamber, and orchestral music.

It was by his organ music that Bach first became
known, and then only by the preludes and fugues. Here
he had a form peculiarly suited to his genius. The prelude gave opportunities for free writing, sometimes
dramatic, sometimes romantic, sometimes sheer delight
in exploiting brilliant figurations and vivid contrasts of
sound. In the fugue his unexampled command over
all technical resources and his unerring instinct for effect
enabled him to sustain a vigorous interest throughout,
to pile climax on climax, to write music which fitted the
organ as a hand a glove. The great preludes and
fugues in A minor, E minor, B minor, the fantasia and
fugue in G minor, the little E minor fugue, as well
as the Passacaglia and the great Toccatas, seem almost
imperishable. A delightful nook in this rich fugue is
the set of six sonatos for clavier with pedals (now almost
exclusively played on the organ) written to perfect the
technique of his brilliant son, William Friedmann.
They are really trios, one line being assigned to each
hand and another to the feet, and all of surpassing
beauty. We have already spoken of the organ chorale
preludes. They form a valuable link between his
vocal church music and his instrumental music, and a
close study of them, from the beautiful and intimate
' Little Organ Book ' to such great fantasies as

THE HERITAGE OF MUSIC

' Vater unser ' and ' Aus tiefer Noth,' helps us to
understand much that might otherwise be obscure in
his church cantatas.   To a certain extent his organ
music has caused misunderstanding.   A quarter of a
century ago, Bach stood for the organ almost
exclusively, and his organ music stood solely for
preludes and fugues ; the chorale preludes were
looked upon as a by-product. Now we are seeing
it all in a better light. Ernest Newman truly remarked a
while ago that if a visitor came from another planet and
read recent Bach literature he would imagine that the
composer was modern. One of the reasons for this is
the attention which has been paid to this branch of his
organ music.

Almost the same thing has been true of his harpsichord
music.   For generations, the Wohltemperirte Klavier
stood for the whole Bach in the minds of pianists, with
the exception of a few of the jolly little gavottes and
bourrées from the suites. This marvellous collection
of preludes and fugues, known in England briefly as
' The 48', the composer's declaration of faith in the
system of tuning the scale falsely known as ' equal temperament,' which permitted the use of all keys, as
opposed to the few available under the older methods,
is an imperishable monument to his genius.   There
is only one dull number, the fugue in A minor
in the first book ; the others are of infinite variety of
mood and style ; one can find music there to meet all
needs, to synchronise with all states of emotion.   It
was after a prolonged study of them that Schumann
said that ' Bach built for all time.'

The preludes, again, are amazing. The Bach-lover,
as he grows in years, turns more and more to these.
The fugue form is to a certain extent stereotyped, but
the form of the preludes is free. They bear undoubtedly
the seeds of many flowers and fruits of the future, besides
forming a glorious garden for present happiness. No

composer ever spoke such widely different thoughts. Compare the romantic E flat minor of the first book with the magnificent orchestral D major of the second, or the exquisitely tender F minor of the second book with the toccata-like B flat of the first. From the ever-wonderful succession of chords of the opening prelude in C, the most perfect harmonic scheme ever devised, to the wistful, almost playfully sad counterpoint of the closing prelude in B minor they speak as no musician ever spoke save Bach.

The eighteen suites (leaving out of consideration the Overture and the smaller sets) have been much neglected in the past. Recitalists have been afraid that their unchanged key and the absence of imposing pianistic effects made them unsuitable for public work. But Mrs. Gordon Woodhouse and Harold Samuel have shown us that it is otherwise, and we may hope that other pianists will turn from the limited set of arrangements of organ works (fine in themselves without a doubt), and make their audiences familiar with the numberless beauties of the charming little French suites, the larger English suites, and the splendid and exhaustive partitas, where the composer summarised the whole possibilities of the classical dance and other short forms common at the time. Without a knowledge of these one only has a one-sided view of his harpsichord music.

It is impossible to pass in review the remainder. Only half has been mentioned ; but whether one considers the exquisite little inventions (almost exclusively considered, unfortunately, as ' studies '), or the romantic Chromatic Fantasia, daring and new even to-day, or the mighty Goldberg Variations, or the fine toccatas, or the delicious short preludes, or the ungrouped fugues and fughettas, or the numbers from the ' Art of Fugue ', not really keyboard music, but available in this medium, one meets with music which is inexhaustible in its charm and variety.

Perhaps one of the most astonishing branches of this music is the six sonatas (or, more properly, three sonatas and three suites) for violin alone. The limitations of the instrument would suggest that his thoughts, too, would be circumscribed. Yet so far did the composer soar above the restrictions that are imposed that there is to be found a wealth of noble ideas. The Chaconne, to take the most familiar number, would seem to be inspired by ·a whole body of strings and not by a single instrument. It is a question whether these sonatas played without the flatter bridge and the loose-haired, arched bow of Bach's time afford a real pleasure to the hearer ; one is always conscious of the need for a more comprehensive medium of expression. One has to fill in and expand by means of one's own imagination where the violin can go so far and no further. They read better than they sound. But to the violinist they are a complete world of beauty, and a training ground whereon his powers may always be proved and tested. The same is true of the three solo sonatas for viol da gamba, although the deeper tone of the violoncello, under the masterly hands of Casals, causes limitations to be less apparent to a listener.

Of the six sonatas for violin and clavier and the three for viol da gamba and clavier, smaller in scale, more intimate, nearer to the ideal of true chamber music, though not so imposing in ideas, the flute sonatas and trios, there is not room to speak here in detail.

Before dealing with his purely orchestral music, we must discuss briefly Bach's conception of the orchestra, as it is so different from that of the great period beginning with Haydn, with which the average music lover is more familiar. Haydn settled a basis for the composition of an orchestra.* He made the foundation of strings. They bore the heat and burden of the day. To them he added

---

*I am not forgetting the work of Gluck and others, and merely quoting the matter in general terms with regard to modern orchestras.

a group of six wind, two each of flute, oboe, and
bassoon, forming the upper medium and lower strata.
The medium register was supplied by two horns,
brilliance by two trumpets, and rhythmic insistence was
obtained by tympani. The wind doubled the strings,
or made small excursions of independence, occasionally
contrasting, occasionally altering the colour, but generally playing a relatively subordinate part. They were
added or subtracted at will. Mozart introduced two
clarinets, reinforcing the upper medium and the medium
as need be. Both composers added three trombones
where power was needed, though never in their symphonies or concertos. Beethoven took the theatre
orchestra of his immediate predecessors as his symphonic
basis, and made the wind and brass more independent.
But the composition of the orchestra was, in the main,
fixed, one always proceeds from strings to the others.
Bach, while he made his strings, plus organ or harpsichord, the foundation for all the accompaniments to his
choruses and for all his larger movements, was not content with a statutory set of wind and brass. He experimented unceasingly with fresh combinations. Every
instrument he could find was pressed into service at one
time or another. The number of different combinations
in the church cantatas is bewildering. One chorus will
be accompanied by strings, two oboes, two flutes ;
another by strings, three oboes and two horns; another by
strings, two oboes, two flutes, three trumpets and tympani.
Almost every cantata contains a fresh combination.* The
lute, the flageolet, the violino piccolo, the violoncello
piccolo, the viol d'amore, the oboe d'amore, and many
others were incorporated into his scores. He stretched
out his hand to the varied collection of different
instruments in existence in his day, and gathered those

*A complete list of his orchestral combinations in the cantatas
will be found in the Appendices to the author's ' Fugitive Notes
on Certain Cantatas and Motets of J.S.Bach' (Oxford University Press).

he needed at the moment. Moreover, he used his wind and brass in an entirely different way from the Viennese school, which, after his death, became the leaders of musical thought. Often he merely doubled the strings, sometimes, no doubt, to obtain a predominance of that piercing nasal quality which was produced by the use of the coarse, reedy oboe of his period, and which had a strong fascination for him, a fascination difficult for us to understand to-day, but which we find also in Handel. But in the majority of cases he treated wind and brass as separate strands ; they were equal partners with the strings, not additional forces. With his love of weaving a many-coloured web he usually gave each a line to itself. An example is shown in the quotation from the B minor Mass earlier in the chapter. Sometimes there may be ten or twelve, or even fifteen, distinct lines, a proceeding never found in Haydn, with whom three or four, or at most five, sufficed. It is one of the perplexing problems of Bach performances to make each audible, because the increased size of our orchestras and our large concert halls obscure flutes or oboes.   Even with orchestras of the size he used himself, there are endless difficulties—a flute cannot vie with the more powerful violins, for instance. Then, again, in the accompaniments to his arias and duets, he frequently forsakes his strings, and chooses only wind or brass and organ, a flute, or a flute and an oboe, or two oboes, or even, in one place, three trumpets and basses against a single voice. An example of a combination new to our modern ears is given supra. These combinations were chosen because he wanted a particular colour, and that colour was maintained right through the number. Instruments did not appear and reappear like the movement of a weaver's shuttle, as we find Haydn and Mozart's practice to be.

He was insatiable in his search for colour, and much of it is marvellously adapted to the shades of emotion he wished to portray. Within the limits of a single cantata he would have several widely different schemes. In No. 175, for instance, the opening numbers, pastoral in character, are accompanied by three flutes ; later comes a command to Christians to open their ears to the word of God, the aria is accompanied by two trumpets and bass. Recent years have witnessed a return to this idea of orchestration ; the chamber orchestras of Stravinsky and his followers had been foreshadowed by Bach. Another peculiarity is his fondness for obtaining brilliance by the addition of three trumpets and tympani, two of the trumpet parts being generally very florid and high-pitched. To our ears they produce a sensation of top-heaviness, but that may be counteracted by an additional strength in the lower and middle parts of the remainder of the orchestra. He would supply this himself at the organ in actual performance.

The only purely orchestral pieces, apart from some twenty odd numbers in the cantatas, are the six Brandenburg Concertos and the four Suites or Overtures. Some of the former are of the old concerto type, where the solo instrument or instruments are only slightly differentiated from the rest of the orchestra ; others are only concertos in the sense of being concerted music. All are for different combinations, in one case only strings, divided into nine parts ; in another, solo harpsichord, violin, and flute, with strings as a background, and so on. They are all fascinating, and are becoming more and more popular. The Suites are not so interesting as a whole, though they contain some delightful music. They are cast in the form of the French Overture, a slow introduction, a fugal movement, and then, not a single dance, as is the case of Handel's opera and oratorio overtures, but a whole series.

It has only been possible, in this brief essay, to glance casually at the many sides of his comprehensive work.

Go where we will in the world of music, the influence of Bach is growing, and wherever his art flourishes there is found a healthy, sound spirit. Whether we listen to the bright little dances of his suites, or to his romantic preludes, or to the busy, vigorous concertos, or to the tremendous Mass, or to the soul-stirring music of the cantatas and the Passions, we feel that here we are face to face with one of the greatest and most potent forces in all art. We never exhaust it ; we never turn from it wearied. His invention may flag at times, his judgment may, at others, be at fault, he may over-estimate the capacity of the human mind, but his message to humanity is the purest, the noblest, the most fruitful that musician has ever delivered.

HENRY PURCELL

THE DRAMATIC COMPOSER OF ENGLAND

(1658-1695)

By GUSTAV HOLST

Save me from my friends —I can protect myself from my enemies.'

HENRY PURCELL, more than anyone, would have been justified in saying this. He has had kinder enemies than any other artist ; for they have only ignored him. In fact, he suffered and suffers still, as a composer, from a lack of *critical* appreciation.

To quote examples of uncritical appreciation, some writers have implied that he was the most important of the Tudor composers, and on the other hand he has been called ' the greatest English imitator of Handel.' He was born about 1658, fifty-five years after Queen Elizabeth's death, and died in 1695, when Handel was ten years of age.

He is generally considered to be England's greatest composer, owing partly to the large amount of music he wrote in his short life, and partly to its variety. This variety is, indeed, noteworthy. Purcell wrote chamber music, church music, and dramatic music. Amongst his chamber music we must include, together with his sonatas, a number of short sacred vocal works, such as the two Evening Hymns. These have real beauty and are far more important musically than his better-known services and anthems which he wrote for Westminster Abbey, where he was organist from 1680 until his death. To judge Purcell by these longer sacred works would be as unfair as to judge Mozart by his Masses. Yet it is only by his church music that Purcell is known to most of his countrymen.

Purcell may have known something of English Tudor music, but its influence on his style is slight. In his day the Tudor choral tradition had vanished, and during the period between its disappearance and the advent of Purcell the state of English music was almost as unsettled as the state of English politics. Chamber music seems to have been cultivated, and there were curious first attempts at opera during the Commonwealth ; but apart from William and Henry Lawes, we hear little of the writing of beautiful music.

Charles II. brought French influence to England. London became a convenient asylum for certain French composers who were driven from the French Court by that master of music and intrigue, the Italian-born Lully. Moreover, Charles sent an English musician, Pelham Humphrey, to study opera under Lully in Paris. Pelham Humphrey subsequently became Purcell's master ; so although Purcell never left England, he was influenced by the French opera tradition, with its insistence on the importance of the ballet and of correct declamation.

As Ernest Walker has said, Purcell ' was of an accommodating disposition ' ; it is easy to trace the effect of the Royal taste on the ' Restoration Anthem', with its spasmodic attempts at dramatic writing, its ornate solos and its *Ritornelli* for violins (the violin was the King's favourite instrument), the whole so remote in style from the sustained dignity and beauty of the work of Byrd and his contemporaries. On the other side of the balance we must put the Royal love of masque and opera, which helped England to produce one of the few supreme dramatic musicians of the world.

It is generally accepted to-day, thanks to Barclay Squire's researches, that Purcell's most famous opera ' Dido and Æneas ' was written about the year 1689 and not nine years before as was previously thought. Even

so it is one of the most original expressions of genius
in all opera. Mozart remains the greatest prodigy in
musical history, but he was brought up in a fine
tradition—in opera, as well as in other music. In
England there was not then, nor has there ever been,
any tradition of opera. Purcell was first a choir-boy
at the Chapel Royal; then he was organist of Westminster Abbey. Yet at the age of about thirty-
one he wrote the only perfect English opera ever
written, and the only opera of the seventeenth century,
as far as I know, that is performed as a whole nowadays,
for the sheer pleasure it gives as opera. Throughout the
whole work not a word is spoken. Between the lovely
airs and choruses there are dialogues, set to easy, free,
and melodious music. Probably the English language
has never been set so perfectly, either before or since.
Playford said of Purcell : ' He had a peculiar genius to
express the energy of English words '. There is no
chance for vocal display in the ordinary sense of the
term, but there is every chance to display powers of
expression simply and beautifully.

The opera is accompanied either by strings or by a
bass to be filled in on the harpsichord. There is beautiful
dramatic and lyrical music, and a perfect sense of
rhythm in setting the English language ; but it is in the
final test of all works of art that ' Dido ' stands supreme
—the test of unity. Many beautiful works fail in this
test—Bach's Christmas Oratorio, for instance. But if
you know ' Dido ' well, you can feel it as a complete
whole. We all know Dido's Lament ; it is often sung by
itself at concerts, but few listeners realise how much they
lose by not hearing all that has gone before. It is impossible to appreciate its full beauty without listening to the
whole opera and perceiving Purcell's power to make one
beauty a stepping-stone to another. Even the Lament is
not more moving than the preceding recitative, ' Thy
hand, Belinda ; darkness shades me', and it is so perfect
that only a real master could have added anything after

it. Yet how incomplete it would be without the final chorus, ' With drooping wings ' !

The libretto by Nahum Tate has been ridiculed for lines such as

' Thus, on the banks of fatal Nile,
Weeps the deceitful crocodile.'

But little or nothing has been said in praise of Tate and Purcell for their power to work up inevitably to the final climax. Then, having achieved it, they stopped. What a lesson for the authors and composers of ' Orfeo', ' Don Giovanni', and ' Fidelio ' !

Having written a perfect opera—the only perfect English opera—Purcell never wrote or even attempted to write another. He never again set the English language to delightful, free, lyrical recitative (except in certain short works), but fell into dull conventional recitative secco that anybody could have written. Above all, he never wrote another big work with any semblance of dramatic unity. Purcell's ' accommodating disposition ' was probably responsible for this. He was at the mercy of his environment.

' Dido ' was written for a girls' school in Chelsea. In any good girls' school in any century one would expect to find a certain standard of taste, and a cultivated sense of language. At the same time, as far as dramatic performances are concerned, all stage effects and all vocal effects must be severely limited. The singers would be expected to pronounce and to phrase their own language well ; but sustained dramatic efforts and any sort of vocal display would be out of the question. ' Dido ' meets these conditions to perfection.

On turning to Purcell's other dramatic works, one realises how little the London theatre has altered since his day. The advertisements of Purcell's later so-called operas read like those of a modern revue—advertisements of enormous expenditure on ' stars', on scenery, on dresses, on lighting, machinery, and other unessential matters. The one great essential of art is lacking equally in Purcell's later dramatic works, and in all ballad-operas, pantomimes, and musical comedies. It is never lacking in any real opera. This great essential is unity of style. One could take the ' Masque of the Seasons ' from Purcell's ' Fairy Queen' and put it into his ' King Arthur', just as people have always taken songs from one ballad-opera or musical comedy and put them into another. It is impossible to treat real opera in this fashion. Imagine the Chorus of Peers from ' Iolanthe ' transplanted into the ' Mikado', or the ' Walkürenritt ' breaking into the second act of ' Tristan' !

Purcell, then, became a successful theatre composer. To be a successful theatre composer in England three qualifications are necessary : a gift of melody, skilful musicianship, and an ' accommodating disposition '. Purcell had all these, and he had genius as well.

Purcell's theatre music (apart from his one genuine opera) falls into three classes :—

(1) Incidental dances and overtures to plays, *e.g.*, ' The Gordian Knot Untied ' and ' The Virtuous Wife '.

(2) Incidental songs and sometimes short choruses, with or without purely instrumental music. Such are ' A Fool's Preferment ', ' The Libertine ', and ' Œdipus '.

(3) Musical interludes (these are sometimes quite elaborate) for solo voices, chorus, and orchestra introduced into plays either as integral parts of the drama or as diversions. Such are ' King Arthur ', ' The Fairy Queen ', and ' Dioclesian '. In the third class we find Purcell at his most characteristic. One example will be sufficient.

' The Fairy Queen ' is an adaptation of the ' Midsummer Night's Dream ' made by a Restoration dramatist. It is interesting and rather terrible to compare it with Shakespeare's original play. Only one point need be mentioned here : all Shakespeare's songs were cut out. However, the anonymous adapter gave Purcell his chance. In addition to overture, ' act-tunes ', dances and isolated songs, there are the following musical interludes :—

(1) A scene of a drunken poet, chased by fairies.
(2) A Masque of Night.
(3) A Masque of the Seasons.
(4) A scene in a Chinese garden.

Not one of these interludes has anything to do with another ; neither have they any connection whatsoever with the ' Midsummer Night's Dream ', but each scene is perfect in itself.

It is surely unnecessary nowadays to dwell on Purcell's gift of melody. According to some it is excelled only by Mozart's. Others hold that Purcell's best melodies— and how numerous they are !—are inferior to none. In addition to his gift of melody there are his sense of harmony, his feeling for orchestral colour, his humour, his intensity, his lyrical power. We can witness their steady growth to perfection as we compare Purcell's earlier with his later works. Yet all these details of composition were subordinate to his amazing power of dramatic characterisation.

This power has been possessed by very few opera composers. Indeed, many do not seem to have been aware of the necessity of cultivating it. They have thought it more important to study the idiosyncrasies of the particular opera singers engaged for a production than to consider the dramatic foundation on which to build the music. Musical characterisation is usually looked upon as a modern factor in opera. One instinctively thinks of Wagner. Both Purcell and Wagner used all their gifts of melody and harmony, all their mastery of orchestral colour, to give life to their characters and situations. But while Wagner painted huge scenes, each consistent in itself and at the same time part of a vaster whole, Purcell was content to paint little cabinet pictures.

But in one way Purcell is a finer stage composer than Wagner : his music is full of movement—of dance. His is the easiest music in all the world to act. Only those can realise fully the truth of this who have experienced the joy of moving to Purcell's music, whether in the ballroom or on the stage or in the garden ; but especially in the garden.

At the end of his life Purcell was master of every branch of musical technique. In all essentials of opera writing, save that of dramatic concentration, he had left 'Dido' far behind. But ' Dido ' still remains his one opera.

If he has never been sufficiently praised for ' Dido ' neither has he been blamed sufficiently for this artistic crime. Any producer of practical ability and imagination will find it easy to make a success of ' Dido.' ' The Fairy Queen,' ' King Arthur,' and ' Dioclesian ' offer almost insuperable difficulties. They are too dramatic for the concert platform, too incoherent for the stage. Producers must be prepared to cut, to alter the disposition of some numbers, to make discreet changes in the words of others, and, ᴧ ᴐve all, to toil and struggle for a scheme that will info:. the work with a semblance of dramatic unity. That success is possible the Cambridge production of ' The Fairy Queen ' in 1920 proved beyond reasonable doubt. It also proved—and Purcell's countrymen were sadly in need of the proof—that England has produced at least one great dramatic composer.

FRANZ JOSEPH HAYDN
(1732-1809)

By Thomas F. Dunhill

JOHN SEBASTIAN BACH is reported to have summed up his ideas of the functions of musical art in a crisp and comprehensive phrase—' the glory of God and a pleasant recreation '.

No composer realised these functions more thoroughly than Joseph Haydn, in whose works they are indivisible. Haydn's avowed aim in music was ' to praise God with a merry heart '. He gave forth what was in him with the passionate conviction that his labours might one day ' be the source from which the weary and worn, or the man burdened with affairs, may derive a few moments' rest and refreshment '. He was so full of joy that the notes flew off ' as from a spindle', and he prayed, with touching naiveté, that he might receive the Divine pardon for serving God cheerfully.

If we begin our study of Haydn's music with this knowledge of his attitude towards his art and his Creator we shall not look for the intensity of emotional content or the deep reverential feeling of J. S. Bach, nor expect anything akin to the large and stately utterance of Handel. The untrammelled spirit of cheerfulness was responsible for something far more important than the almost innumerable collections of symphonies, quartets, and sonatas to which Haydn signed his name, and which he adorned with such pious inscriptions as ' Soli Deo Gloria ', ' Laus Deo ', or ' In Nomine Domini '.

The work of such a man as Haydn could no longer move comfortably when clad in the severer forms which his giant predecessors had adopted for their own needs. His native happiness of mind was no doubt the incentive that led him to seek for new methods of composition in which the austerities of an older school were discarded

in order that he might gain greater ease in expression·
And since these new methods were of commanding importance in the progress of music, and destined almost
to transform the whole face of musical art, it is not only
in Haydn's own compositions that the changes he evolved
were of moment. Indeed, one is tempted to set forth
a new paraphrase—' What should they know of Haydn
who only Haydn know ? '—before urging the wider
recognition by a forgetful generation of this truly remarkable figure in the history of music.

As regards Haydn's own compositions, musical
students of the present day may be said to have a fairly
clear idea of their characteristics without possessing a
very comprehensive knowledge of their scope. The
opportunities of hearing performances of certain works
by Haydn are by no means infrequent, but out of the vast
quantity of music which he composed only a small per-
centage survives—four or five symphonies, the violoncello concerto, a goodly number of string quartets, a
few piano sonatas, and solo songs ; these are almost all.
Even the oratorio ' The Creation ' and the cantata, ' The
Seasons ', once popular choral works, are seldom performed, and arouse little enthusiasm.

On the whole, however, posterity has been just to
Haydn. The works we know best are those in which the
essentially human mirthful spirit of the man is most
clearly revealed. For the highest type of religious music
he was imperfectly equipped. His settings of sacred
words lack dignity and solemnity. They neither scale
heights nor probe depths. We must remember that he
did not come under the strong Protestant influences
which moved Bach and Handel so powerfully. The
Catholic Church of his time, at all events in Central
Europe, had temporarily abandoned the pure principles
of Palestrina, and was swayed by baneful secular and
operatic conventions in music. Haydn, as a typical
Catholic of his day, could not quite cast them aside. His

music for the church was ornamental and slightly superficial, and as such could hardly be expected to outlive the fashions of the age.

But the works of Haydn which we rejoice to remember to-day have an air of lively innocence which is ever fresh and renewable. They are also strangely full of wonderful anticipations of the music of later years.

It is significant that an affectionate sobriquet bestowed upon the composer during his lifetime has survived to this day, for he is still known as ' Papa Haydn'. His position in musical history is such that he must be regarded in more than one sense as a father. If the most rigid critics may deny him the title of ' the father of instrumental music', he was assuredly the father of the most significant and the most living types of such music. He was the father of the solo sonata, of the symphony, of the string quartet. He was assuredly the father of orchestration as we know it, for before his time a perfectly balanced orchestra was practically unknown. It was Haydn who first distributed the instruments into groups of wood-wind, brass, and strings, and it was Haydn who first realised the delicate colouring that could be obtained by the use of separate instruments as eloquent solo voices in the orchestra. So momentous were the developments he inaugurated, and so widespread were his immediate influences, that to latter-day musicians the prefix ' Papa ' is especially significant, and it is not surprising to find that composers of all nations unite in claiming direct descent from him.

To arrive at a fuller understanding of the historical importance of Haydn's work it is necessary to take into account the achievements of some of the composers who immediately preceded him, and especially of the composer who, by foreshadowing certain important developments in musical form, gave a definite cue to his successor. This composer was Carl Philipp Emanuel Bach, the third son of the great J. S. Bach.

As Sir Henry Hadow has pointed out in his excellent volume on the Viennese Period,* Emanuel Bach marked out the ground and laid the foundations ; he did not ' foresee the full capabilities of the superstructure'. If Emanuel Bach was the innovator, it was Haydn who first showed the vital genius to apply. Emanuel Bach, commencing his career at the climax of the greatest polyphonic period in musical history, was thoroughly grounded in the methods perfected by his illustrious father. He saw, apparently, that the culmination of music of contrapuntal character had been reached ; he tried to set forth on a new journey, but was entangled in the network of the style he sought to replace. The elegant new forms were not destined to flourish when so encumbered. The severities of detailed texture had to be relaxed in order to secure the lightness, the ease of movement, the clarity necessary to give life and freedom to the new style of art. Emanuel Bach had neither the genius nor the suppleness of mind to transform the face of music in the way that his successor did.

What, then, were the special qualities which Haydn brought to his work that were to effect this transformation of character ? Well, to begin with, Haydn's subjects or melodies were more symmetrically shaped, more neatly rounded and polished, and less encumbered by figuration. There was an air of pleasantry and rusticity in many of his themes, which gave an easy-going gaiety to the music. He dispensed with complexities of every kind, both textual and rhythmical. There was nothing difficult to listen to ; all was transparently flowing and natural. Yet such was the vitality of his genius that he succeeded almost always in steering clear of any tendency towards triviality or flippancy.

It is true that Haydn transferred the chief interest in instrumental music from studied texture to frank melody,

---

* The Oxford History of Music, Vol. v. (Clarendon Press).

and that an accompaniment of simple chords or chord-figures replaced contrapuntal richness. It might have been thought that this was, in a definite measure, an historical set-back, but Haydn was shrewd enough to see that even the most inspired complacency was not enough to sustain the interest of his hearers. So, when he abandoned the elaborations of counterpoint which had hitherto supplied the needful intellectual appeal in music, Haydn put a very definite scheme of design in its place. Instead of presenting a constant interweaving of outlines, and overlapping threads of melody (as J. S. Bach had done), he devoted attention to the ordered sequence of different, and often contrasted, ideas, keeping the interests of the listeners alive by the happy relationship of one section of a movement to another, and encouraging expectancy for repetitions. He sought to appeal by a continuous chain of melodic sections rather than to concentrate upon the ingenuities of which each section was composed. In a word, the symmetry of shape which was the main feature of Haydn's themes was preserved, on a larger scale, throughout an entire movement. And so each movement became in itself an orderly pattern consisting of a sequence of smaller orderly patterns, all clearly designed and set out so as to balance properly each with each.

Of course, this new scheme was not evolved all at once, and in Haydn's early works we find only the merest skeleton of the sonata form, as the scheme came to be called. His first care was for an ordered sequence of keys, for he realised that to employ only a limited number of harmonies, which were all related to one keynote, or centre, would be a very wearisome procedure. But if the keynote was altered from time to time these self-same relationships obviously provided an entirely new set of chords. Complexity was thus replaced by variety. There was less exploration, but more change of scene.

Later on, Haydn introduced changes of mood as well as changes of tonality. Two definitely contrasted subjects were balanced one with another, and, at the conclusion of the first section of a movement, some enterprising expeditions were made into more or less remote keys, bringing a spirit of adventure into the music and making the home-coming to a settled third section, or recapitulation, increasingly welcome. Last of all, an important feature was made of a peroration, or coda, in which the main themes were presented in a new light or given some fresh brilliance or piquancy of utterance.

The developments just described were the most important of those for which Haydn was mainly responsible. His more extended quick movements were almost always constructed in this manner. But in his slow movements he did not generally use such an elaborately wrought scheme, whilst for his playful and dance-like finales he often adopted a far simpler ' rondo ' pattern, in which the chief theme recurred over and over again in full, with episodes of slighter interest sandwiched between the repetitions. He also borrowed from the Suites of earlier composers the stately measure called a minuet, placing it either before or after the slow movement (sometimes both before and after) for the sake of additional variety. The minuet, as Haydn found it, was, however, very different from the movement of that name which he evolved and handed on. The character of the minuet of the old dance suites suggests dignified deportment. It is essentially aristocratic. Haydn did not attempt to preserve this air of high-bred dignity, but fashioned something of an altogether more vigorous type. Occasionally he was content with a graceful and flowing melody, but more often he gave to these measures a humorous and somewhat *bourgeois* character. The following examples, from two of his most familiar string quartets, are typical. A few bars of each are sufficient to show how strong was the rhythmic energy Haydn imparted to these movements.

By quickening the *tempo* and increasing the vitality of the minuet Haydn led the way to the ' scherzo,' which became so prominent a feature in Beethoven's works later on.

These various innovations and adaptations, gathered together and grouped as outlined above, constitute the sonata form of four movements as we know it. Their constructive excellences and their sequence were evolved by Haydn almost unaided. They were handed on as live novelties to Mozart and Beethoven, who, with greater inventive powers and possibly a wider outlook, enriched this organic creation to such an extent that it ultimately became the most important structural basis of all orchestral music and all instrumental chamber music.

To dwell with too much insistence upon Haydn's influence over other composers, however, would be to risk conveying the impression that his music had less vitality than theirs, or that his works had ceased to be valued for their own sake. Such a view would be entirely erroneous and unjust. It is true that at the present time, in company with Handel, he is suffering temporary neglect, whilst J. S. Bach and Mozart, recently much underrated, are enjoying a fashionable revival. But there is no sign of any serious diminution of interest in Haydn's music amongst real music-lovers. On the contrary, a great deal of attention has been paid of late, by cultured musicians, to the question of his nationality and its effect upon his style.

When we find undoubted authorities such as the late Sir Hubert Parry and Sir Henry Hadow at variance upon such an important matter we are tempted to recall the words of Pope, ' Who shall decide when doctors disagree ? ' Parry declares, in his *Art of Music*, that ' Haydn is throughout as Teutonic in spirit and manner as it was possible to be'. Hadow says, in ' A Croatian Composer', ' he was a Slav by race and a Slav by temper, and his music is too genuine to present itself in foreign guise'. Neither of these writers can be regarded lightly as superficial observers. Both have shown an intimate knowledge of Haydn's music. How is it possible to reconcile these two opposing views, so emphatically expressed ? Let us examine the facts, however, and see what conclusions are possible.

Sir Henry Hadow, who has made special efforts to trace several of Haydn's themes to their sources, is convinced that the composer made extensive use of Croatian folk-music in many of his works.* We find that Parry, in *Style in Musical Art* (a far more recent book than his *Art of Music*) shows some disposition to acknowledge these researches.

Now, it is customary to divide serious instrumental music into two categories, the classical and the romantic —the latter type of music beginning when the former ceased to satisfy the need of composers for freedom of poetic expression. It is customary, also, to point to Haydn as a pioneer amongst the classicists, but Parry

*W. H. Hadow, 'A Croatian Composer.'

(in *Style in Musical Art*) claims him as an early romanticist, despite the clearly defined patterns in which his ideas were presented to the listener. Parry's arguments are interesting and not to be ignored. He points out that Haydn was but a few generations removed from the undiluted simplicities of the Croats, from whom it is admitted he is descended, and that ' the peasant quality which is so vividly and pertinaciously in evidence in everything he did takes his work out of the region of cultured classicism, about which there always is a slight suggestion of the atmosphere of courtliness and etiquette and gentility'. ' Haydn's position in connection with courtly people,' he continues, ' was rendered possible by the quaint fact that just at his time it was fashionable to take a languid poetic interest in rusticity and peasant life. Some of the members of the highest society had just discovered that the lower orders were human beings, and it amused them to see how people who had not been so fortunate as themselves revealed the workings of familiar human traits in uncourtly terms.'

Haydn's surroundings in his early and most impressionable years were certainly of the humblest kind. He was twenty-eight years of age when his acceptance of the post of Capellmeister to the princely family of Esterhaz brought him into close and continuous contact with the courtly world to which Parry alludes. And even then it must be remembered that in this position he was little more than a servant. He did not by any means live on equal terms with the members of the society into which he was thrust. Thus the natural brightness and primitive freshness of his ideas were but little tarnished by the circumstance that he was forced to mould them into the polite and decorous conventions of symphony and quartet, and so forth, in order to please his patrons.

It is probable that, in most instances, the fragments of folk-melody which are found in Haydn's works were

used unconsciously rather than deliberately. The jolly
dances and peasant songs, or at least the lilt of them, had
remained in his memory since his early boyhood ; they
pervaded his thoughts and danced their way through his
brain as he composed. One particular type of rhythmical
measure in 2-4 time, which again and again makes its
appearance in the Finales of Haydn's quartets, has been
identified by Sir Henry Hadow and others as a variant
of a Slavonic dance called the ' Kolo '. But Haydn's
dainty treatment of these wild tunes is far more personal
than national and he cannot be accounted a ' national-
istic ' composer in the sense that later writers such as
Grieg or Dvořák (who likewise seldom consciously
adapted real folk-music) may be represented to be. The
out-and-out nationalist aims at reproducing the living
spirit of his native music. Haydn seldom did this. His
thematic outlines may have been Croatian, but the
geniality of their presentation seems to be pure Viennese
Haydn rather than either Croatian or Teutonic.

The whole question is so interesting to the student of
music that it may be valuable to set forth some of the
themes in question and examine them.

A prolonged search through Haydn's compositions
would not reveal three tunes more thoroughly characteristic of the composer's personal genius than those of
which the following are the opening bars :—

No. 1 is a part of the principal subject from the Quartet in D, Op. 17, No. 6. If, as is claimed, this is a variant of a Croatian folk-tune it is so entirely changed in character, by the addition of notes which give new curves to the melodic line, that it is scarcely more like its supposed forerunner than the theme of the Variations in Beethoven's Septet is like ' The British Grenadiers', an accidental resemblance which has occasionally been noticed. Here is the folk-tune, as quoted by Hadow :—

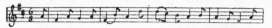

The case of No. 2 is decidedly more convincing. This is the main subject of the Finale of the well-known Symphony in D (No. 7 of the Salamon set), and the folk-tune given by Hadow as its origin has undoubtedly an identical note-shape.

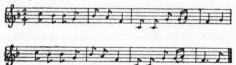

There is no suggestion of the broad dignity of Haydn's melody in the above, but it seems likely that the composer's memory may have dictated the rhythm and choice of notes in this particular instance.

If No. 3, which is the opening of the Andante from the Symphony in E flat (known as the ' Paukenwirbel '), is the direct descendant of the tune given below, then one can only say that reminiscence-hunting may be a very ingenious parlour game, but it does not add very much to our knowledge of a composer's character or methods.

Haydn's appropriation of the ' Kolo ' measure is, however, undoubtedly an interesting discovery. In the Quartet in C major, Op. 33, No. 3, there is a prolonged melody beginning thus :—

which is, without question, identical for the first four bars, both in notes and style, with a genuine and authentic ' Kolo '. It is also not to be disputed that Haydn composed a large number of movements of a similar type, though there seem to be no further evidences of actual quotations to be found in them, at all events amongst the published compositions of his maturity. It would seem that he adopted the ' Kolo,' as he adopted the Minuet, moulding it anew for his own uses and finding in it a congenial mode of expression.

How far what seems rather a faint survival of national instincts coloured the stream of Haydn's music each listener must decide for himself. It seems fairly certain that the flow of his ideas was neither quickened nor impeded by considerations of this kind, and it is obvious that he set no store upon his supposed indebtedness to traditional melodies, since he gave no hint of an acknowledgment which one may reasonably presume he would have been proud to make. He had a notoriously poor memory. It is reported that when, in later life, he was asked to assist in the preparation of a thematic catalogue of his music, Haydn was quite unable to say whether several works which were attributed to him were of his composition or not ! The creative brain is generally too much occupied with what it is engaged upon at the moment to concern itself with recollections of the past.

Few composers of any age were more truly progressive than Haydn, and none has shown more complete assurance at each successive stage of development. Every close student of his music must be struck by the composer's alertness in seizing upon each new opportunity which came his way to expand his musical outlook. In studying his works chronologically one can clearly trace the improvement in the playing of instruments which led him by gradual degrees to demand more from his performers. As he trained the members of his own orchestra at Esterhaz to greater perfection he made full use of their increased skill, scoring his works with more enterprise and experimenting with many new effects which such technical improvement made possible.

But perhaps the most striking and unusual feature of Haydn's progress was his willingness to absorb and profit by the achievements of his youngers. This is only paralleled by one other instance in musical history—that of Verdi.

We shall be able to trace these influences best if we study Haydn's string quartets in sequence. The string quartet, as Otto Jahn said, was Haydn's natural mode of expressing his feelings, and if we place side by side, for comparison's sake, any typical movement of his early style and one from a work of his old age we shall see how marvellously his feelings altered, and his gifts ripened, after he had become acquainted with the music of Mozart. In his early years Haydn wrote quartets which served Mozart as models. In his later years Haydn himself learnt all sorts of secrets from his younger contemporary, whom he long outlived.

So advanced in character are some of Haydn's mature movements that they may be regarded as connecting links between Mozart and Beethoven in his middle period.* As a characteristic example one cannot do better than quote a few bars from the second movement of Haydn's Quartet in G, Op. 54, No. 1 (overleaf).

*See the author's treatise on *Chamber Music* (Macmillan), Chapter II.

Such a romantic passage as this, with its strikingly unexpected change of key, is a perfect illustration of Haydn's mastery over methods which normally belong to a later age in music. It helps us to realise the significance of Parry's contention that Haydn's progress was ' a little epitome of the history of musical evolution'.

From whatever standpoint we prefer to look upon Haydn's achievements we must acknowledge him as a paramount figure in the art of the eighteenth century, the century which saw the rise of instrumental music to what may be described as an advanced stage of formal perfection. His stature is not diminished by the circumstance that cultivated music is no longer the monopoly of a privileged princely class. Much may be argued against the artificial system of ' patronage ' under which Haydn and his contemporaries laboured, but at least the system resulted in what has been called ' the spiritual homogeneity of the group who practised it.'† Some of the supreme creative work of all time was then accomplished under conditions which would seem to us to-day to be stifling rather than stimulating.

Haydn's beautiful music has now passed from the hands of the nobility to the people. It has stood the

---

†Daniel Gregory Mason, *Contemporary Composers*, ' Democracy and Music.' (New York. The Macmillan Co.).

test. It has had its share in softening the crudities incidental to democratic upheavals in art. It is no mere
reminder of the fashions of a bygone day, for its simplicity is of the kind that has a permanent hold upon
humanity.

An exquisite modern poet, who understands music as
few poets have done, has declared that

‘ The simple days are dead, the rich tides roll,
   And we, the inheritors of toil and tears,
   Utter the ampler message of the soul.’

This is true. But it is equally true that our heritage
includes an appreciation of ideal beauty which has been
handed down to us untarnished by time or change.
Haydn, who was an obedient conformist of those simpler
days of patronage and servitude, has become one of the
chief priests of ideal beauty for us, and his utterances
despite all transitions and the turmoil of this restless
generation, are not destined to be lightly forgotten or
unvalued.

WOLFGANG AMADEUS MOZART
(1756-1791)

By W. J. TURNER

MR. BERNARD SHAW once remarked that nothing could be more uncharacteristic of Mozart than the portraits of the beautiful young man exhibited above his name in all the music shops of the world to-day. These portraits show Mozart as the most handsome, the most regular-featured of all great composers. These ' classic ' proportions seem at first sight to be peculiarly appropriate to a composer who is to-day universally admired as the classic of classics. Where else in music shall we find those qualities of serenity, limpidity, simplicity, lucidity, which we concentrate in one adjective Mozartian ? It is impossible to find a parallel to that flawless perfection. Whether we take a whole opera—such as *The Marriage of Figaro*—or a mere scrap scribbled impromptu on the page of a visitors' book— such as the Gigue written in 1789 for the Leipzig organist, Engel—we are confronted with a completely finished musical composition in which there is not a superfluous bar, not a redundant or meaningless note. There is no ' waste ' in Mozart—no overlapping, no exaggeration, no strain, no vagueness, no distortion, no suggestion. He is so simple that he is meaningless. His music *disappears*, like the air we breathe on a transparent day. Everybody who has really appreciated Mozart will admit that at one time or another they have felt a Mozart masterpiece as one would feel a still, bright, perfect, cloudless day. Such a day has no meaning, none of the suggestiveness, the ' atmosphere', the character of a day of cloud or storm, or of any day in which there is a mixture of warring elements whose significance has yet to appear. Such a day does not provoke or in the faintest degree suggest one mood rather than another. It is infinitely protean. It means just what you mean.

It is intangible, immaterial—fitting your spirit like a glove. Thus, as Sir Charles Stanford has said, when you are a child Mozart speaks to you as a child—no music could be more simple, more child-like—but when you are a man you find to your astonishment that this music which seemed child-like is completely adult and masculine. At every age this pure pellucid day, this intangible transparency, awaits you and envelops you in its unruffled light. *Then* suddenly there will pass through you a tremor of terror. A moment comes when that tranquillity, that perfection will take on a ghastly ambiguity. That music still suggests nothing, nothing at all ; it is just infinitely ambiguous. Then you remember the phrase of a German critic who wrote of the ' demoniacal clang ' of Mozart. Then you look at a genuine portrait of Mozart, and instead of that smooth Praxitelean young beauty you see a straight jutting profile with a too-prominent nose and an extraordinary salience of the upper lip, and for an instant you feel as if you have had a revelation. But that revelation escapes you as suddenly as it came, and you are left face to face with a mask whose directness and clarity is completely baffling.

In endeavouring to explain Mozart to oneself, it is well to remember first of all that he was the most remarkable example of a child prodigy that has ever been known. He played the hardsichord in public at five years old. At seven he composed, and played on the harpsichord, the organ, and the violin. In 1764, at the age of eight, after touring Europe, he came to London and played before the Royal Family ; in London he published his third set of sonatas and wrote an anthem for four voices entitled *God is Our Refuge*, which was presented to the British Museum. At the age of ten he wrote an oratorio which had a great success in Holland, and a year later, in Vienna, he wrote an *opera bouffe*, *La Finta Semplice*, for the Emperor Joseph II. At fourteen he was taken to Italy by his father, and in Rome

during Holy Week he went to the Sistine Chapel to hear
the famous *Miserere* of Gregorio Allegri. Immediately
on returning to his lodging he wrote down the *Miserere*
from memory note for note. The same year he was sub-
jected to the severest possible examination by the
Bologna Accademia Filarmonica, passed it successfully,
and was awarded the degree of ' compositore', although
the regulations did not admit of any candidates under
twenty years of age. This exercise is No. 86 in Köchel's
catalogue, and, in Professor Donald Tovey's words, is
' written in the severe ecclesiastical style of the six-
teenth century', and abounds in ' points of ingenious
imitation and device'. In 1770, at the age of fourteen,
he wrote an opera entitled *Mitridate Re di Ponto* for La
Scala, of Milan. The orchestra of La Scala was at that
time the largest in Europe ; Mozart directed it seated at
the harpsichord as the fashion then was. The opera was
received with enthusiasm, and ran for twenty nights.

From the age of fourteen onwards Mozart poured
forth a constant stream of compositions of all kinds.
What is astonishing is that this immense early produc-
tivity seems in no way to have harmed the natural
growth of his mind, for although there are pieces of
church music written before the age of fifteen which the
best critics claim to rank as masterpieces, yet there is
perceptible in his music a real development of his natural
powers which ends only with his death.

It is suggested by some writers that the fact that
Mozart acquired at the age of fourteen a technique equal
to, if not surpassing, that of any living composer explains
why he was able to pass through the critical years of
adolescence from fourteen to twenty in ceaseless musical
composition without straining his mind. For Mozart
had to acquire the usual education, and his letters suggest
—as later his invention in the *Seraglio* of the character of
Osmin, words and all, proves—that he had great literary
ability and possibly the same inexhaustible fertility in

language that he had in music. But Mozart's intellectual force was a quality inherent in the structure of his mind. One day the physiologists will be able to show us in a physiological generalisation Mozart's peculiar gift for form. Many writers on æsthetics think music is the most abstract of the arts, but it is certainly true that Mozart's are the purest works in music. One may speak of a movement of Mozart just as a mathematician might speak of a beautiful proposition of Euclid. Whereas in the music of most composers it is a case of content *and* structure, it is with Mozart a case of structure only, for there is no perceptible content—*ubi materia ibi geometria*. Nowhere, perhaps, is this more strikingly shown than in the overture to the *Marriage of Figaro*. I would suggest to the reader that he should buy the gramophone records of this overture and of Rossini's overture to *The Barber of Seville*, and compare them. The difference is astonishing. Rossini was born the year after Mozart's death ; he also had the advantage of following instead of preceding Beethoven, and he was a composer of striking natural genius. But, after *Figaro*, listen to the *Barber of Seville* overture, with its alluring tunefulness over its easy *tum-ti, tum-ti, tum-ti, tum-ti* bass, and you will be struck with its straggling formlessness. Its tunes are very engaging, but you can carry them away with you and hear them mentally on a penny whistle, a cornet, or any instrument you like. They are like bright threads in a commonplace piece of stuff which you can pull out without compunction as there is no design to spoil. But you can do nothing of the sort with the *Figaro* overture. There are no bright threads to pull out. There is no melodic content as such. You cannot even hear the music in your memory apart from the rush of the strings and the accents of the wood wind. It cannot be played upon the piano. Take away a note of it and the whole is completely disintegrated. Nor can anyone put his hand upon his heart and say what feeling that music arouses in his breast. It is completely without expression, as expression is vulgarly understood ; but the oftener you hear it the more excited you become, the more passionate grow your asseverations that there was never music like this before or since. Its effect upon the mind is out of all proportion to its impingement on the senses. To hear it is as though one had been present at a miracle and had seen a mountain of matter blown into a transparent bubble and float vanishing into the sky. Your desire to hear that Overture again and again and again is the simple but intense desire to see the miracle repeated. It is an astonishing experience, and it is an experience which only Mozart can give us.

It would be useless to attempt to explain this peculiar intellectual gift which was Mozart's in a degree that separates him from all other composers. It must just be stated and left. But there are certain facts known about Mozart which are so relevant to this point that they should be mentioned now. He was exceptionally good at dancing and playing billiards, which were his two chief pleasures. He was small, but his limbs, feet, and hands were beautifully proportioned. He composed away from any musical instrument entirely in his head, and could complete the whole of a work, from the first note to the last and then write it down—often some weeks or more later—from memory. Thus the overture to *Don Giovanni*, which was written on the night of October 28th, 1787, for the first performance of the opera in Prague on the next day, while his wife kept him awake by telling him fairy stories, was not composed on that night but merely copied out from memory. He would often compose at meals, and while composing would take his napkin by two corners and continually fold and refold it very neatly and exactly. To me this is all extraordinarily illuminating. Conciseness—even conciseness so unparalleled and amazing as Mozart's— is not surprising in a composer who could work in this

way. One also cannot but think that his invariable
serenity and good temper—upon which all who knew him
have left comment—was yet another sign of perfect
physical and mental poise. It is on record that Mozart
never used glasses and that his eyesight was perfect at
his death in spite of the strain which manuscript music
imposes. This, also, is not without significance. Mozart
may be bracketed with Schubert as one of the two composers whose fertility in melodic invention exceeds all
others, but the listener never feels that Mozart is being
swept along the current of his own emotions as he feels
Schubert is. In listening to such works as Schubert's
Octet or his ' Unfinished ' Symphony, one is conscious
sometimes of a dissolution, almost a liquefaction, of the
composer's sensibility, which streams into the music like
treacle. It is this that makes Schubert's music often so
formless. The composer is simply melting helplessly
away, and it seems as if only death can conclude the
process. Yet melting, tender, exquisitely sweet as
Schubert's melodies can be, they are never intrinsically
sweeter or tenderer than Mozart's in themselves, but
only in their effect. They seem sweeter because of the
absence of that intellectuality, that lucid precision which
was so integral a part of Mozart's mind. There are
passages in Mozart's pianoforte concertos which are so
piercing in their intense sweetness that I have often
stopped playing and laughed aloud with excess of
pleasure ; but Mozart's mental grip never loosens ; he
never abandons himself to any one sense ; even at his
most ecstatic moments his mind is vigorous, alert, and on
the wing. It is from this astounding elasticity that his
conciseness largely derives. Most artists are unable to
tear themselves away from their most delightful discoveries ; they linger on them and handle them fondly,
but not Mozart. He dives unerringly on to his finest
ideas like a bird of prey, and once an idea is seized he
soars off again with undiminished power.

Yet impossible as it is in Mozart's music to separate form from content—which is his great, his unique intellectual distinction, the quality in which he surpasses all other composers—we can range his forms in a hierarchy of value. The overture to *Figaro* is perfect. There is nothing to be altered, there is not a note we could wish different, and nobody but Mozart could have written it ; but, nevertheless, the overture to *The Magic Flute* is a finer work. It also is perfect, but it is artistically greater than *Figaro*. Wherein is it greater ? Well, I believe we shall go least astray if we make the comparison in purely quantitative terms. The Overture to *The Magic Flute* is a greater composition than the overture to *Figaro* because while form and content are equally one, while ' matter ' has once again been turned to ' form ', more matter has been involved in the operation. It was a bigger and more difficult bubble to blow.

I am conscious that some readers will dislike the manner in which I have put this comparison of *Figaro* with *The Magic Flute*. They will wonder why I do not use the familiar terms : *Figaro* is a comic opera, *The Magic Flute* is a more serious work. It expresses Mozart's religious feeling, his idealism ; that is why, they will say, *The Magic Flute* overture is superior. Such expressions, I admit, are not without meaning, but they are misleading. The world is full of music which is none the less worthless because it is ' serious ' or ' religious '. What we can say is that there is present in the music of *The Magic Flute* a quality which is not present in *Figaro*, and a quality which we instinctively feel to be infinitely more precious. That ' infinitely ' is a concession to my own feeling. I hope it will appease the fanatical admirers of Beethoven, but my reason urges me to take it out. However, it must be recognised that Beethoven almost consistently attempted to blow bigger bubbles than Mozart. That he so frequently failed, that his bubbles so often burst instead of sailing off beautifully, as Mozart's do, into the upper regions of the mind, will not prevent his admirers ranking him instead of Mozart as the greatest of all musicians. I do not really object to this very seriously, because one or two of Beethoven's biggest bubbles do float off successfully, although I confess I always watch them with anxiety, never with that utter confidence which Mozart inspires. But when we remember that Mozart died at the age of thirty-five, and reflect upon such works as *Don Giovanni*, the *Requiem*, the *Magic Flute*, and much of his earlier church music, it is permissible to believe that he would have successfully achieved even bigger things.

Personally, I would go farther. I very much doubt if Beethoven or any other composer has exceeded Mozart in vital energy. The last movement of Beethoven's Seventh Symphony has been called the ' apotheosis of the dance ', and in actual ' sound and fury ' it far exceeds anything Mozart ever wrote ; but I do not feel there is as quick, as tense a ' rush ' in it as there is in the *Figaro* overture ; there is only a bigger volume of noise. It is the rumble of thunder compared with the flash of lightning. Nor is there in all Beethoven's great and intensely dramatic overtures anything more impressive, more dramatically effective than the use made of the opening chords in the *Magic Flute* overture ; but Mozart secures this dramatic intensity with a far greater economy of sound. He never bludgeons the senses into recognition of his powers, as so many inferior composers do ; he appeals directly to the imagination.

It is not astonishing that a mind so well-balanced as Mozart's should show so great a sense of humour. In this he surpasses all other composers, and as the sense of humour is essentially intellectual, it is natural that Mozart, the most intellectual of composers, should be the greatest master of comic opera. But what is altogether unexpected is his power to make one's flesh creep. Nothing has ever been written of such truly diabolical verve as the aria for the Queen of the Night in the *Magic Flute*. It is the rarest event to find a light soprano who can sing this at all ; it is certain that we shall never have it sung so as to do full justice to its startlingly cold-blooded ferocity. And yet that aria has the smooth, glassy surface of a mere bit of coloratura virtuosity ; but it is the surface of ice beneath which is a fathomless black water. This sinister ambiguity is a quality quite apart from the more familiar power of striking the imagination which he shows in the music which announces and accompanies the entrance of the statue at the supper-party in the last act of *Don Giovanni*. This is the most famous of Mozart's dramatic touches, and nobody can deny that there is not a more thrilling moment than this in the whole of Wagner's *Ring*, or, indeed, in any opera that has ever been written. Yet I would like to insist that there is another and even more troubling quality in Mozart's music. Linked with the ' demoniacal clang ' which is probably the result of that bareness which makes Mozart's music appear a mere rhythmical skeleton beside the work of more sensuous composers such as Brahms and Wagner (but a skeleton of electric vitality !), there is a profoundly disturbing melancholy. It is never active in Mozart's work as it is frequently in the work of Tchaikovsky, in Brahms, in Chopin, and even in Beethoven. It is a still, unplumbed melancholy underlying even his brightest and most vivacious movements. It is this which gives his music that ambiguity to which I drew attention at the beginning of this essay. It would be an interesting psychological study to try to discover its meaning. It may be that Mozart's life was a profoundly unhappy one—he was certainly unfortunate in his environment, far more unfortunate than Beethoven, for he never had Beethoven's comparative financial security, nor did he ever enjoy such appreciative and discriminating friends. It is probable that his extreme sensitiveness in unfavourable surroundings caused him great suffering, and that he was unfortunate in his relations with women ; but such in varying degree are the trials of all artists of genius, and I do not think they will account for the peculiar, all-pervading, transparent gloom of Mozart's music. I am not even sure that ' gloom ' and ' melancholy ' are the right words to use. Mozart is very mysterious—far more mysterious than Beethoven, because his music seems to express much less of his human character. I believe that Mozart's personal life was a failure. In his last years he abandoned himself to frivolous gaiety. Without being dissipated, he wasted his time and strength upon masked balls, dancing, feasting, and idle gallantry. It is impossible to believe that he found such a life satisfactory. Why, then, did he pursue it ? Mozart was not without that sense of spiritual life which we call religious. On the contrary, he had this sense as highly developed as his sense of humour—he was no La Rochefoucauld. The *Requiem*, *The Magic Flute*, *Don Giovanni*, the *Twelfth Mass*, and a great deal of purely instrumental music exist to prove it. If it were not so, Mozart would be enormously less important. But Mozart obviously lacked that quiet, steady, flaming faith which burns so intensely in Bach and Beethoven. This is the secret of that all-pervading gloom, that quiet hopelessness. I do not mean, merely, that Mozart was a child of the eighteenth century and consequently a realist and a sceptic. The true eighteenth-century man of the world is not troubled by any religious feelings at all ; he entirely lacks spiritual sensibility. All men are materialists, because all life is ' matter', even if that ' matter ' resolve itself into positive and negative electricity—though God alone knows what that means ! But ' matter ' varies in its sentient power. One piece of matter, ' Mr. A ' can see but cannot hear, he is deaf, for him sounds do not exist ; another piece of matter ' Mr. B ' hears but cannot see ; another, ' Mr. C ' hears *and* sees but is colour-blind : for him colours do not exist, yet he, living among the blind and deaf, may easily convince himself that he misses nothing, and that these ' colours ' of which a few odd people talk, are fantastic or sentimental illusions. This is the position of the true eighteenth-century ' materialist '. Mozart was not one of these ; he was vividly aware of the spiritual colours of life, they were to him as concrete as heat and cold. But something else was lacking. I am conscious of it, but I do not quite know how to describe it. I can only point to Beethoven's Ninth Symphony and declare that I find it unmistakably present there. Mozart could not have written the last movement of that symphony. He was not capable of it. It expresses an emotion he had never felt. To describe this emotion as ' joy ' is utterly inadequate and ridiculous. It is a spiritual sublimity which surpasses in value all other human emotions, and which only the few supreme spirits of this earth have ever expressed. In many millions of years from now, men—if there are still men or descendants of men living on this planet—may be able to explain in biological terms the value of this emotion ; or, rather, it will have become intelligible to them—as the value of the abstract feeling for justice is to-day becoming intelligible. At present it is the rare emotional possession of the few, but nothing can prevent its slowly dominating mankind. Its power is irresistible because it is latent in us all. Bach and Beethoven knew this, and therefore—to use the extraordinarily apt and suggestive words of the Jacobean translators of the old Hebrew folk-tales—they ' walked with God '. Mozart did not. Mozart danced with the masked daughters of Vienna and wasted his spirit, not in passion or in sudden excesses of lust—which might not have harmed him, which might even have been beneficial to him—but in the aimless dissipation of the man without faith. This spiritual ' faith ' in which Beethoven and Bach lived is altogether different from that romantic faith in themselves which came into fashion for artists and men of genius in Europe at the beginning of the nineteenth century, when Napoleon began to talk about his ' star ' and Byron set the fashion of extravagant, egoistic gestures. Bach had none of this, and in so far as Beethoven indulged in it it did him harm. Mozart was not handicapped through having lived before the invention of that comfortable padded cell of the soul, that lotus-island, the Nietzschean vanity of the superman-artist ; and of all artists who have ever lived Mozart was least likely to fall a victim to such a snare. He had too penetrating an intelligence, too keen a sense of humour. No, he was deficient in an active power which Beethoven and Bach possessed, and I think he was deficient in nothing else. In all else he was indeed superior to Beethoven and Bach, and, consequently, to all others.

But now that I have put my finger on what I believe to be the radical weakness of Mozart, and have given my explanation of the melancholy of his music—namely, that Mozart had extreme spiritual sensitiveness but no spiritual faith in life (and by that I do not mean acceptance of any theological dogma)—I think I can give a different interpretation of one of Mozart's apparent failures. In Professor Donald Tovey's brilliant article on ' Sonata Form ' in the *Encyclopædia Britannica*, he says : ' The sonata style never lost with him (Mozart) its dramatic character, but while it was capable of pathos, excitement and even vehemence, it could not concern itself with catastrophes and tragic climaxes '. He then goes on to say that the G minor Symphony shows poignant feeling, but that it is not an embodiment of sad experiences. So far Professor Tovey, although writing about the ' sonata form ', is accusing Mozart of a lack of emotional content, but then he continues : ' In the still more profound and pathetic G minor quintet we see Mozart for once transcending his limits. The slow movement rises to a height not surpassed by Beethoven

himself until his second period ; *an adequate finale is
unattainable with Mozart's resources, and he knows it.*'
But in what way, may one ask, has Mozart transcended
his limits in this work if the slow movement only rises
to a height surpassed by Beethoven in his *second* period
and his resources do not admit of his writing an
adequate finale ?

That the slow movement of the G minor quintet is surpassed by Beethoven in his second period I should be
inclined to deny.   That the technical resources of the
man who wrote that wonderful allegro, that astonishing
minuet, that rich and tragic slow movement, and those
poignant introductory bars were inadequate to a satisfactory finale is to me unbelievable.   That Mozart—
whose technical mastery at every point surpasses Beethoven's in the opinion of, I should imagine, ninety-nine per
cent. of scholars—should have been incapable of satis-
factorily *concluding* an admitted masterpiece through
lack of technical resource is completely unconvincing.
What, then, does Professor Tovey mean ?   Let us
examine that last movement of the G minor quintet.
What is wrong with it ?   In my opinion, this : Mozart
has written a really great work, he has taken plenty of
room, the design of the quintet is magnificently spacious,
and he can fill it.   Not only has he all the technical
resources necessary—to talk of Mozart ever lacking technical resources seems to me ludicrous—but he is in the
rich, abundant, creative mood to fill it, and so to fill it
that it strikes Professor Tovey as ' profound and
pathetic '—words which he does not use lightly.   The
third movement, *Adagio*, is tragic in its intensity.   But
what, then, happens ?   Mozart concludes with a finale,
light, sparkling, and gay, but once more masking an
abyss of black melancholy.   A finale that is utterly
inadequate—admitted !   But why inadequate ?   It is not
technically inadequate.   To spin that light-hearted
gossamer *allegro* so that, after what we had heard, it

should captivate and delude, not shock and disgust, the listener, called for that technical skill which Mozart alone possessed. But, still, inadequate ! That finale is beyond all denial inadequate. Why ? Because after the poignant, heart-breaking intensity of the slow movement some affirmation of the soul is inexorably demanded. *Mozart could not make that affirmation.* He could not even attempt to make it. If he had attempted but had failed, *then* we could speak of inadequate resources. But he had no faith, he could not lift up his heart and sing from the bottom of that abyss, he could not stretch his wings and rise up out of it, he could only shrug his shoulders and blow us another bubble. Therefore, and therefore only, he is not the world's greatest composer.

FRANZ SCHUBERT
(1797-1828)
By Donald Francis Tovey

FRANZ SCHUBERT, the youngest of five sur-
vivors of the fourteen children of a parish schoolmaster, was born at Vienna on January 31st, 1797,
and died there on November 19th, 1828. It is not
plausible to write optimistically of a life thus cut short
before its struggles with poverty have achieved more
than moments of present success and remote hopes of
future security. And musical biographies are specially
intractable material for writers and readers who wish to
take a view of life which is neither dismal nor patronising.
The musician is usually quite as sociable as most artists ;
but his art is more of a mystery to the world at large, even
where it is most praised, than any other art ; and the
biographer finds singularly little help from the musician's
contact with other interesting people. In the vast scheme
of Goethe's general culture music had as high a place as
a man with no ear for anything but verse could be
expected to give it ; but the one famous meeting
between Beethoven and Goethe reveals nothing except
that Goethe disliked Beethoven's manners nearly as
much as Lord Chesterfield disliked Johnson's, and that
Beethoven more than suspected Goethe of being a snob.
Beethoven is easily the most interesting personality in
purely musical biography ; nor perhaps need he be
denied that supremacy even if we regard Wagner as a
mere musician. Schubert, Beethoven's junior by seventeen years, was a shy man, and almost every anecdote
that is told of him shows him in some pathetic position
of failure to make his way. Let me tell a new one. There
is a curious English musical dictionary published in 1827
which may sometimes be found in the fourpenny box
outside a second-hand bookshop ; and in this dictionary
Beethoven is given one of the largest articles and treated

as unquestionably the greatest composer of the day (though on the evidence only of his less dangerous works). Such was Beethoven's fame in the year of his death. Schubert died in the next year. There are five Schuberts in this dictionary, but Franz Schubert is not among them. When I showed this dictionary to Joachim he remarked that it was a pity that there was not a Franz Schubert in it ; because as a matter of fact there was another Franz Schubert early in the nineteenth century, whose publisher once wrote to him enclosing a song that had just been issued by another firm, as being by Franz Schubert, which, if true, constituted a breach of agreement which the publisher was the less ready to credit since the song was not only marked as Opus 1, but entirely lacked the smoothness of Herr Schubert's accomplished and esteemed pen. Herr Schubert replied with some stiffness that he was glad his publisher did not feel ready to impute to him the authorship of this wretched production. The ' *Machwerk* ' in question was Schubert's *Erlkönig*.

From such portents it is easy to infer a tragic picture of neglected and hopeless genius. But these are accidents, thrown into undue prominence by the crowning accident of early death from typhus fever in poor circumstances. Modern sanitation, to say nothing of modern medicine, has made typhus fever a rare cause of death. But we are unduly optimistic if we imagine that a musical genius of Schubert's calibre has a better chance of success before thirty-one at the present day. When we are invited to show indignation at the barbarity of an age which made Schubert consent to part with a dozen of his finest songs at a krone apiece, and with his great E flat Trio for about seventeen shillings and sixpence, we may as well begin by asking the Carnegie Trustees what their experience shows them as to the modern composer's opportunities for getting his works published at all. Schubert's early death during a struggle with poverty is too sad for us to waste our emotion on details which indicate, if they indicate anything, that he lived at a period of exceptional opportunities for young and obscure men of musical genius. In literary biography a brave standard of tragic and moral values was established, at all events for English readers, by the giant who in his own person brought forth the exodus of literature from Grub Street and gave the death-blow to the system of patronage. Musical biography did not begin to attract the attention of otherwise cultured people until the dogmas of the Eccentricity of Genius and the Virtues of the Deserving Poor had brought into our moral currency a new kind of patronage, equally remote from good breeding and good science. Biography is not to the purpose of the present essay ; and in any case a musician's work is, more than that of most artists, far more important than the events of his life. All the more necessary, then, is it to dismiss from our minds certain prepossessions which originated at a time when music, not being taken seriously by the educated Englishman, was alternately revered as a religious mystery and set forth biographically and historically as a charitable investigation in slum-life. If Forster had written his ' Life and Times of Goldsmith ' on the lines that have determined popular notions of the lives of Beethoven and Schubert, he would have produced one of the dismallest books in the English language. The bare facts of that delightful biography amount to a career far more miserable than the facts about Schubert. Sir George Grove played a distinguished part in collecting both the works and the biographical records of Schubert ; and his article in the ' Dictionary of Music and Musicians ' is, with all its indignation at Schubert's fate, such a summary of Schubert's friendships, hopes, interests and activities as can leave the careful reader no excuse for imagining that the pathos of Schubert's life was the pathos of misery. But Grove's enthusiasm in his researches left him no

leisure to realise the need of warning the general reader
explicitly against the prevalent dismal tone of early nine-
teenth-century musical biographies ; and in any short
biographical survey the heartrending facts about the
deaths of Mozart, Beethoven and Schubert inevitably
dominate the narrative. On the other hand, works on a
larger scale, which might restore the balance by a fuller
record of the composer's conversation and daily life,
find no Johnsonian club-records to help them. It is
remarkable that within the compass of his dictionary
article Grove has achieved an attractive picture of Schubert, incessantly composing ; the acknowledged tyrant
of a host of adoring friends ; hopeless and helpless in
argument, but the possessor of the glorious nickname of
' Kanevas,' since his invariable question about any pro-
spective new acquaintance was, ' Kann er was ? ' or
' What's he good at ? '*

On the other hand, Schubert presented an elusive
problem to the enlightened and musical Viennese aristocracy that did so well by Beethoven. In Beethoven's
republican pride Archdukes could recognise the call of
' noblesse oblige ' without the need of his superb gesture
when (being questioned in the law-courts as to the prefix
' van ' in his name) he pointed to his head and heart,
saying, ' My nobility is *here* and *here*.' But the difficulty
with Schubert was that he evidently preferred the
servants' hall, where he, the son of a parish schoolmaster and sometime schoolmaster himself, could be at
friendly ease with everybody, to the drawing-room of
Count Johann Esterhazy at Zselesz, where ' no one cares
for true Art, unless now and again the Countess.' It is
the more necessary to take warning against indulging in
too miserable a view of Schubert's struggle with poverty,
since Grove himself is stung by the tragedy of the end

*This, though not a literal translation, is the only idomatic English
I can find for a locution in which ' Können,' the ability, is intimately
linked with ' Kennen,' the knowledge.

into an outburst of anger at Schubert's friends. The anger is not ungenerous, and nobody will wish to minimise the tragedy. But *is* it clear that ' with his astonishing power of production the commonest care would have ensured him a good living '—even in those days when a publisher could actually be found for a setting of the *Erlkönig* with an accompaniment which the finest pianists of to-day cannot master without either long practice or some way of evading its difficulties ? The worst of this angry view of Schubert's outward circumstances is that it proceeds from and fosters an unwarrantable optimism as to the conditions of modern musical life. There will never be many Schuberts, even among men of genius ; but in all the arts there have been, before and since, and there are now and will be in future, many worse tragedies. The conclusion, then, remains that there is not the slightest reason to hope that now or in future, a genius of Schubert's calibre will have any better chance of recognition before the age of thirty-one. Even in Utopia there will be room for accidents.

In approaching Schubert's work something has been gained when we have discarded notions that confuse pathos with misery and mischance with culpable neglect. But more serious difficulties await us in the criteria of form and style by which his work has been judged. Here, again, it would be as misleading a paradox to assert that Schubert was a perfect master of musical form as to assert that his career was prosperous ; but we have also here to deal with current errors far more radical and definite than the vague false proportions of a biographic treatment true as to fact, the result of patient research, and mistaken only in the inexperienced emotional tone of a more comfortable phase of life and culture.

Certain criteria of musical form have been fixed with an illusory decision by the extraordinary number and perfection of a series of instrumental compositions by three great masters whose lives overlapped each other

and whose mature works were all produced within the
eighty years beginning at the middle of the eighteenth
century. No great misunderstanding need have arisen
from thus basing our laws of musical form on the works
of the Haydn-Mozart-Beethoven triumvirate (as we base
the laws of Greek tragedy on what we know of Æschylus,
Sophocles and Euripides), if it were not for the fact
that purely musical phenomena are difficult to describe
in any but technical words. The description of a
developed musical form is, even with the aid of technical
terms, a bulky statement which fills the mind to repletion
without giving much real information. When we say
that the ground-plan of most cathedrals is cruciform,
nobody imagines that the statement is either abstruse or
indicative of a large number of conventional rules and
restraints on the architect's liberty. Add to it the mention of a spire, dome, or towers, and specify the aisles,
and still you will have nothing which anybody supposes
to be profoundly technical. Even the orientation of the
building raises no question greatly beyond the intelligence of a child who knows his right hand from his left.
But these architectural facts already amount to notions
fully as definite as all that musical text-books have ever
inculcated as to sonata form. If elementary architectural
concepts were definable only in mathematical terms we
might over-estimate their artificiality as grossly as we at
present over-estimate the rigidity of the art-forms of
classical music. But in reality the sense of key-relationship in music is on the same level of thought as the elementary topographical sense that enables us to enjoy the
symmetries of architecture. The method and scope
change from age to age ; an ancient Greek would be even
more shocked than an eighteenth-century Englishman
of ' classical ' taste at the barbarities of Gothic architecture ; and Palestrina would, on first acquaintance, find
the harmonic banality and coarseness of Mozart and of
all classical instrumental music so shocking that he

would hardly notice that Beethoven, Schubert, or even Wagner could aggravate or modify the anarchy. Such is the normal first impression of the art of a later period as seen from the point of view of an earlier period. It is thus no question here of ' immutable laws of art ' ; but it is a question of permanent categories. If these categories are describable only in such untranslated technical terms as *counterpoint* and *tonality*, and if such vernacular words as *harmony*, *rhythm*, and *form* develop technical meanings which are at once narrow and ill-defined, who shall set limits to the possibilities of plausible nonsense in musical history and education ?

Schubert's masters at the *Convict* or court-chapel choir-school have been severely blamed for neglecting his education and allowing him to compose without restraint. One of these masters left on record the honest remark that when he tried to teach Schubert anything, he found the boy knew it already. It is evidently dangerous to leave such remarks lying about where the directors of later institutes of musical education can get at them. But we are not justified in inferring that the master really taught Schubert nothing. And there is abundant evidence that the child taught himself with remarkable concentration, if not with severity. One of the most trying tasks ever imposed on a young musician is that still recommended by some very high authorities, which consists of composing an instrumental movement that follows, phrase by phrase, the proportions and modulations of a selected classical model. It might be objected to this exercise that it is unlikely to reveal the inner necessity of the original form of a purely instrumental piece ; but this objection would lose force if the exercise were ever applied to vocal, and especially to dramatic music, with its cogent outward necessities. Now the earliest song of Schubert that we possess is ' Hagar's Klage,' an enormous rigmarole with at least twelve movements and innumerable changes of key ;

evidently (one would guess) a typical example of childish diffuseness. It turns out, however, to be accurately modelled, modulations and all, on a setting of the same poem by Zumsteeg, a composer of some historical importance as a pioneer in the art of setting dramatic narrative for voice with pianoforte accompaniment. The same is the case with several other songs ; and Mandy-czewski has printed three of Zumsteeg's original settings in his complete edition of Schubert's songs, so that we can see how this child of thirteen was spending his time. Zumsteeg, by the way, was no fool. Yet even within the limits of *Hagar's Klage* Schubert makes decisive pro-gress, beginning by following his model closely until about the middle of the work. At this point Zumsteeg's energy begins to flag, and the child's energy begins to rise. Schubert's declamation improves, and before he has finished his long task he has achieved a sense of climax and a rounding-off which Zumsteeg hardly seems to have imagined possible. Song-writing, whether on a large or a small scale, was still in its infancy. A few masterpieces appear sporadically among the experiments, themselves few and heterogeneous, of Haydn, Mozart and Beethoven. The real development of the art-forms of song was worked out by the child Schubert with the same fierce concentration as that with which the child Mozart laid the foundations of his sonata forms.

Within four years from this first attempt to ' play the sedulous ape,' Schubert had written three stout volumes of songs of all shapes and sizes, besides a still larger quantity of instrumental music. A professional copyist might wonder how the bulk was achieved by one penman within the time. And as the songs lead up to and include *Gretchen am Spinnrade* and *Erlkönig*, it seems futile to blame Schubert's teachers for not teaching him more before he was seventeen. The maturity of this famous couple of masterpieces remains as miraculous when we know the mass of work by which the boy trained himself for them as when we know them only in isolation. *Gretchen am Spinnrade*, the earlier of the two, is an even more astonishing achievement than *Erlkönig*. There is no difficulty in understanding how the possibilities of *Erlkönig* would fire the imagination of any boy, though only a genius could control to artistic form the imagination thus fired. Schubert's *Erlkönig* is as eminently a masterpiece in musical form as in powerful illustration of the poem. It has the singular luck to be rivalled, and to some tastes surpassed by Loewe's setting, a work not much later in date but more in touch with modern methods. Loewe brings out the rationalistic vein of Goethe's ballad by setting the Erl-king's words to a mere ghostly bugle-call which never leaves the notes of its one chord. Schubert uses melodies as pretty as the Erl-king's promises. In other words, Loewe's point of view is that of the father assuring the fever-stricken child that the Erl-king, with his daughter and his whisperings, are nothing but the marsh-mists and the wind in the trees ; while Schubert, like the child, remains unconvinced by the explanation. His terror is the child's ; Loewe's terror is the father's. Schubert has already, at the age of seventeen, mastered one of his cardinal principles of song-writing, which is that wherever some permanent feature can be found in the background of the poem, that feature shall dominate the background of the music. The result is that, after all, he naïvely achieves a more complete setting of the poem with his purely musical apparatus than Loewe with his rational adroitness. Loewe has almost forgotten that the father, with his child in his arms, is riding at full gallop in the hope of reaching shelter before the marsh-fever takes its toll. Schubert, composing, like Homer, ' with his eye on the object,' represents the outward and visible situation by means of an ' accompaniment ' the adequate performance of which is one of the rarest *tours de force* in pianoforte playing. (Liszt's transcription of *Erlkönig* as a concert-

solo is far easier, for the added fireworks give relief to
the player's wrists.) But Schubert's accompaniment also
realises the inward and spiritual situation. With the
Erl-king's speeches the accompaniment, while still
maintaining its pace, takes forms which instantly transfer
the sense of movement from that of a thing seen by the
spectator to that of the dazed and frightened child in the
rider's arms. To some critics this may seem a small
point ; but it is decisive, not of the superiority of one
version over the other, but of the completeness of
Schubert's view. Against it all cavil at the ' prettiness '
of the Erl-king's melodies is as futile as a cavil against
the prettiness of the Erl-king's words. Schubert at
seventeen is a mature master of the ironies of tragedy and
of nature. He is also a better realist than Loewe. The
change in the point of view at the Erl-king's speeches is
a matter of fact ; nobody but the child heard them, and
only the father or tha narrator could have recognised
that they had no more substance than can be musically
represented by Loewe's chord of G major. This does
not dispose of Loewe's achievement as a work of genius
on lines inadequately recognised until recent times ; but
it shows the futility of attacking a great composer like
Schubert on the *a priori* assumption that the declamation
and illustration of words is at variance with the claims
of purely musical form. When we have got rid of this
assumption we shall be in a better position to see the
true origins of the classical forms of music, and, inci-
dentally, to follow the methods by which Schubert provided himself with a musical education.

Gretchen am Spinnrade is a far more astonishing
achievement for a boy of seventeen than *Erlkönig*. If,
for the sake of argument, we summon up the naïve
impertinence to ask where this shy choir-boy, absorbed
incessantly in writing and only just out of school, could
have obtained the experience, not of Faust, but of the
victim of Faust and Mephistopheles, the answer is not

E

easily guessed ; for *Faust*, though published, had not yet been presented on the stage. But plenty of good drama was cultivated in Viennese theatres, and we need not suppose that Schubert avoided it. He then kept his eye on the object, in this case the spinning-wheel. And he knew, as Parry has admirably pointed out in ' The Art of Music,' not only that the climax comes at the words ' Und ach ! sein Kuss ! ' but that with that climax the spinning is interrupted, and resumed only with difficulty. With these points settled, all that remains to be postulated is the possession of a noble and totally unsophisticated style, together with some individual power of modulation to secure variety in simplicity throughout a song which is too dramatic to be set to repetitions of a single strophic melody. The style Schubert already had ; the individual power of modulation shows itself at the third line of the poem. Before Schubert, only Beethoven would have thought of moving from D minor to C major and straight back again without treating C as the dominant of F. This modulation is here entirely Schubert's own, for the influence of Beethoven on Schubert had not at this time produced in him any direct result beyond a decided opinion that Beethoven was responsible for the ' bizarrerie ' of most contemporary music. Beethoven and Schubert were, in fact, developing the resources of key-relationship on idential principles ; but this fact is not one that ever appears in the guise of any external points of their styles. Schubert's idolatry at this time was devoted to Mozart ; and in the art-forms of song there was even less room for Mozart's style than for Beethoven's. With the forms of opera and of instrumental music the position was very different ; and, now that we have illustrated Schubert's amazing early maturity in the pioneer work of the song with pianoforte accompaniment, it is time to direct our attention to his work in other and older art-forms.

If one half of the six hundred odd songs of Schubert's

whole life's work are to be regarded as waste products, then Schubert, as a song-writer, must rank as an economical and concentrated artist. To estimate the wastage as high as one half is the limit of severity. By this I do not mean to imply that three hundred of Schubert's songs are masterpieces. In all such matters the fruitful criterion is not perfection but intrinsic significance ; and certainly at least three hundred of Schubert's songs have intrinsic significance. Most of the waste products have, on the other hand, historic significance, as we have seen in the case of *Hagar's Klage*. What, then, is the position of the equally vast bulk of Schubert's juvenile work in larger and older forms ?

Here, if anywhere, we may suspect, as Schubert's contemporaries already complained, that Schubert would have been the better of a firmer guiding hand. But it is no easy matter to name anybody who could have done better for Schubert than his adoring and bewildered masters at the *Convict*. It is a great mistake to suppose that any master living in 1810 could teach a young composer of instrumental music the genuine art-forms of Haydn and Mozart. There was Beethoven, who was enormously expanding and apparently revolutionising those forms ; there was Mozart's best pupil Hummel, who was inflating certain safe and imitable procedures of Mozart's by means of a pianoforte technique far too brilliant for anything those procedures had in purpose ; and there was Spohr, who was doing much the same thing far better than Hummel by means of a really beautiful violin technique as yet unspoilt by his cloying later mannerisms. These were, to all appearance, the great masters in such forms ; and they are, in fact, almost the only names prominent enough for modern criticism to scoff at. The great Cherubini was totally outside the classical tradition of instrumental music ; Clementi had already retired to London in 1810, and was probably remembered in Vienna mainly by the hard brilliance of his technique in the days of his 'tournament' with Mozart in 1781. On what lines were the art-forms of instrumental music taught in Schubert's boyhood? I have never seen this question asked, and do not expect to see it answered. All I know is that to this day it would be invidious to specify the few text-books on these forms that do not consist mainly of platitudes deviating only into such mis-statements as must make the book demoralising to any observant child who tries to learn from it. In Schubert's day there was certainly no more a received method of teaching the art-forms of Mozart than there is to-day a received method of teaching those of Wagner and Richard Strauss. The only item of musical education which Beethoven's teacher Albrechtsberger called 'composition' was what is now called 'counterpoint'; it was not as yet in the shocking tangle of arbitrary and unenlightened rule-of-thumb to which it degenerated during the later nineteenth century; but it was already dangerously remote from its original living sixteenth-century practice, no less than from the art-language of instrumental music. Sir George Grove is very angry with one of Schubert's older friends for encouraging his larger efforts when ' he had better have taught him some counterpoint.' Later on, Grove very rightly draws attention to the magnificence of Schubert's basses. That settles the question : a composer whose basses are magnificent is a great contrapuntist, even if (like Wagner) he never published a fugue in his life. Nor is the case weakened by Schubert producing some obviously unsuccessful fugues towards the end of his short career ; and still less is it weakened by the fact of the awakening which the reading of the works of Handel effected in him, and the resulting determination to go through a course of counterpoint with Sechter, a project frustrated by Schubert's own untimely death. The grammatical exercise nowadays called counterpoint contributes nothing beyond brick-making towards the architecture of a fugue ; and the text-book rules of fugue as an art-form are usually based on a scheme, best known in the form drawn up by Cherubini in his text-book, which completely ignores both Handel (who has, in fact, no scheme that could be generalised), and Bach, whose last work, *Die Kunst des Fuge*, was a series of scientifically classified fugues. Doubtless in Schubert's days at the *Convict* ' counterpoint ' was among the things which his honest teachers ' found he knew already.' From Sechter he hoped to get something very different from a belated filling-up of gaps in his primary schooling. Sechter was a researching scholar who knew his six-teenth century. Even Beethoven was attracted by him, long after he had, for somewhat similar reasons, left Haydn for the more painstaking and systematic Albrechtsberger, who, being neither a genius nor sympa-thetic to Beethoven, nevertheless knew how to explain matters of scholarship. It may surprise some readers to know that within living memory Brahms, whose early works already show him to be easily the greatest contra-puntist since Mozart, took keen pleasure, after he was fifty, in working at counterpoint with Nottebohm, the scholar to whom we owe the deciphering of Beethoven's sketch-books. Real scholarship will always attract men of genius ; but it is almost as rare as genius itself. The sanity of true genius may, as often as not, rightly revolt against tradition ; but there is no revolting against knowledge.

Now, just as Schubert's juvenile work in song-writing culminates at seventeen in *Gretchen am Spinnrade* and *Erlkönig*, so does the equally huge pile of work in larger forms culminate, at the same age, in the *Mass in F*. The doyen of English theorists, the late Ebenezer Prout, has called this work the most remarkable first Mass next to the First Mass of Beethoven ; thereby paying a pious tribute to the greatest of musical names ; for the most remarkable thing about Beethoven's First Mass is that Beethoven, entering on the full swing of his ' second period,' should have spared the energy to finish a work which contains hardly a feature that expresses anything but inhibitions. Schubert's First Mass is, in its way, a not less astonishing phenomenon than *Erlkönig* ; and it is far more perfect in form, and even in style, than the ambitious efforts of his later years, the Masses in A flat and E flat. Prout quotes one of the fugues *in extenso*, and dubs it a very creditable performance, open to no criticism except that the voices are too low at the opening. I am not acquainted with any models Schubert can have had for the very definite style of church music he here achieves. Possibly he had heard a mass or two by Cherubini, whom Beethoven considered the greatest composer of the age, who visited Vienna in the train of Napoleon, and whose church music is the only first-rate work of the period that shows the faintest resemblance to the peculiar fragrant piety of Schubert's Masses. There is nothing remotely like it in the church music of either Mozart or Haydn. The triumphant performance of this important choral and orchestral work by the choir of Schubert's school was an experience such as very few modern conservatoire students can obtain at the age of seventeen. A year afterwards Schubert wrote a more ' effective ' *Dona Nobis* in the form of a vigorous final fugue. In the same way English Doctors of Music have been known to spoil a poetically conceived oratorio or cantata by a final fugue, in order to satisfy the examiners. In the critical edition of Schubert's complete works this second *Dona Nobis* is rightly relegated to the appendix.

We must return to Schubert's Masses later. Some readers may be surprised to hear that the next topic that concerns us with Schubert at seventeen is his operas. His first, *Des Teufels Lustschloss*, is historically more important than appearances might indicate. The libretto seems hopelessly silly, but it stands under the name of Kotzebue, who was a writer of quite clever comedies which Jane Austen would have enjoyed ; and its idea is traceable back to *The Castle of Otranto*, much as parts of *Northanger Abbey* are traceable to *The Mysteries of Udolpho*. Kotzebue, however, has here failed to show any of his sense of humour, and Schubert never attempted burlesque ; his slightly later imitations of Rossini (the overtures ' in Italian style ') developing into sincere flattery rather than caricature. But the interesting thing about the music of *Des Teufels Lustschloss*, apart from one or two successful passages, is that the young Schubert took the trouble to revise it and to go to Salieri for lessons in Italian operatic style and method. Herein he followed the example of Beethoven, who had gone to Salieri for the same purpose some twenty years earlier, and who, while grumbling that Haydn had taught him nothing, took pride and pleasure in calling himself Salieri's pupil. No view of either Beethoven's or Schubert's development can be trustworthy which fails to account for the zest into which these mighty men of genius put themselves into Salieri's hands. Salieri had the misfortune to have shown jealousy of Mozart ; and it seems certain that at a time when a word from him to the Emperor might have improved Mozart's position, Salieri not only missed the opportunity but intrigued against him. Be this as it may, his retribution was appalling. Mozart died young and in straitened circumstances, and gossip said that Salieri had poisoned him. This was a wild slander ; but even within living memory Rimsky-Korsakov wrote an opera *Mozart and Salieri* which I do not know except in very charming quotations, but which only the vainest of hopes could expect to deal with anything so dramatically ineffective as a refutation of the slander. On Salieri himself the slander must have weighed cruelly ; for when he was dying he sent for Moscheles in order to say these words— ' I did not poison Mozart.' So even the friendship of Beethoven and Schubert, both of whom must have heard and contemptuously ignored this inhuman gossip,

did not avail to bring peace to the old man's mind.
Now, what was it that Salieri could teach these great
composers ? Here the significant point in Salieri's history is that when Gluck, at the end of his life, found
himself unable to carry out his last project, an opera
entitled *Les Danaides*, he handed the task over to Salieri.
This proves that he could trust Salieri to set dramatic
situations as well as words. And the reader may verify
this without taking the trouble to investigate Salieri's
own work further than by playing the theme of one of the
best of Beethoven's early sets of variations, those upon
' *La stessa, la stessissima*,' from Salieri's *Falstaff*. Any
opera on the subject of Falstaff must take its plot from
The Merry Wives of Windsor ; for no coherent story
can be made from the genuine Falstaff of the two parts
of *King Henry the Fourth*, though it may be possible to
transfer his best speeches to the perfunctory dupe of the
merry wives, as we may learn from Boito and Verdi.
Now, the first situation in *The Merry Wives of Windsor*
is the meeting of Mrs. Ford and Mrs. Page after they
have received identical love-letters from Falstaff. ' *La
stessa, la stessissima* '—here you see them comparing
notes (' the same, the very same ! ') in Salieri's theme as
recorded in simple pianoforte terms by Beethoven. You
can see them pointing from one letter to the other in
symmetrical phrases ; and in the disruption of symmetry with the truncated second part of the tune you
can identify the burst of laughter, the quick scolding
phrase in which vengeance is vowed, and the derisive
triumphant gesture with which the letters are flourished
in the air. You can see also that though Salieri shows no
profound musical invention in this trivial affair, he is no
formalist. To Beethoven and Schubert it was unimportant that Salieri was jealous of the brilliance of
Mozart and warned his pupils against the poetry of
Goethe. In these high matters they could take care of
themselves ; Salieri was neither a preoccupied man of

genius nor a pedant, but a clever and highly-cultured
Italian musician with the will and the power to give
practical and interesting information.

The fruit of Salieri's teaching is clearly shown in
Schubert's early operas. The outward course of events
is that the operatic stage had a fascination for Schubert,
that grew in proportion to the disappointments it brought
on him. As his talent for work on a large scale matured
so did his grasp of dramatic movement in theatre-music
weaken, and the only operas which it has recently been
found possible to rescue from the wreckage of his
fourteen efforts in this art-form are the one-act *Der
Vierjährige Posten*, written soon after the Mass in F, and
Die Verschworenen, written in 1820 and showing how he
applied his riper musical style to the technique of
Salieri. We must return to the operas and their grave
defects later ; at present our concern is to note that
while Schubert's whole development and the mightiest
influences of his time drew him steadily and fatally away
from the solution of the problem of dramatic movement
in stage-music, he had nevertheless as a mere boy eagerly
and successfully learnt from Salieri an admirable light
theatrical style ; a thing totally different from the style
of his songs. He could not set an action to music ; but
he could set a dialogue. His own contemporaries said
of him that he could set an advertisement to music ; and
the statement has a higher truth than the implication
that words did not matter to him. It means that he had
exhaustively mastered the inwardness of musical sym-
bolism ; and Salieri was the last teacher of the great
Italian tradition that had steadily viewed music from
that centre ever since the time of Palestrina and earlier.
Pseudo-classicism, opposing itself to helpless experiment and *a priori* theory, occupied the whole field of
musical education as soon as teachers formed the futile
ambition to teach ' composition ' in larger and more
abstract senses than that of musical rhetoric.

Schubert's boyhood, then, culminated in two of his most powerful songs, a uniquely charming piece of church-music, and an almost equally pretty one-act opera (*Der Vierjährige Posten*). In his early instrumental music there is nothing so important, though the quantity is not less enormous. The earliest pieces, including the earliest string quartets, are fantasies of such ubiquitous rambling that the catalogue-maker cannot specify their keys. Some of them may possibly be regarded as Zumsteeg ballads without words ; but why should we allow the young Schubert no child's-play at all ? Music paper was always as necessary to him as food and coals ; the *Convict* afforded very insufficient supplies of all three. The mastery he so early attained in vocal music already stultifies all aspersions on his early training ; and his early instrumental works do not alter the case. We are right in thinking that his maturest works in large instrumental forms are diffuse and inconsistent ; but, apart from the earliest child's-play, the quartets and symphonies of his adolescence show, as often as not, the opposite tendency, being for the most part stiff exercises in the outward forms of Mozart with a certain boyish charm of hero-worship in their melodies. The stiffness is anything but Mozartean ; it is, in fact, the typical angularity of a conscientious student. Six symphonies, about a dozen string quartets, another dozen of pianoforte sonatas, and a vast number of fragments, show him pursuing a consistent line of work, of observation and experiment ; if with ideas in his head, then so much the better for the result ; if without, then so much the better for the practice. It is quite a mistake to suppose that any contemporary master could have pointed out to Schubert where he went wrong. Beethoven himself, in whom Schubert's work aroused a lively interest which would assuredly have led to historic consequences if both composers had lived a few years longer, made no criticisms on points of form, though he had before him some of the larger works, on which he could and would, with time for reflection, have spoken out of the fullness of his own experience. At all events Schubert's instrumental music did not begin to go definitely ' wrong ' until it began to be as definitely and prophetically right as his best songs. There is nothing of first-rate importance to mention here until we reach the work of his last nine years of life. Our discussion up to this point has aimed at removing certain grave current misconceptions and substituting for them a more reasoned account of Schubert's early development. The ground being thus cleared, we need not attempt any chronological or otherwise systematic account of the rest of Schubert's works ; it will suffice to quote, for the most part from well-known masterpieces, such points as illustrate the full range of his musical thought up to the time of his death.

The first instrumental work which shows his peculiar power beginning to rise up against his greatest weakness of form is the ambitious quintet in A major for the unusual combination of pianoforte, violin, viola, violoncello and double bass. It is known as the ' Forellenquintet ' because the fourth of its five movements (the most perfect, though not the most important) is a set of variations on his pretty song *Die Forelle* (' The Trout '). The Scherzo is another successful movement in one of those small melodic and sectional forms which nobody denies to be thoroughly within Schubert's grasp. But the important things are the first movement, the slow movement in F, and the Finale. In all three cases the first half of the movement is the boldly drawn exposition of a design on the grandest scale, while the rest, with the exception of a well-managed modicum of development in the first movement, is a mere exact recapitulation of this exposition starting in such a key as to end in the tonic. In the first movement and in the finale Schubert adds insult to the crudity of this procedure by giving the usual direction that the exposition shall be repeated !

Now, the sonata forms, which are here in question, depend largely on the balance and distinction between three typical organic members ; an exposition, a development, and a recapitulation. Of these, the most delicate is the recapitulation, on which the symmetry of the whole depends. In works like the *Forellen-quintet* Schubert was exhausted by the effort of his grand expositions and fell back with relief upon a mere copyist's task by way of recapitulation. This was wrong ; but the *a priori* theorist is not less wrong who regards extensive recapitulation as a weakness in the classical schemes. There is no surer touchstone of Schubert's, as of Mozart's, Beethoven's, and Brahms's, treatment of form, than the precise way in which their recapitulations differ from their expositions ; and where Schubert is at the height of his power this difference is of classical accuracy and subtlety. Technicalities may be avoided by means of the following generalisation. Whenever a composer with a true sense of form conceives anything in the nature of exposition he inevitably conceives therewith some notion of its possible effect in returning after other matters or in the course of recapitulation. The question of its return or recapitulation, whether finally answered positively or negatively, is inherent in the original idea. In the simplest typical case we may imagine the composer thinking, ' How splendid this will sound when it sails in again at another pitch and at home in the tonic ! ' This simple notion may become too familiar for the composer to notice it, but it will guide him even in the extreme case where an exact recapitulation is all that is required. This case actually occurs in genuine works, and is there as much the result of subtle balance as in the cases of utmost variation. Whether in exact repetition or in free variation, the true conception of this musical symmetry is thus essentially dramatic, and has nothing in common either with such effrontery as the fold-up forms of Schubert's *Forellen-quintet* or with arbitrary short cuts and divergences attempted for the sake of variety with no clear conviction that if the later statements are right the original statements were not wrong or superfluous. Now, when Schubert is at the height of his power in large forms we may know it by the returns to his main themes. Two great movements notorious for their redundancies and diffuseness are the first movement of the string quartet in G major and the first movement of the piano-forte sonata in B flat, Schubert's last composition. In both of them the whole interest converges upon the return to what is called the First Subject, involving the return to the main key after the wanderings of a long and dramatic development. The method of that return is entirely different in the two cases ; both passages may rank with the most sublime inspirations of Beethoven. In the G major quartet the return has an overpowering pathos, which is the more surprising since the tone of the whole movement, though at the acme of romance and picturesqueness, is by no means tragic. Yet this passage is the most ' inevitable ' as well as the most unexpected part of the whole design. The original First Subject began with a soft major chord which swelled out and exploded in an energetic phrase in the minor key. The next phrase repeated this event on the dominant. In the return, which is long expected, the soft tonic chord is minor, and the energetic phrase is calm and in the major key. The subsequent theme is not less wonderfully transferred in another way. In the B flat sonata the return is more subtle. The whole movement, as in the case of the G major quartet, runs a course not unusual in Schubert's large designs ; opening with a sublime theme of the utmost calmness and breadth ; descending, by means of a good though abrupt dramatic stroke, from the sublime to the picturesque, and then drifting from the picturesque through prettiness to a garrulous frivolity. But then comes meditation. The frivolous theme itself begins to gather energy in the course of the development.

It originates a dramatic passage which begins picturesquely, and rises from the picturesque to the
sublime. When the calm has become ethereal a distant
thunder is heard. That thunder had been twice heard
during the opening of the movement. At present the
key (D minor) is not far from the tonic. The main
theme appears softly at a high pitch, harmonised in this
neighbouring key. The distant thunder rolls again, and
the harmony glides into the tonic. The theme now
appears, still higher, in the tonic. An ordinary artist
would use this as the real return and think himself clever.
But Schubert's distant thunder rolls yet again, and the
harmony relapses into D minor. The tonic will have
no real weight at such a juncture until it has been adequately prepared by its dominant. The theme is
resumed in D minor ; the harmony takes the necessary
direction, and expectancy is now aroused and kept duly
excited, for a return to the First Subject in full. Accordingly, this return is one in which transformations would
be out of place ; and so Schubert's recapitulation of his
First Subject is unvaried until the peculiarities of his
transition themes compel the modulations to take a new
course.

At the risk of entering into further technicalities, we
must now consider Schubert's dealings with what the
idiotic terminology of sonata-form calls the Second
Subject. The grounds for this term appear to be that
there are no rules whatever to determine how many
themes a sonata-exposition shall contain, nor how its
themes shall be distributed ; but that whatever is contained in or about the tonic key, from the outset to the
first decisive change of key shall be called the First
Subject, and that whatever is contained from that decisive
change of key to the end of the Exposition shall be called
the Second Subject. The material that effects the decisive change of key will obviously be called the Transition.
But as for what and where the different themes are,

Haydn may run a whole Exposition on one theme, Mozart may reserve one of his best themes for the Development, and Beethoven may have one-and-a-half themes in his First Subject, a very definite new theme for his Transition, five-and-a-half themes in his Second Subject, and still a new one in the course of his Development. And in all three composers you will have no reason to expect any two works to be alike ; and all three composers may adopt each other's procedures.

The real fixed points in the matter are, that there is at the outset a mass of material clearly establishing the tonic key ; that there then follows a decisive transition to another key ; and that in that other key another mass of material completes the exposition. In any case, the exposition asserts its keys in order to maintain them.

Schubert's First Subjects are generally of magnificent breadth, and the length of his big movements is not actually greater than their openings imply. If Beethoven had to set to work from any one of Schubert's finest openings two things are certain : that he would have produced quite as long a movement, and that its materials would have been very differently distributed, especially as regards the continuation of the Second Subject. Up to that point all is well with Schubert (the present summary is no occasion to specify the exception that might be cited). His Transition is usually an abrupt and sometimes primitive dramatic stroke ; whereas with Mozart it is, when not merely formal, an occasion of magnificent musical draughtsmanship such as Schubert achieved for another purpose in the passage in the B flat sonata which we have just discussed. Schubert, in avoiding the problems of such draughtsmanship, is only doing as Beethoven often did in his best early works ; for Beethoven, too, found it easier to be either clever or abrupt at this juncture than to achieve Mozart's calm breadth of transition until his own style and scale of form had passed altogether beyond Mozart's horizon. Meanwhile, why should he or Schubert reject more startling methods which perfectly suit the circumstances of their early works (for Schubert did not know that his early works were going to be his last) ? An author is perfectly justified in simply saying, ' Then a strange thing happened ' on two conditions ; first, that what happens is really strange ; secondly, that the strange event is not a mere device of the author to get out of a difficulty.

Schubert's strange event is usually the beginning of his Second Subject in a quite unexpected key, remote from that in which it is going to continue. The masterly examples are to be found in the following first movements : in the great String Quartet in C ; in the Symphony in C ; the E flat Trio ; the ' Grand Duo ' for pianoforte *à quatre mains* ; and, once more, the Sonata in B flat. This last case is on the border-line ; but the device is a true art-form, widely different from the things in Beethoven which may have suggested it (see Beethoven's Sonatas, Op. 10, No. 3 and Op. 28) ; and Schubert's ways of bringing the unexpected key round to the orthodox one are thoroughly masterly. The trouble begins after this problem is solved. Then Schubert, feeling that the rest of his exposition must not be less spacious than its enormous opening, fills up most of what he guesses to be the required interval with a vigorous discussion of the matter already in hand. Even if the discussion does not lead him too far afield, it inevitably tends to obliterate the vital distinction between exposition and development, a distinction universal in the arts (at least, in all those that have time as one of their dimensions) quite irrespective of their names and shapes. The cruellest irony in this situation is that Schubert, whether he knew it or not, is only following or anticipating the advice so constantly given nowadays to orthodox young composers ' to stick to the main themes and not dissipate energy on a multitude of new ones.'

Schubert is commonly cited as the awful example of such dissipation, which is supposed to lead to the bottomless pit of Liszt's *Symphonic Poems*. But these nefarious works are, in point of fact, fanatical efforts to evolve a new kind of music out of transformations of a single musical germ. And the first and greatest of symphonic poems on Liszt's principles happens to be Schubert's *Wanderer-Phantasie*, a masterpiece of independent form which the *Lisztianer* were desperately anxious to explain away.

The real classical procedure with the continuation of a big Second Subject, the procedure of Mozart and Beethoven, is to produce a series of new sentences, all conspicuously shorter than the main themes, but not less sharply contrasted in length and shape among themselves. If the key of the Second Subject is not remote, one of these themes will probably have a strong admixture of a remote key within its own single phrase. This instantly serves all the purpose of Schubert's widest digressions. I have here sometimes called these items ' themes,' and sometimes ' sentences.' It does not matter a pin whether they are new themes or old ; what matters is that they have the manner of exposition and not of development. They are epigrams, not discussions. That is why they make paragraphs that will bear recapitulation in the later stages of the movement, while Schubert's expositions will not, though there is no other means of dealing with them. Schubert himself achieves the right kind of paragraph to perfection in the unique case of the Unfinished Symphony ; the very case which is most often quoted against him as illustrating his besetting sin of ' vain repetitions,' because its admirably terse and rhythmically uneven phrases persistently recur to the same theme. But Haydn, Mozart and Beethoven would have recognised that Schubert had in this case grasped the secret of their own technique.

So far, then, we already see that it is no mechanical matter to sift ' right ' and ' wrong ' from Schubert's

instrumental form, even with the earlier great masters
to guide us. But when we find (as, for instance, in the
first movement of the great C major Symphony) that
some of the most obviously wrong digressions contain
the profoundest, most beautiful and most inevitable
passages, then it is time to suspect that Schubert, like
other great classics, is pressing his way towards new
forms. In any case, where a work of art, or a human
being, has ubiquitous great quantities together with a
manifest lack of unity, there may be great difficulty (and,
perhaps, small profit) in determining which of its conflicting personalities is the more real. If the progress is
(as we have seen in the Sonata in B flat) from the sublime
to the garrulous, we shall naturally appeal from Schubert
garrulous to Schubert sublime ; but in the C major
Symphony the whole tone is sublime, and nowhere more
so than in the grotesque finale which fell on a blind spot
in Bülow's sense of values. It is impossible in a summary non-technical statement to demonstrate what were
the new forms towards which Schubert was tending ;
and the mechanical triviality of the accepted doctrines of
sonata-form makes even a detailed technical demonstration more difficult than work on an unexplored subject.
I must therefore beg permission to leave this matter
with the dogmatic statement that the fruition of Schubert's new instrumental forms is to be found in Brahms,
especially in the group of works culminating in the Pianoforte Quintet, Op. 34. Whoever has once begun to
notice the profound influence of Schubert on these undisputed masterpieces, and especially on this quintet,
the ripest and weightest of the group, will be surprised
at the blindness which, following the lead of Hanslick,
ascribes Brahms's forms mainly to the direct influence
of the last quartets of Beethoven. Of course, the
influence of the later works of Beethoven is just as clearly
there as the influence of Schumann is definitely not
there. Schumann's interest in Brahms would have been

but tepid if what Schumann saw in him had not been the very powers he felt to be lacking in his own work. These powers are characteristic of the instrumental art-forms of Haydn, Mozart and Beethoven ; and they determine the fitness of a certain range of musical thought to be cast in sonata forms, and, conversely, the fitness of sonata forms to deal with that range, or to adapt themselves to a more extended range of musical thought. Schumann soon felt a lack of these special powers, and, being a very clever man, created for his larger works a kind of mosaic style, in which he imitates sonata forms only in so far as mosaics imitate pictures. He thus creates a province for himself, and must be understood on his own terms. But Schubert's larger works belong to the main stream of musical history ; their weaknesses are relaxations of their powers, and Schubert has no devices (unless we count the absurdities of the Forellen-quintet) for turning them into an artificial method with a point of its own. Hence it is as easy for a later master in the main stream of musical thought to absorb and develop the essentials of Schubert's ideas as it is for a poet similarly situated to absorb the essentials of Shakespeare's. Neither Shakespeare nor Schubert will ever be understood by any critic or artist who regards their weaknesses and inequalities as proof that they are artists of less than the highest rank. Even if a great artist can be ' written down by himself,' one work of art cannot be written down by another ; and even if the artist produces no single work without flaws, yet the highest qualities attained in important parts of a great work are as indestructible by weaknesses elsewhere as if the weaknesses were the accidents of physical ruin. I see no reason to conclude that Shakespeare had at the age of thirty-one attained either a greater mastery or a wider range than Schubert. Up to that point is seems clear to me that Shakespeare, Schubert and Keats are artists not unlike in achievement and calibre.

Other elements in Schubert's sonata forms are in much the same condition as his expositions ; a condition in which weakness in the actual context is often indistinguishable from new power in some future art. The part of a sonata movement known specially as the Development is, of course, already at an almost hopeless disadvantage in Schubert because his Exposition will have already digressed into developments of its own. But nothing could be wider of the mark than the orthodox statement that Schubert is weak in this part of his form. His best developments are in themselves magnificent ; but he has in some four or five cases committed an indiscretion which is a characteristically youthful result of the impression made upon him by the first movement of Beethoven's *Eroica* Symphony, the development of which produces a brilliant cumulative effect in its earlier stages by reproducing its first topic in another key after an energetic different line of argument has been worked out. This procedure Beethoven handles so tersely as to give a feeling of enormous breadth to a development elsewhere crowded with other matters ; but when Schubert decides to resume his first topic in this manner he has no room for much beyond a plain transposed reproduction of the two pages of argument it has already cost him. After thus repeating his argument he generally has in store some stroke of genius by which its end shall bring about a beautiful return to the tonic ; and the most primitive of Schubert's developments is more highly organised than that of the first movement of Schumann's Quintet, in which Schubert's simplest plan is very successfully carried out in terms no so much of a mosaic as of a Dutch-tile fireplace. In this case it is so clear that to doubt Schumann's success is merely to question the whole postulate of his quintet, that we have here an interesting proof how much safer it is to yield to temptation when working on an obviously artificial basis than when working on highly organic lines. The most notorious of Schubert's developments is that in the first movement of the E flat Trio ; where he goes over his argument, itself a cumulative slow *crescendo*, three times. When the third statement begins its effect is, at the moment, disastrous, but it leads grandly enough to the return to the main theme in the tonic ; and thus even here what is wrong is not the scheme in itself, but the impossible scale on which it is worked. In the first movement of the C major String Quintet, where the process consists of twice two stages, the one lyric and the other (on the same theme) energetic, the total impressions is by no means unsuccessful, though processional rather than dramatic. There is no reason why it should not indicate a new type of form, such as Schumann actually produced, with less than his usual hardness of outline, in his D minor Symphony.

In both the E flat Trio and the string quintet there can be no doubt as to the magnificence of the harmonies and changes of key, not only from one moment to the next, but as an entire scheme. This is still more eminently the case with the considerable number of Schubert's developments, some of them long and some short, that have no redundancy in their plan. I have already described the wonderful end of the development in Schubert's last composition, the Sonata in B flat ; the whole development is a masterpiece, the more remarkable in that it all arises from the weakest part of the exposition. It would be a mistake to ascribe any part of its effect to its origin in that weakness ; Schubert, in the year of his death, had not yet attained the power of Shakespeare and Beethoven in blending tragedy and comedy ; though he had long overcome his early resentment against Beethoven's use of that power. It is impossible to set limits to what he might have achieved in a longer life ; both Beethoven and Shakespeare were older than Schubert before they could be sure of finding the right continuation and the right contrast to any note as sublime as that of Schubert's greatest openings.

At least two of Schubert's first movements may be considered flawless ; at all events, that is by far the best assumption on which to interpret them. The first movement of the Unfinished Symphony has already been cited ; its development is in superb dramatic contrast to the exposition, and nothing can be more characteristic of the greatest composers than the subtlety, pointed out by Sir George Grove, of alluding to the syncopated accompaniment of the ' second subject ' without the theme itself. The other masterpiece among Schubert's first movements is little known, and not easily accessible. It is the first movement of an unfinished pianoforte sonata in C, not included in the usual collections of his pianoforte works. Perhaps it is the most subtle thing he ever wrote. To describe it would involve a full account of Schubert's whole range of harmonic ideas, which are here sounded to their utmost depths. And these depths are not such that later artistic developments can make them seem shallow. Schubert's harmonic range is the same as Beethoven's ; but his great modulations would sound as bold in a Wagner opera as in a Beethoven symphony. We have now seen in what ways the weaknesses of Schubert's expositions and developments are intimately involved in tendencies towards new kinds of form ; and it remains to consider his recapitulations and codas. When Schubert's instrumental works are at their best his handling of the recapitulation (that is to say, of what follows after his development has returned to the tonic) is of the highest order of mastery where the original material permits. He shows an acumen not less than Beethoven's in working out inevitable but unexpected results from the fact that his ' second subject ' (or his transition to it) did not begin in the key in which it was destined to settle. To describe these results would be too technical a procedure ; but the reader may go far to convince himself of their importance by taking the

cases of the Unfinished Symphony and the C major
Symphony and comparing what actually happens in the
recapitulation with what would have been the course of
modulations with a plain transposition of the ' second
subject ' into such a key as would lead to the tonic automatically.   The externals of these two cases are obvious
enough ; behind them lies an art, unknown to text-books
on musical form, but as vital and subtle as the *entasis*
of a Greek temple, whereby every apparently straight
line has its curve and every column its imperceptible
narrowing towards the centre.   There is nothing surprising in the fact that with Schubert such art may be
found in works notorious for obvious faults of structure.

Since the indiscretions of Schubert's expositions,
though they may spoil the effect of his developments, do
not prevent him from almost always developing magnificently and sometimes faultlessly, we may say that up to
the end of the recapitulation Schubert's energy stands
the strain of his most impracticable designs.   Further it
seldom goes, and the codas of his first movements, with
the solitary exception of that in the C major Symphony,
are all in the manner of an expiring flame, often
supremely beautiful, sometimes abruptly dramatic, but
never revealing new energies like the great codas of
Beethoven.   In the codas of finales Schubert's energy is
capable of expansion, for the enormous sprawling forms
of the typical Schubert finales are the outcome of a sheer
irresponsibility that has involved him in little or no
strain, though he often shows invention of the highest
order in their main themes.   Here, again, there are two
exceptional masterpieces of form, in both of which the
grotesque is the veil of the sublime ; the finales of the
string quintet and the C major Symphony.

But the mention of Schubert's finales opens up the
whole question of his range of style.   In the present discussion I have been compelled to make frequent use of
the word ' sublime,' not by way of mere reaction against

the current impression that Schubert is a composer of secondary importance in his larger works, but by way of accurate definition. The only qualification the term needs is that in Schubert it is still associated with the picturesque and the unexpected ; it is, in fact, as sublime as any artist's earlier works can be. No one calls the clear night-sky picturesque ; and when Beethoven was inspired by it to write the slow movement of his E minor quartet he was older than Schubert lived to be. It is, however, one thing to write under the direct inspiration of the night-sky, and another thing to set a description of it to music ; and there is a wonderful song for tenor solo with male voice chorus and pianoforte, in which the pianoforte part, representing the innumerable multitude of stars, achieves the sublime by Schubert's characteristic picturesqueness. In the voice parts Schubert is, of course, already an older and more experienced artist ; more experienced, in fact, than Beethoven ; and so in this way, as in many others from *Erlkönig* onwards, the spacing of the words and the turns of melody are as severe and indistinguishable from familiar forms or formulas as the lines of a Greek temple. Now, it is in this matter of the sublime use of formulas that we can trace gradations in Schubert's style. When he begins a big instrumental piece with a formal gesture (as in the big A major sonata and the *Forellen-quintet*), his intention and achievement are usually grandiose ; and this applies to most of his argumentative sequences and processes of development. He can seldom rise above the grandiose when either his musical forms or his verbal subjects give him a sense of responsibility. On official occasions he is rustic, if not awkward ; and though the beautiful features of his last two Masses (in A flat and E flat) outweigh the clumsiness of their officially necessary fugues, it is perhaps only in the *Incarnatus* of the A flat Mass that his church music reveals the depths of the Schubert vein of imagination. In a *Kyrie* or a *Benedictus* there is a vein of beauty which rises far above, but which is not incompatible with, a vein of rather too comfortable piety prevalent in the religious poetry of the period ; and we have an excellent opportunity for measuring the difference between the wrong and the right stimulus to the imagination of a rustic tone-poet by comparing Schubert's grandiose song, *Die Allmacht*, a fine opportunity for singers, with its origin, as to modulations and general aspirations, in the aria known in English as *In native worth* in Haydn's *Creation*. Here it is Haydn, another rustic composer, who quietly reaches the sublime in describing man made in God's image ; while Schubert, dealing with verses that begin with the Almighty speaking through thunder-storms and end with the heart of man, achieves Haydn's finest modulation twice in a plainly repeated passage instead of once as a divinely unexpected variation.

It is tempting, but dangerous, to draw inferences, unsupported by musical facts, from the statistics of Schubert's song-texts. Every great musician, even if he be as voluble as Wagner on matters of general culture, is quicker to seize upon a fine musical possibility in a poem than to perceive that the words which gave it to him will not bear scrutiny. For no false sentiment can deceive except by claiming to be a true sentiment. It is therefore unprofitable to draw inferences as to Schubert's limitations from the merits of the poems he set to music. His friend Mayrhofer, who was said to toss him song after song across a table to be set as fast as the next poem could be written, was no Goethe, nor does he compare with the unpretentious Wilhelm Müller ; yet most of the Mayrhofer songs rank with the Goethe and Wilhelm Müller songs among the greatest of Schubert's or any musician's achievements in lyric music. At his own best Mayrhofer will ' do ' ; but his *Viola, eine Blumenballade* would have had no more chance of coming within Jeffrey's notice than Mac-aulay's ' Tears of Sensibility,' had that parody (which was plausible enough to worry his father into horrid doubts) been intended seriously.   Yet *Viola* inspired Schubert at the height of his power to one of the last of his very long songs, a masterpiece of form, using every suggestion of the words to purposes of an imagination as true as Wordsworth's.

Müller, the poet of Schubert's two great song-cycles, we are in some danger of underrating ; he deserves at all events full credit for the quality ascribed by Pope to Homer and by Johnson to Thomson, of always writing ' with his eye on the object ' ; and his style is absolutely free from affectation. It is, like all German poetry of its class, untranslatable without disastrous injustice.   German poetry at the turn of the eighteenth to the nineteenth century had the good fortune to blossom out with no Augustan tradition, and hence with no cleavage between poetic and prose diction ; with the result that, apart from the philosophy of his Nature-worship, the propaganda of Wordsworth could have had no meaning to a German poet.   A simple test case will suffice.   An English composer, Loder, happens to have produced a really beautiful setting of an English version of *Wohin ?* one of the most typical songs of *Die Schöne Müllerin*, set by Schubert with the utmost simplicity and continuity of flow, like that of the stream the youth is following till it leads him to his fate.   The mere fact that Loder's setting is in nine-eight time shows how the English composer is driven to an elaborate rhythm in order to convey any acceptable degree of distinction to a text that translates ' so wunderhell ' by ' so wondrous bright.'   It is a sheer impossibility to avoid such wrong notes in any English or French translation of Müller's poetry.

The cumulative pathos of *Die Schöne Müllerin* owes its force to the radiant happiness which culminates in the middle of the song-cycle, when the young miller

in his *Wanderjahr* is accepted by his beloved miller's
daughter, who afterwards deserts him. The story of the
Winterreise is as simple, but is not directly told ; all we
know is that the wanderer sets forth in mid-winter to
leave the town where his beloved has jilted him, and
that everything he sees reflects back upon lost happiness
and forward to death that will not come. The text of
each song is a straightforward verse description of some
common scene of country life, but this suggests none but
misleading analogies to a student of English poetry.
Crabbe, according to Macaulay, has a pathos which can
make a hardened and cynical reader cry like a child ;
but nobody ever thought of setting Crabbe to music.
Thomson, the pioneer of simple truth to Nature, was
so far from impressing Haydn as a kindred spirit that
it was only after a long and direct protest against the
project as a prosaic and philistine affair that Haydn was
persuaded to compose *The Seasons*. Wordsworth's
Nature is a pantheism always indicated above and behind
his Lucy Grays and Alice Fells. Tennyson's rural
scenes have squirearchy around them and aristocracy
above them, through which the Higher Pantheism pene-
trates with difficulty. The English reader who wishes
to capture the inspiration of Schubert's overpowering
pathos in *Trockne Blumen* or *Des Baches Wiegenlied* (the
lullaby of the brook for the young miller who has
drowned himself) will find the nearest analogy to it in
Herrick's *Mad Maid's Song*. There is no room for
character-drawing, no philosophy, no pantheism ; but
purely the presentation of a sorrow such as unhinges the
reason of a young miller or a country lass, in terms of the
common sights and sounds around the sufferer which
assume a primitive animistic relation to the sorrow.

These two song-cycles, *Die Schöne Müllerin* and *Der
Winterreise*, must be taken as two single works. To
regard them as forty-four single songs will only lead us
to the endless shallows of a criticism occupied with

questions of which is the prettiest, the most important, or the most distinguished. The prettiness and perfection of any single member does, no doubt, seem sufficient to itself, like Loder's setting of an English version of *Wohin ?* but the cumulative effect of the whole cycle is overwhelmingly greater than the sum of its parts. Even taken by itself, *Trockne Blumen* has a pathos that makes us grudge Schubert forgiveness for subsequently writing on it a set of variations, which was a bad thing to do ; and writing them for flute, which was worse ; and making some of them brilliant, which was blasphemous. But in its context *Trockne Blumen* is a song which many a singer has found difficult to learn because its pathos destroys all control of the voice.

The final song, *Des Baches Wiegenlied,* is not less difficult, and its supreme art lies in its being merely strophic, with melody and accompaniment unaltered throughout all its stanzas. The criticism of vocal music will never attain what should be regarded as its ordinary professional competence until it recognises that the merely strophic song with a single melody for all stanzas is no mere labour-saving device, but, as Brahms always maintained, the highest accomplishment of the song-composer's invention, compared to which the declamatory song is child's play. Schubert himself has produced too many masterpieces of declamatory song, such as *Der Wanderer, Der Doppelgänger,* and *Tod und das Mädchen,* not to stultify any theory of song-writing that does not accept Wagner and Hugo Wolf as masters of the theory of musical declamation ; but a criticism that regards that theory as constituting the whole, or even the highest art of vocal music, is fundamentally incapable of understanding verse. If Sullivan had not been a consummate craftsmen we should have had our declamatory theorists pointing out that Gilbert's metrical novelties were *a priori* incapable of any treatment more lyrical than that of *Das Rheingold.* Very different is the theory of the masters of lyric melody, whose view of declamation was not confined to prose. Weber writes to his librettist : ' Mind you give me plenty of trouble with unexpected rhythms and strange inversions ; nothing so stimulates the composer's invention and drives him out of the common grooves.' Schubert had from childhood practised the musical handling of all kinds of sentence, so that, unlike Weber, he presents us with results in which it is impossible to guess the difficulties. In his six hundred songs there is, no doubt, as Brahms said, something to be learnt from each one ; but it will not always be easy to learn it unless you have Brahms's knowledge to begin with. Of course, there is no more infallibility with Schubert than there is with Shakespeare ; *Erlkönig* and *Gretchen am Spinnrade* stand alone in four volumes of early work ; *Die Forelle*, after two strophes, perfectly realising in melody and accompaniment the picture and mood of the darting trout in the clear stream, shows none of Schubert's later skill when, in the last stanza, the music makes a perfunctory effort to follow the narrative ; and even in the later years there are songs, not always despised by singers, from which Brahms himself could have learnt little but the fact that Schubert was always keeping his pen in practice, whether or not he had anything in his head at the moment. The most summary critical sifting of this material would require a volume, with an introductory essay on principles of musical word-setting that have never been formulated in text-books.

One technical principle, not difficult to understand, suffices to dispose of any *a priori* objections to what has been called the 'lazy' method of the strophic song with the same tune to all stanzas. The objection rests on an ignorant belief in the bar-stroke as a genuine and rigid musical unit, together with the idea that no other basis of accent counts. Composers with poor rhythmic invention produce melodies in accordance with these limitations ; and they are rightly afraid of deviating from them, since they cannot do so with conviction. But great masters like Schubert play with all possible occasions of musical accent as great poets play with verse accent ; and the various occasions of accent coincide only in order to mark special points. The first notes of the first song in *Winterreise* show the method at once. The first note is off the beat (in anacrusis) ; but is higher than the second. The beat comes on the second, which is an expressive discord. The height of the first note provides enough accent to fit any prosodic inversion without interrupting by declamatory pedantries the dogged march of the jilted lover as he leaves the town of his joy and sorrow. But the note is not so high as to make an accent where the iambic feet of the verse are normal. Then the sensitive discord on the first of the bar asserts itself.

Schubert is not less masterly in the handling of paragraphs as wholes. He never over-punctuates, as is the inveterate tendency of the conscientiously declamatory composers. *Dass sie hier gewesen*, a series of statements that the air, the flowers, etc., prove that the beloved has been there, is set by Schubert, strophically, to a musical paragraph beginning outside the key and corresponding in every point of musical analysis to the grammatic structure of the poem, so that it is as impossible to lose the thread of its series of dependent clauses as to misunderstand its sentiment. In the first of the *Schwanengesang* (a publisher's title for a selection of Schubert's latest songs) *Rauschendes Bachlein*, the *Bachlein* continues its movement while the thought of the beloved hanging her head in a pensive mood is expressed at a tempo twice as slow as that of the rest of the setting. In short, Schubert the song-writer is as great a master of movement (which is form) as Mozart or Beethoven. All his structural devices seem so absurdly simple, when pointed out, that only the cumulative effect of their number, variety and efficiency will suffice to undo the injuries that our understanding of Schubert's art has suffered from over-emphasis on his incapacity to theorise in words, and from academic ignorance of the nature of musical art-forms on a large scale. Vogl, the singer, who, in Schubert's own lifetime, recognised and produced his songs, spoke of his insight into poetry as ' clairvoyant ' ; and that praise was useful in its day. At present we cannot too strongly emphasise the fact that, clairvoyance or com-monsense, Schubert's mastery in his songs includes an immense technique consciously developed and polished from childhood in over six hundred extant examples, many of them several times re-written. His inability to explain himself in verbal or analytic theory is the inability of a master to explain an art to people who, thinking they know all about it, do not, in fact, know that it exists. From Salieri Schubert learnt Italian declamation and operatic gesture with a thoroughness which, musically, stood him in good stead so long as his dramatic ambitions and his uncritical good nature to poetaster friends did not betray him into wasting pre-cious time and fine music on hopeless blood-and-thunder like *Fierrabras* and *Alfonso und Estrella*. Zumsteeg, the pioneer of long ballads, he outpaced, as we have seen, in the very act of making a musical paraphrase as a self-taught boyish exercise. The sporadic non-operatic lyrics of Mozart and Beethoven can hardly account for any measurable fraction of Schubert's range of song-forms ; you might as well try to account for Shakespeare by his parentage. It is easier to trace Schubert's emo-tional power to contemporary influences than so to trace his technique. Too much has been made of his adverse criticisms of Weber and Beethoven ; these are the honest first impressions of a fearless young artist, shy only in the actual presence of persons formidable by position or attainment. Many an artist has spoken resentfully of things that have profoundly influenced his work even

before he learnt to enjoy them.   Beethoven, for his
part, on his deathbed recognised Schubert as a kindred
spirit ; and he had no love of things incompatible with
the sublime.   When all the pretty and picturesque
things, and even all the dramatic things in Schubert's
songs, have had their due ; even after *Der Doppelgänger*, which many consider the greatest of his songs,
has been revered for its awful transcendence of Heine's
grim pathos ; still the full measure of Schubert is
revealed when, unoppressed by ceremonies and official
responsibilities, he joins Beethoven and Wordsworth in
Nature-worship.   The classical interests of Goethe and
Schiller contribute largely to this strain, and Schubert
is magnificently himself when dealing with Greek subjects, and with ' cosmic emotion,' as   in   Mayrhofer's
Auflösung (a glorious opportunity for a big soprano
voice, unaccountably neglected), or, in a less remote
vein, the great long *Waldesnacht*.

It is in this mightly framework that the sorrows of
the Miller and the banished Winter Traveller become
universal ; and the calm of *Du bist die Ruh* is as mystic
as the glory of Beatrice's eyes which drew Dante from
heaven to higher heaven.

LUDWIG VAN BEETHOVEN
(1770–1827)

By Herbert Thompson

A Chronology of Beethoven's Career

1770	December 16th. Born at Bonn, on the Rhine, where his grandfather, Ludwig van Beethoven, and his father, Johann, were musicians in the Court of the Elector of Cologne.
1781	Became pupil of Neefe, organist at the Electoral Court.
1782	First published composition : nine variations on a march by Dressler.
1784	Appointed Assistant Court Organist.
1785	Composition of three pianoforte quartets.
1787	Visits Vienna and has a few lessons from Mozart. Death of his mother. Becomes acquainted with the von Breunings and Count Waldstein.
1791	Death of Mozart.
1792	Haydn passes through Bonn, and Beethoven submits a cantata to him.
1791–2	Composes three pianoforte trios (Op. 1).
1792	November. Leaves Bonn and makes his permanent home in Vienna. Studies under Haydn and Albrechtsberger. Death of his father.
1795	First pianoforte Concerto, in C.
1796	Composes the song ' Adelaide '.
1798	Difficulty in hearing first shows itself. (This increased very gradually till, in 1814, he gave up playing in concerted music ; in 1816 he had to use an ear trumpet ; in 1822 had to cease conducting ; and in 1824, at the first performance of the Choral Symphony, had to be turned round in order to realise that the audience was applauding. After this his conversation was chiefly conducted by writing.)

F

1800   The Septet (Op. 20) and First Symphony (Op. 21), in C major, performed at the first concert given in Vienna for his own benefit.

1800   Composition of his only oratorio, ' The Mount of Olives' (Op. 85), the ' Prometheus ' Ballet, and the third pianoforte Concerto (Op. 37) in C minor, and completion of first set of six string quartets (Op. 18).

1801   Pianoforte Sonata in C sharp minor (Op. 27, No. 62) (commonly known, from a criticism by Rellstab, as the ' Moonlight ').

1802   Second Symphony (Op. 36), in D major.

1803   The Sonata (Op. 53) dedicated to Count Waldstein, and the ' Kreutzer ' Sonata (Op. 47) for violin and pianoforte.

1803–4   The ' Eroica' Symphony, in E flat major (Op. 55).

1804–5   Composition of ' Fidelio'. (First performance, 20th November, 1805 ; revised version performed 23rd May, 1814.)

1806   Composition of the three ' Rasoumovsky ' Quartets (Op. 59), the Fourth Symphony, in B flat major (Op. 60), the Violin Concerto (Op. 61), and fourth Pianoforte Concerto, in G (Op. 58).

1807   ' Coriolan ' Overture.   Mass in C (Op. 86).

1808   Fifth Symphony, in C minor (Op. 67), and Sixth (Pastoral) Symphony, in F major (Op. 68).

1809   Fifth Pianoforte Concerto, in E flat (Op. 73).

1809   Death of Haydn.

1809–10   Egmont music (Op. 84).

1812   Seventh Symphony, in A major (Op. 92), and Eighth Symphony, in F major (Op. 93).

1818–22   Missa Solemnis, in D major (Op. 123). (First performed 7th March, 1824.)

1822   Last Pianoforte Sonata, in C minor (Op. 111).

1822–23   Ninth (Choral) Symphony, in D minor (Op. 125).

1825–6   The ' Posthumous ' String Quartets.

1827   March 26th.   Died in Vienna, aged 56.

BEETHOVEN: ORIGINS

THIS is not a biography of Ludwig van Beethoven, but before we contemplate his art it is necessary to form some conception of his origin. As the 'van' in his name implies, he was of Flemish ancestry, but to style him bluntly a 'Dutchman', as has recently* been done, is to overstate the case. His grandfather was a Belgian, but he migrated to Bonn in 1732 (thirty-eight years before the composer's birth), married a German, as did his son Johann, the composer's father. So it will be seen how much more German than Flemish blood ran in Beethoven's veins, while he himself was by birth, education, and surroundings entirely German, and seems never, save for an excursion, as a boy of 11, to Holland, to have quitted German (or Austrian) territory throughout his life. And—which is more important— his artistic ancestry is distinctively of the German school : through Mozart, Haydn (an Austrian), and Carl Philipp Emanuel Bach he can trace his descent from the greatest of purely German masters, J. S. Bach. And, if one trusts to his most typical works, it is surely quite impossible to imagine any composer of his time save one of the German school writing his symphonies or chamber music.

For the main incidents in Beethoven's career reference must be made to the chronology prefixed to this essay. In glancing through it the preponderance of symphonies, concertos, string quartets, and pianoforte sonatas will be noticed, and this points to what will generally be considered as marking the distinctive place he takes in the history of music, for these are all works couched in the form associated with the sonata. The main constructive lines of this important form in 'abstract' music had been laid down by his immediate predecessors, of whom the three composers just referred

---

*Stanford & Forsyth, 'A History of Music', 1916, p. 235.

to, C. P. E. Bach, Haydn, and Mozart, are the most important, and upon their structure he laid the top-stone. Beethoven's name will always be associated with the symphony, and his nine symphonies are, on the whole, his most representative works. An appreciation of them makes an understanding of the nature of his art and of its place in history comparatively clear.

THE GROWTH OF 'SONATA' FORM

Before going into any detailed consideration of the symphonies, however, it is necessary that we should have some idea of the main structural lines on which they, as well as all Beethoven's chamber music, were formulated. While Bach was perfecting the polyphonic style, another was being organised which for a time seemed likely to supplant it. The polyphonic method was, shortly, to make a melody, through its repetition by another voice or instrument, serve as its own accompaniment. It therefore required either several instruments or voices, or else an instrument like the organ, on which several parts could be played at once. The perfecting of the violin by great Italian masters of the seventeenth cen-tury (Stradivari, who marks the culminating point of the school, produced his best work in the early years of the eighteenth century) was coincident with the rise of a school of Italian violinist-composers, contemporaries of Bach, who wrote solo music suited for their instrument. Pieces by such great virtuosi as Geminiani (b. 1680), Veracini (b. 1685), Tartini (b. 1692), and Locatelli (b. 1693) are still frequently heard in our concert rooms, and illustrate the type of music which, when developed by the German masters, was for a long time to oust the older polyphonic style of instrumental music.

The violin is essentially a melodic, or monophonic, instrument, and it must be allowed that even Bach's remarkable contrapuntal compositions for the solo violin, effective as they are, do some violence to its nature. So, to make their violin pieces artistic and interesting in design, the Italian composers had to adopt a very different method from that which was suitable for, say, the organ or harpsichord. Their music must, in the nature of things, consist mainly of a single thread of melody, to which the accompaniment, if any, must be given to another instrument, and be entirely subordinate, consisting chiefly of a few chords emphasising the harmony. How subordinate the accompaniment was is shown by the fact that it was not the custom to write it out, but only to give the bass note and indicate by figures the rest of the chord, the exact form of which was left to the discretion of the performer.

Dance tunes and songs were the most obvious sources to which the violin-composers could turn for material, and, indeed, the simple ballad tune contains the germs of a more complex design, which, in the hands of these composers, was materially advanced towards the modern 'sonata form'. A typical ballad tune may be resolved into three sections : a clause of assertion, a second in which a sense of contrast is secured by the adoption of a different, but related, key, and a third in which finality is given by a return to the original phrase and key. In this early violin music we find these principles elaborated. The leading phrases were developed into well-defined subjects, the clearer appreciation of tonality, that is, of the key-system, enabled the composers to employ it as a means of contrast, and they modulated from the section in the primary key to another in a related one, and introduced sections in a freer and more discursive style before returning to recapitulate in the original key, and so wind up. In the arrangement of the successive movements of which their 'sonatas' consisted they foreshadowed the plan of later works. It was, for instance, usual to open with a slow introduction, a call to attention, serious in character, which was followed by a quick movement, generally the most elaborate section of the work, and, since it had an appeal to make to the hearer's intellect, finding its appropriate place in the forefront of the work, before his attention was likely to flag. Then, by way of contrast and relief, came the slow movement, appealing more to the emotion than the intellect ; and, finally, not to put too great a strain upon the hearer, the sonata would end with a movement of lighter calibre, bright and gay in character.

Of Bach's numerous sons, Carl Philipp Emanuel (1714–1788) was, as a composer, distinguished enough to achieve a personality of his own, in spite of being over-weighted by so great a name. He was so prominent a figure in the time of transition between the close of the polyphonic period with his father, and the beginning of the harmonic period associated with Haydn and his successors, that he has often been styled ' the inventor of the sonata', and though this is not quite true in substance or in fact, his sonatas are among the most characteristic of their time. His specific musical gift was not great, and for this reason he had the more need to lay stress upon artistic construction, and in the form of his sonatas he is the immediate precursor of Haydn (1732–1809) who, with the still younger Mozart (1756–1791), brings us into contact with Beethoven. As Haydn and Mozart practically settled the form of the symphony which Beethoven was to adopt and perfect, it will be well to sketch briefly the typical symphony as it left their hands.

It frequently opened with a slow introduction, but this was from the first a matter of purely individual fancy. Haydn adopted it more often than not ; in a list of 40 of his most important symphonies, given in Grove's Dictionary, 25 have an introduction in slow time, while of Mozart's 49 symphonies only four have such an exordium. It was not an independent movement, but

as a rule little more than a ' call to attention', preparing
the hearer for the first movement proper, and frequently
foreshadowing its opening subject.

This first movement was in quick time, and in
' sonata ' form. It opened with the ' exposition ' of the
two main themes. The first was given out in the key of
the symphony, and when it had been fully stated there
was often a conventional flourish, which had no particular meaning beyond pointing unmistakably to the
close of one stage in the music. Wagner likened it very
happily to the rattling of the dishes between the courses
of a banquet. To follow out this simile, the next course
was represented by the second subject. This was always
in a different key, related to the first, yet sufficiently contrasted to give a new impression. In character the two
subjects were not, in the earlier symphonies, always very
distinct, and sometimes we even find the second subject
actually derived from the first, but it was soon realised
that it was well to contrast them in form and character,
as well as in key. By degrees an almost universal practice arose of making the first subject rugged and vigorous,
the second sympathetic and fluent, and this became so
much the rule that one frequently finds the second subject referred to in general terms as 'the *cantabile* subject'. A typical and familiar instance is afforded by
Beethoven's C minor Symphony, where the first subject
is a brusque phrase—' Fate knocking at the door '—and
the second a suave, pleading melody, as opposite in mood
as it is possible to imagine. These ' subjects ' are not
necessarily short phrases ; they may branch off into
accessory phrases, but the one feature which distinguishes each subject as a whole is its key. In this
opening section, the ' exposition', it is essential, in order
that the hearer may follow the design, that its chief
elements should be clearly stated. This was, naturally,
of greater importance in the time of Haydn, when the
symphonic structure was only just settled, and was,

therefore, less quickly apprehended.   Later on, when
musicians had grown accustomed to the form, they were
no longer satisfied with the plain and clearly cut lines of
the early symphony, and demanded a greater elasticity
and subtlety, yet under all the complexity in which composers, from Beethoven onwards, indulged, there is the
same broad principle of design.   The importance of
making the texts of the discourse clearly understood
before proceeding to discuss them led to the custom
of repeating the exposition section, in order that it might
be the more firmly fixed in the hearer's mind.   This was
practically invariable in Haydn and Mozart's time ;
Beethoven omitted the ' repeat ' in his last symphony
(1823), no doubt because of the exceptional dimensions
of the work, and frequently did the same in his later
pianoforte sonatas.   In more recent times the necessity
of going twice over the same ground is less felt, not only
because the musician has grown more sensitive to any
indications of design in a familiar form, but because, as
Sir Hubert Parry put it, ' the progress of music towards
a more passionately emotional phase makes it noticeably
anomalous to go through the same exciting crises twice
over'.   As the necessity of repetition is obviously not so
pressing in works that are familiar, the practice has
grown among conductors of not observing the repeats in
the older symphonies, and, so long as this does not inter-
fere with the proportions of the movement, there is much
to be said for it.

Having thus set forth the subjects of his movement,
the composer proceeds to discuss them in all their
aspects, in what is known variously as the ' working-
out', or ' free fantasia', or ' development ' section.   Up
to now he has made it his business to be clear and definite
in his statement, now he plays about his subject as his
fancy dictates.   He still sticks to his text, for though he
may allow himself a certain amount of digression in the
introduction of new matter, this will, as a rule, be found

to spring naturally from his main subjects. For the most
part, however, he will be content to ' develop ' his
original matter, to place it in a different light by a multitude of devices.   Thus he may take one of his principal
subjects and separate it into its constituent parts.   He
may vary it by changes of rhythm, of harmony, of accompaniment.   He may present it in different keys, and
change its ' colour ' by giving it to different instruments,
and may, in short, do anything he choses to secure
variety so long as the result is not incongruous with
the main idea. ' Variety in unity ' is, indeed, an aim
which, as we shall find more and more, was strictly
observed as the symphony was developed by Beethoven,
as regards both the collective impression of the several
movements and the conduct of each separate movement.
The freedom allowed the composer in this ' working-
out ' section is, of course, far removed from anything like
licence, but its æsthetic value in the scheme is obvious,
since it affords a necessary relief after the plain and
direct statement which has preceded it.   It may be as
fanciful as you please, but it must have a logical basis,
and must insensibly lead to an effective return of the
principal subjects in what is known as the ' recapitulation'.   In this concluding section a sense of finality is
secured by returning to the original matter in the key
of the opening.   Both first and second subjects are
restated, but with this distinction, that both are now in
the main key of the movement, which is thus strongly
asserted.   They may be, and generally are, followed by a
peroration known as a coda.   This was originally no
more than a brilliant flourish based on the notes of the
final chord, and Beethoven was the first composer to
make it of real artistic significance.   The length and
importance of the coda to the first movement of the
' Eroica ' Symphony (1805) is one of the features which
make that work a new departure of epoch-making
importance in the history of the symphony.

The first movement of a symphony is fairly constant
in form, the second is more variable. It is usually a slow
movement, of a more or less emotional character, but in
structure may follow many different types. Being in
character akin to the operatic aria, it frequently follows
its lines. In this case it may consist of a sustained
melody of a lyrical type, succeeded by a contrasted
section more declamatory and agitated in character, after
which there is a return to the original melody. In one
of his last string quartets Beethoven expressly styles the
slow movement a ' Cavatina', and in Tchaikovsky's
Fourth Symphony it bears the heading ' In the style of
a Canzona'. One alternative is to introduce an air and
a series of variations, though this is more frequently
assigned to the final movement, as by Beethoven in the
' Eroica', and by Brahms in his Fourth Symphony. In
the slow movement of the Choral Symphony Beethoven
introduces variations along with other features, and in
the ' Eroica ' a funeral march. Another form which a
slow movement may assume is a simplified version of
the first movement just described, and yet another is the
rondo, the consideration of which may be left till we
come to the finale, in which it is most frequently employed.

The third movement is in the earlier symphonies a
minuet, which, from Beethoven's time onwards, was
transformed into a ' scherzo', which is still its most
usual form. The minuet is a graceful dance of French
origin in triple measure. It was occasionally but
not invariably introduced into the ' Suites ' of the
eighteenth century, the period when it was still danced
in the ball-room. Its courtly, formal grace was most
happily caught by Mozart, who left many examples, of
which the minuet in the first act of ' Don Giovanni '
(1787) and that in the Symphony in E flat (1788) may be
cited as familiar and typical. A second minuet tune is
customarily added by way of a pendant to the first, and

THE HERITAGE OF MUSIC 133

this, from the fact that it used to be written in three-part harmony, came to be known as the ' trio '*. As employed in the symphony, this section consisted of a minuet, then a trio in a related key, after which the minuet was repeated. From the minuet Beethoven evolved the scherzo (*i.e.*, a ' jest '), a movement constructed on exactly the same lines, but very different in character, substituting humour for grace, and generally in a quicker time. He did not entirely abandon the minuet, which appears in three out of his nine symphonies, while of later composers, Mendelssohn introduced a distinctively Mozartean minuet in his ' Italian ' Symphony (1833), and Schumann in his E flat Symphony (1850) has for his second movement a scherzo, which is more like a minuet, but perhaps equally suggestive of the lazy swing of the German ' Ländler ' or slow waltz.

The last movement, the ' finale,' is as varied in form as the slow movement, but the general tendency, at least in the earlier composers, was to make it lighter in calibre than what had gone before, the natural feeling being that, after the hearer's attention had been absorbed by complex music in the opening movement and by emotional music in the slow movement, he was ready for relaxation, and it would not be politic to run the risk of exhausting him. For this reason the rondo was found peculiarly suitable for a finale. It is simple and fairly obvious in structure, consisting of a principal subject, followed by a succession of other subjects in related keys, the presentation of each of which is always succeeded by a return to the principal subject, the whole concluding with a coda. The gaiety which was thought fitting in a finale was happily expressed in a series of lively melodies, thus strung together, while the recur-

---

*If this were not a serious book, it might be permissible to suggest that the three-part section was designed to afford the fourth musician an opportunity to go round and collect from the audience.

rence of the main subject gave it a sense of unity, but the form continued to be employed even when a loftier mood was invoked, as happened in later times, when the dignity of the symphony as an art-form came to be more fully realised. It has already been told how the variation form has been employed for the finale, and frequently recourse is had to ' first movement ' form.

BEETHOVEN'S SYMPHONIES

With Beethoven we arrive at a great epoch in music, and particularly in symphonic music, the type with which his name is most closely associated and for which he accomplished so much. He was a youth of 19 at the time of the French Revolution, and there is no doubt that ideas of ' freedom, equality, and fraternity ' affected both his life and his art. Instead of being the servant of princes, as were Haydn and Mozart, he associated with them as their equal ; he even, on a famous occasion, declined to bow to royalty, and his admiration for Napoleon as First Consul was changed to disgust when he assumed the title of Emperor. It is, perhaps, a mere coincidence, but a suggestive one, that if one examines a series of portraits of the great composers, Beethoven is the first to discard the wig and wear his own hair, which assumed an unrestrained freedom quite characteristic of his personality. And, when we remember that the pig-tail, or ' Zopf', supplied a nickname for the most formal period in music, the coincidence is the more striking. Beethoven, as we have seen, came of a Netherlandish ancestry on the paternal side, but the family had become thoroughly Germanised before his appearance. The influence of his northern ancestry may be felt in his serious view of his art, while his long residence among the light-hearted Viennese (from 1792 till his death in 1827) no doubt helped to give it grace and vitality. His hard experiences as a boy, with a harsh and intemperate father, and at an early age the cares of the whole family, helped to make him independent, while at a later time the gradual approach of deafness, which in the end became total, tended to make him draw more and more within himself, and care less for outside opinion. His rough humour, finding a vent in crude practical jokes, and his intense love of the open air may be instanced as other personal idiosyncrasies that had a strong influence on his art. Like most strong natures, he developed very slowly, forming in this respect a strong contrast to his great predecessor Mozart, who began as an infant prodigy, and resembling Verdi and Wagner, whose art developed almost to the close of their long lives. He wrote his first generally acknowledged symphony when he was thirty, at which age Mozart had written forty-five. It may be admitted, however, that if the symphonies are weighed instead of being counted the contrast will not be so striking, for it must be remembered that Mozart's early efforts are of a very primitive type—mere symphonic embryos. The fluency with which Mozart poured forth his ideas is in equally strong opposition to the laborious manner in which Beethoven revised and polished his themes before he found them suited to his purpose. No doubt Mozart's finest themes underwent in his mind a process analogous to that which we can see going on in Beethoven's sketch books, but it is impossible not to realise that Mozart was far less self-critical, and would often, when original inspiration failed, be satisfied with a mere commonplace. Beethoven, in his early works, was often satisfied if his melody was euphonious, but as he matured he became more and more anxious to make it significant, and in his most characteristic later works there is hardly a phrase that has not individuality and meaning.

Like every other great genius, Beethoven built on the firm foundation of his predecessors, and he came at a critical moment. Sir Hubert Parry, in his *Art of*

Music, puts it thus : ' It was his good fortune that the sonata form had been so perfectly organised and that the musical public had been made so perfectly familiar with it, that they were ready to follow every suggestion and indication of the principle of form ; and even to grasp what he aimed at when he purposely presumed on their familiarity with it to build fresh subtleties and new devices upon the well-known lines ; and even to emphasise the points by making progressions in directions which seemed to ignore them.' Haydn and Mozart had, in their latest symphonies, completed a logical and perfectly balanced structure ; Beethoven's task was to accept it and vitalise it, he had in it a mould in which he could pour the strongest human emotion.

His nine symphonies are of such importance to an understanding of his art that it is worth while to take them in order and attempt very briefly to trace their most striking characteristics.*   After experimenting in many types of composition, of which some of the chief examples were mentioned in the chronology already given, he completed, early in 1800, his FIRST SYMPHONY in C.†

It follows the lines of Mozart's and Haydn's symphonies closely, and is written for the fullest orchestra they employed, including the clarinets, which they had used only in their latest works. Beethoven follows Haydn's favourite method of beginning with a slow introduction, but in the very first bar he gives some evidence of his independence, since he begins with a discord, and brought upon his head the wrath of the pedagogues of the day by so doing ! The introduction, ten bars in

---

*For further details the reader will do well to turn to the late Sir George Grove's *Beethoven and his nine Symphonies* (London, 2nd edition, 1896), and the other writers mentioned in the condensed bibliography at the end of this essay.

†Professor Fritz Stein discovered at Jena, in or about 1906, the parts of a symphony which, on good if not conclusive grounds, has been ascribed to Beethoven, and may well be one of the early essays in symphonic writing which are said to have been made by him.

length, leads into an allegro, very much in the accepted style of the final. The first and second subjects are more strongly contrasted than was usually the case, at any rate with Haydn,

but the close of the first is marked in the customary conventional way by the noisy type of passage which Wagner, as has been pointed out, likened to the 'clatter of the dishes between the courses'. The sudden drops from fortissimo to pianissimo, though not without precedent, are sufficiently characteristic of Beethoven to call for notice, and still more individual is the introduction of a long coda of 40 bars. The custom of ending a movement with a few bars' meaningless flourish, for the purpose of emphasising its conclusion, was common enough, and occasionally it was made something more interesting than a mere perfunctory finish, as by Mozart in the 'Jupiter' Symphony, but it was Beethoven who, in his determination to make every portion of the movement significant, gave the coda a greater artistic importance in the scheme than it had ever possessed before. The second movement is a very graceful Andante, based on a very attractive subject, which Beethoven makes a feint, but only a feint, of treating fugally.

It used, by the way, to be said of Beethoven, almost as a reproach, that he 'could not write a fugue', but though neither his genius nor the tendencies of his period lay in

that direction, he proved many times that he could
employ fugal methods most effectively as incidents in a
larger scheme.   In this andante a novel feature is the
independent use of the drum in a solo part.   Hitherto it
had been employed chiefly to strengthen the ensemble,
and as the natural bass to the trumpet parts, but Beethoven gave it an individuality that was quite new.   In this
case the two drums are tuned, not to the keynote of the
movement, F, and its dominant C, as was the almost
invariable custom, but to C and G, an innovation of considerable importance, since it led to a much greater
freedom and variety in the employment of the instrument.   Though the third movement is still entitled
' Menuetto ' and ' Trio', it is essentially of the ' Scherzo '
type which Beethoven introduced into symphony.   It
departs from the courtly grace of the minuet and becomes
more hurried, abrupt, and energetic, and is made a
vehicle for the humour that was one of his characteristics.   Haydn is said to have expressed the wish that
some one would write a new minuet, and, as he lived for
nine years after the first performance of this symphony,
he may have had a chance of realising that his wish was
granted.   In the Trio, or alternative section of the
minuet, we have an instance of the ' dialogues ' between
the wind and the strings which Beethoven so often introduced.   The finale is, in accordance with the almost
invariable custom of the Viennese school, of much
lighter calibre than the earlier movements.   In this
section, again, Beethoven loved to air his humour, and
in the false starts that precede the opening subject we
have an instance of this.   One conductor, it is said, had
so profound a sense of the gravity of a symphony that
he always omitted these opening bars, for fear they might
make the audience laugh !   The spirit of the movement
never flags, but it occasionally approaches triviality,
especially in the second subject, and many of the passages are, for Beethoven, distinctly conventional in cut.

THE HERITAGE OF MUSIC 139

The SECOND SYMPHONY in D (1802) is still immature Beethoven, but is rather bigger in scale than the first. It is for the same orchestra as the first, and again opens with a slow introduction, while the Allegro con brio into which it leads has still a certain ' square-cut ' form that is typical of the earlier symphonies. Save for one of those sudden and unexpected interruptions that became one of Beethoven's most marked characteristics, and gave his music its peculiar romantic feeling, the movement is mature chiefly in the sense that it shows a thorough mastery of technique, for there are only glimpses of the strong individuality that was first to be fully manifested in the Third Symphony. The slow movement is an illustration of Beethoven's power as a melodist, for whilst its tunes are as pure and beautiful as any of Mozart's, there is an added warmth and richness in their treatment. It is as if Beethoven wished to show the world what could be done on the lines of his predecessors before he applied himself to the task of extending these far beyond what they had accomplished. The two remaining movements, Scherzo and Finale, are more distinctive of the composer than any we have yet come across. They are full of the abrupt transitions, of the wilful caprice which, when the symphony was first heard in 1803, must have seemed almost a violation of artistic decorum. The fire and energy of these two movements are still remarkable, and in the finale we have one thoroughly characteristic touch, where the master suddenly passes from jest to earnest. This is in the ' Coda', which is analogous to the peroration of a discourse, or the epilogue of a drama, and is a feature which Beethoven developed into one of the most significant parts of a movement, for which he often reserved some of his most individual inspirations.

The THIRD SYMPHONY (' Eroica ') in E flat (1804) forms a landmark, not only in Beethoven's career, but in the history of modern music, the importance of which cannot easily be exaggerated. About the time when he was engaged upon the Second Symphony, Beethoven is said to have declared his intention to take ' a new road ' in his art. He was a man of his time, and it was a time when ideas of freedom and the expression of individuality were in the air. The French Revolution, occurring at the most susceptible time of his life, fanned his republican sympathies, and affected not only the general character and course of his music, but helped to some extent to shape this particular symphony, in which he first gave full rein to his imagination. Its title is due to a well-known incident. It was originally intended as a tribute to Napoleon Buonaparte, for whom, in the earlier phases of his career, Beethoven had a great admiration. Hardly was the score completed than the news came that Napoleon had accepted the title of Emperor, whereupon Beethoven, in disgust, tore up the dedication, and removed the name ' Buonaparte ' from the title, which afterwards ran, ' Sinfonia Eroica, composed to celebrate the memory of a great man '. The importance of this for our purpose lies in the circumstance that Beethoven was in the first instance inspired to write the work by an impulse which had its origin outside the range of music. It is to that extent an example of what is known as ' programme music', of which we shall have a more thorough-going instance when we come to the Sixth (' Pastoral ') Symphony. For the present it is enough to realise that Beethoven, in writing the Eroica Symphony, was not simply endeavouring to produce a series of sound-patterns, charming the senses by sensuous beauty of melody and interesting the intellect by a well-balanced design, but was striving to reproduce in terms of music the poetic significance he found in the character and career of a famous personality. His specific intention in the several movements he never revealed, save that, when he heard of Napoleon's death, he said ' I have already composed the proper music for that catastrophe', meaning, of course, the slow movement, which is expressly styled in the score, ' Marcia Funèbre'. Any other details in the picture we are left to supply for ourselves. The main fact, however, that the Symphony was, in Beethoven's own words, ' written on Buonaparte', means that a new element was added to its composition, giving it that touch of humanity which distinguishes it from its predecessors.

In the general lines of its structure the Symphony follows its predecessors, but in length it exceeds all previous symphonies. The orchestra employed is the same as before, with the exception that a third horn is added to the score. Two loud chords from the whole orchestra usher in the principal theme, which affords but little premonition of the force of the movement, and the opening phrase of which is, indeed, curiously anticipated in one of Mozart's boyish efforts, the overture to the operetta, ' Bastien et Bastienne '.

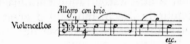

It is in the way in which the comparatively simple materials are developed that we find the enormous advance which the ' Eroica ' represents. The movement no longer presents any appearance of artificiality—it is, of course, highly ' artificial ' in the true sense of the word—it suggests more a natural growth in which one subject leads naturally and inevitably to another. The more or less formal passages which separated the significant ones—the first and second subjects, for instance— have become an organic feature in the whole ; there is an enhanced freedom and a much stronger expression of invicuality. There is one notable episode, a series of strident discords, big chords for the full orchestra fortissimo, which, without their context, could only be regarded as ugly, but are explicable, and readily accepted, as part of a strongly emotional tone-picture. In the century that has elapsed since the ' Eroica ' was written we have gone further and further in pursuit of characteristic expression in music, but when one thinks how out of place such an outburst would seem in a Haydn or Mozart symphony one can form some impression of the gulf which separates them from the new territory in which Beethoven was the pioneer. One other point may be mentioned in this first movement, the coda, which in length and character goes far beyond anything that had been done before. Originally, as has been mentioned more than once, this was little more than a flourish to give emphasis and finality to the conclusion of the movement, but Beethoven expanded it—in this case to the extent of 140 bars—and made it an eloquent peroration, based on what has gone before, but presenting it in a new light, and often with fresh details. No doubt Beethoven, whose fertile imagination must have made him often wish to go beyond the set forms, welcomed an additional opportunity for giving free rein to his fancy, but while he allowed himself full scope, his logical mind would not permit him to be irrelevant. As soloist in his own pianoforte concertos, he must, as the greatest extemporaneous player of his time, have found in the freedom of the customary cadenza—usually interpolated just before the close of the movement—a congenial opportunity, and one can imagine that this gave him the cue for enlarging the scope of what had before been a perfunctory flourish, and making it a fanciful excursion on materials already heard. (To avoid misapprehension it should be added that there is no structural analogy between coda and cadenza.).

The second movement, which bears the title ' Marcia Funèbre', explains itself, both as a symphonic slow movement and in its connexion with the heroic subject of the work. In its noble, elegiac mood nothing to approach it had been done by earlier composers, and since Beethoven's time the second movement of Brahms's ' German

Requiem ' and the Trauermarsch of Wagner s ' Götter-
dämmerung ' are perhaps the only compositions of the
kind that are on the same plane of solemn grandeur. The
scherzo is a further development of the type of movement which Beethoven made peculiarly his own. It
transcends the scherzo of the Second Symphony in
piquancy, and the divorce from the suave minuet is em-
phasised by dislocation of the accents, and especially by
the interpolation of four bars in duple measure, interrupt-
the regular ' three-in-a-bar ' of the movement. The last
movement introduces a form quite new in symphony.
Its structure has been the subject of great discussion,
but for the present purpose it may be described as a
succession of freely treated variations on an air from his
own ' Prometheus ' ballet (1800). As a whole, it has
hardly the same distinction as the earlier portions of the
symphony, but the note of elevation in a section in slower
time (poco andante) brings it into harmony with the
general scheme of the work.

The FOURTH SYMPHONY in B flat (1806) may be
treated more briefly, for though it is a thoroughly
characteristic work in a lighter mood, it displays fewer
essentially novel features than the Eroica. Its chief
characteristic is a gaiety which we shall find equalled
only by the Eighth. That it was new enough in spirit,
however, to prove embarrassing to the musicians of the
time is shown by the sarcastic *jeu d'esprit* written by
Weber, who was then quite young enough to have known
better. There are glimpses of triviality—a canon, in
which the clarinet and bassoon imitate each other, is,

indeed, as near actual commonplace as Beethoven ever
got in his more important works—but the mixture

of poetry and humour presents the composer in his
happiest mood, and there are many instances of his
power of investing the several instruments with
personalities of their own, and especially of making them
converse together with an effect sometimes eloquent,
often exceedingly humorous. This is particularly noteworthy in the adagio, which is based on a melody of
exceptionally pure and tender beauty, with which is
associated a persistent figure, strongly rhythmical in
character, heard first on one instrument, then
another, and used sometimes as an accompaniment,
sometimes alone, and frequently with a distinctly
humorous effect, which is, however, never inappropriate
to the situation.

In the next movement Beethoven returns to the name
' minuet', but here again the strong syncopation and the
generally breezy character of the music make it a distinct
scherzo.   An original point is the addition of three bars
at the close by way of coda, in which, as Schumann said,
' the horns have just one more question to put', and it is
characteristic of a certain type of criticism that this
delightful touch was objected to as a superfluity !   The
finale is as frisky a movement as was ever penned, full of
high spirits and without a cloud to disturb its serenity.
It has the light-hearted charm of Mozart, with a certain
freakish humour peculiar to Beethoven.

   THE FIFTH SYMPHONY in C minor (c. 1808) is, with
its twin the ' Pastoral ', the most widely known of any
of the nine, and in it we have undoubtedly the quin-
tessence of Beethoven.   The short, abrupt theme of
four notes which forms the principal subject of the first
movement is an emblem of the extraordinary compact-

ness of the movement as a whole. Economy of means could hardly be carried further, yet one feels that the composer has said everything he wanted to. Beethoven, as we can well believe, habitually composed with ' a picture '—that is, some definite poetic conception—in his mind, and in this case he gave us a clue by saying that this opening phrase was his way of suggesting ' Fate knocking at the door '.

This is quite consistent with another statement, to the effect that the germ of this vigorous theme was the note of a bird he heard in the Prater. We can the more easily believe in this insignificant source, since in this instance, as in so many others, Beethoven's sketch books demonstrate the very ordinary character the theme assumed when it first occurred to his mind. In this one feels that the orchestra, as it then existed, hardly sufficed to express Beethoven's ideas. Mozart's ideas, and the orchestra for which he wrote, were perfectly adapted to one another, and this is one of the reasons why his later symphonies give such an impression of flawless perfection. Beethoven, on the other hand, seemed to make a distinct individuality of each instrument, and expected it to take its own characteristic part in the music, giving it significant themes as well as mere ' filling in'. Many instruments (*e.g.* trumpets and horns) were, with their imperfect scales, severely limited, and one often feels that Beethoven was sorely embarrassed by their deficiencies. As Weingartner says, ' the horns and trumpets often came to a standstill simply because it was impossible to obtain a suitable sound for a given chord on the instruments of that time, and that for the same reason they often break off the melodial design entrusted to them, and either proceed merely with harmonic notes, or pause altogether. We see that these instruments are often obliged to make dangerous and apparently aimless leaps because they could follow the progress of the musical representation in no other way. Finally, we see that sometimes the most important part becomes quite inaudible because it is entrusted to instruments which are drowned by others with a louder sound playing a much less important part.'* This last question of balance of tone was no doubt made more difficult by Beethoven's deafness, which by this time (1808), though not at its worst, must have hindered his appreciation of niceties of this kind, and driven him to depend on the experience acquired in his youth. The various instruments of the orchestra have been so much improved since Beethoven's time, and composers like Berlioz, Wagner, Rimsky-Korsakov, and Strauss have done so much to study their effective employment that the unbiassed hearer cannot fail to notice in Beethoven's music passages which lack the brilliance or sonority which they seem to demand, and for this reason a sense of historical perspective is necessary in order that we may make a due allowance for the disadvantages under which he laboured.

The strongly dramatic character of the first movement of the C minor Symphony is due in part to the strong contrast between the first and second subjects. This apparently obvious source of effect was not so much observed by the earlier composers (especially Haydn), but Beethoven and his successors made full use of it, and the precedent set here, where the overwhelming force of one subject finds it foil in the tender pleading of the other, has been observed by all later composers. After the stern and compelling force of the first movement, the andante seeks to charm by its lyrical grace, and succeeds, but it is not so individual as the scherzo, which

---

*On the performance of Beethoven's Symphonies, Breitkopf and Härtel, 1907.

is among Beethoven's most characteristic movements.

(a) Opening phrase

Bass strings *pp*   Violins *pp*

(b) Subject given to horns

Horns *ff*

(c) (Trio: opening phrase:)

Violoncellos & double basses *f*

Its note of mystery in the opening phrases for the bass
strings, contrasted with the tense energy of the subject
given to the horns, and the extraordinary gambols of the
double basses in the trio, are among the features which
make it, with all its familiarity, so fresh and even surprising in its appeal to the hearer. It is certainly among
the most original inspirations that ever came to a composer. Equally original is the idea of linking the scherzo
to the finale, and the whole trend of symphonic music in
modern times shows that this is no mere caprice, but
an indication of a desire for greater continuity and
coherence in design. This transitional passage, which
looks so simple on paper, is a stroke of genius. As Sir
Hubert Parry has said, ' the whole of the scherzo of the
C minor Symphony is as near being miraculous as
human work can be ; but one of its most absorbing
moments is the part where for fifteen bars there is
nothing going on but an insignificant chord continuously
held by low strings, and a pianissimo rhythmic beat of
the drum. Taken out of its context it would be perfectly
meaningless. As Beethoven has used it, it is infinitely
more impressive than the greatest noise Meyerbeer and
his fellows ever succeeded in making.'*
    This mysterious passage leads without a break into
the finale, a sort of triumphal march, which bursts upon

*The Art of Music, ch. xii.

the ear in the brightness of the major key, and with the full force of the orchestra (Beethoven here employs, for the first time in symphony, trombones, piccolo, and double bassoon), and effects a contrast that would seem too obvious were it not so well contrived. The finale itself is not so distinguished as the preceding movements, but an episode of great originality and charm is a brief return to a theme of the scherzo, for which, it seems, Haydn furnishes a precedent, but which we may perhaps regard as another indication of a desire to look upon a symphony as a complete and indivisible organism, and not as a series of movements with no logical connection. At any rate, this method of ' cross reference ' has been made use of frequently by later composers, from Schumann to Brahms.

The close of the symphony is a striking instance of a peculiar mannerism—Beethoven's determination to leave no doubt of the conclusiveness of his ending by emphasising the final cadence as much as possible, the chord of C major being reiterated with a persistence that verges upon monotony.

THE SIXTH OR ' PASTORAL ' SYMPHONY in F (1808) is of historical interest as the great classical example of ' programme music ' in symphony. There is no doubt that Mendelssohn was speaking the truth when he asserted that ' since Beethoven had taken the step he did in the Pastoral Symphony it was impossible to keep clear of it ', and he furnished a proof of the truth of his words by his ' Italian ' and ' Scotch ' Symphonies, his ' Fingal's Cave ' and ' Midsummer Night's Dream ' Overtures. There was, indeed, nothing new in the idea of making a series of aspects of pastoral life the motive of an instrumental work. Composers in all ages have been curiously alike in protesting against the principles of programme music, while making more or less tentative efforts in the forbidden direction, and, as it happens a symphony by an obscure composer named Knecht

published in or about 1784, has a series of movements
bearing descriptions almost identical with Beethoven's.
The originality was in the manner in which the idea was
carried out, which far transcends anything of the kind
that had been accomplished before. Beethoven had, to
begin with, an intense sympathy for Nature, and he
had at his command a subtle and flexible means of
expression in the orchestra, whose resources he had done
so much to develop. At the head of this symphony he
set the sentence, ' More an expression of feeling than
painting', an axiom which, characteristically enough, he
violates in at least two episodes in the course of the work.
In construction we find, as in the Fifth Symphony, one
movement run into another, for the scherzo which
represents a village festivity, is interrupted by an
episode, quite foreign to the normal scheme of a symphony, representing a storm, and this in its turn merges
into a finale described as a Shepherd's Song of Thanksgiving after the storm. The first movement has a complacent, easy-going character quite suggestive of country
life. The slow movement, ' By the Brook', is not only a
wonderfully vivid presentment of its theme, but is one
of Beethoven's subtlest pieces of orchestration, the use
of two solo violoncellos, muted, to suggest the murmur
of the stream, being an early, if not the earliest, instance
of this method of employing the instrument in the
orchestra. It is at the end of this movement that we
have the direct imitation of nightingale, quail, and
cuckoo that contradicts the composer's own description of the symphony, and there is more realism in the
storm music, where the violoncellos play groups of five
ascending semiquavers whilst the double basses have
only four, a passage incapable of analysis but producing
just that undefined rumble that is so suggestive of distant
thunder. As in the Fifth Symphony, trombones and
piccolo are introduced, being reserved to add to the
colour and force of the storm scene.

THE SEVENTH SYMPHONY in A major (1812) presents few novel features of construction, but is one of the biggest and most vigorous, and perhaps the best sustained, of all the nine. Its outstanding characteristic is its tremendous, unflagging rhythmical energy and its sudden transitions, qualities which have caused it to be described variously as ' The Romantic Symphony ' (Grove) and ' The Apotheosis of the Dance ' (Wagner). In it Beethoven reverts to the smaller orchestra, having no use for trombones or piccolos, but he contrives to give a wonderful impression of bigness of scale. The music pulsates with vigour, and the measured tread of the allegretto :—

is sustained without a break from beginning to end. A marked rhythm is, of course, to be expected in the scherzo, a fine and thoroughly characteristic movement, with a strongly contrasted trio, in slower time, and containing some striking features. The quaint melody is said, on fairly good authority, to be from a pilgrim's hymn, but the employment of its first three notes :

is highly original, the reiteration of the phrase by the horns in syncopation—that is, against the normal accents of the movement—being a particularly individual and beautiful touch. The finale is a piece of boisterous humour in what the composer would have styled his most ' unbuttoned ' mood. In the coda, which is of exceptional dimensions, there is, however, the note of elevation to which Beethoven accustoms us, and the gigantic climax which is worked up near the close is among the most impressive passages in all the symphonies.

THE EIGHTH SYMPHONY in F (1812) is perhaps the most light-hearted of all the nine. Its only rival in this respect is the fourth, but there is in the adagio of that symphony an element of seriousness which has no counterpart in the playful allegretto of the later work. Grace as well as gaiety characterise the Eighth Symphony, but this does not mean that there is any retrogression, for it is as characteristic and original as any of its predecessors. The scherzo, certainly, gives place to a ' Tempo di Menuetto', which has more than an echo of Mozart's peculiar grace, but it is full of very individual touches. The trio section, in which the two horns have the subject, with a rather florid accompaniment for the violoncellos, is original, but one must confess that the effect is so little satisfying to the ear that the hearer is sorely tempted to regard it as one of those miscalculations which Beethoven's deafness prevented him from realising. The brief allegretto is a charming miniature, wrought with the utmost delicacy of touch, and though here, again, in the conventional final cadence, we seem to have a reversion to an older type, it is obviously done by way of a joke. That Beethoven regarded it in this light is indicated by the fact that he used the opening theme as the subject of a humorous canon in honour of Maelzel, the inventor of the metronome, the ticking of which is suggested by the detached chords of the accompaniment.

The story runs that the Italian cadence at the close was intended as a sly dig at Rossini, but that composer's popularity in Vienna was not achieved till a later date ; in 1812 he was only 20, and hardly known outside Italy. In the finale Beethoven tunes his kettledrums in octaves, a new departure that enables them to take a prominent share in the humour of this remarkable movement, one of the most brilliant and characteristic things he ever wrote. The coda is even more extended than those of the Eroica (first movement) and Seventh Symphony (finale), and is in Beethoven's most fanciful, unrestrained mood, full of those surprises which seemed so violent to his contemporaries, brought up as they had been on the stricter etiquette of an older school.

THE NINTH (CHORAL) SYMPHONY in D minor (1823) comes after a gap of eleven years, to complete the sum of Beethoven's symphonies. It is in scope and character the biggest of them all, and as regards the three instrumental movements, the greatest. There is in the first movement and the slow movement a note of elevation which has rarely been approached, and never surpassed, either before or since in any kind of music. There is a tremendous, rather austere dignity about the former, and here, as elsewhere, Beethoven reserves some of his finest ideas for the great Coda, especially one passage where the strings,

moving about in a chromatic figure, form the mysterious background to a wailing theme for the wood-wind that has an unspeakably solemn and deeply moving effect. The scherzo is the greatest example of this type of his own creation. Its tremendous, unflagging rhythmical energy is sustained and enhanced by the octave figure of three notes

OPENING BARS OF SCHERZO

that, in one instrument or another, is absent from hardly a single bar, and is most characteristic in its effect when given to the drums, which here, as in the Eighth Symphony, are tuned in octaves. The trio, heralded by a note on the trombone, silent hitherto, is contrasted, not only by being in the major key, but by the smoother, more sustained character of its themes. In the slow movement, which consists of alternating adagio and andante sections, one seems to probe the depths of Beethoven's emotional nature. In nothing, save perhaps some passages in the still later ' posthumous ' string quartets, does his genius seem freer from the restraints of convention or custom. It is not that he runs counter to any principles of form or design in music, but that he has so absorbed them that they are a part of himself and he need not consciously consider them. Just as Titian and our own G. F. Watts often in their latest works seemed careless of the niceties of draughtsmanship, yet could never unlearn the discipline of their youth, so Beethoven, while giving the freest rein to his fancy, was never neglectful of construction, save in the eyes of the pedants of his generation, who measured his stupendous creations with their little foot-rules, and shook their heads over his vagaries. There is no pause indicated at the close of the slow movement, and it seems at least highly probable that the omission was intentional, and that Beethoven wished to give as dramatic an effect as possible to the finale by making it come without any break after the exquisitely tender close of the Adagio. It opens with a strident outburst, the purpose of which becomes apparent when, later on, the baritone enters with the recitative, ' O Friends, no more these sounds ! But let us sing something pleasanter and more joyful ! ' Before we come to this, however, a theme worthy of the occasion has to be found, and the composer reviews the chief subjects of the previous movements, dismissing them all in turn, and then propounding a beautiful and characteristic melody, composed almost entirely of consecutive notes, which is, as it were received with acclamation by the rest of the orchestra :

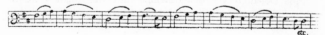

The object of this preamble is to give point to the introduction of Schiller's ' Ode to Joy ', which Beethoven,
thirty years before, had announced his intention to set to
music.   No candid critic, however devoted an admirer
of Beethoven, can conscientiously affirm that this finale,
in which a quartet of solo vocalists and a chorus take part,
is an entirely worthy successor to the three superb
movements that have preceded it.*   Beethoven was not
at home in writing for the human voice ; technically, his
vocal music was ineffective, and from the purely æsthetic
point of view it shows little or none of the sympathy
which makes his orchestral compositions so delightful.
There is an adagio episode in this finale that must be
excepted from this criticism, for it has a majesty quite
in keeping with the symphony as a whole, but with this
exception one must leave the finale with the remark that
it is less happy than its context.   But if it must be
allowed to be less convincing than the preceding movements, the scheme of the series of movements of which
the finale consists has many points of interest.   It
afforded a new precedent, in the introduction of a
chorus in a symphony, and in the reference to themes
from previous movements supplied another indication
of the growing desire to establish a logical connection
between the various sections of a symphony, to which
reference has already been made.   The terrific hullabaloo
that preludes the finale (on its repetition the opening
chord includes every note in the minor scale !) is itself
a sign of the times, when character was being sought
even at the expense of formal beauty.   After this, one
could no longer object to a passage because it was ugly
in itself ; it became necessary to go further, and inquire
what relation it bore to its context.

---

*Prof. Donald Tovey, in a searching and sympathetic analysis of
the Symphony (*Beethoven's Ninth Symphony, an essay in Musical
Analysis*, Edinburgh, 1922), has put the case for the finale very
persuasively

The orchestra employed by Beethoven is larger than had ever before been introduced into symphony. It includes four horns (for which some exceptionally trying passages are provided in the slow movement), three trombones, a double-bassoon, and in the finale a piccolo' triangle, cymbals, and big drum.

Beethoven may be said to have vitalised the symphony ; he breathed life and emotional warmth in the formally beautiful structure which Haydn and Mozart left behind them. Beginning where they left off, he made it the vehicle of expressing strong individual feeling, and for the first time we find in it a perfect balance of design and expression. Sir Hubert Parry's summary of what Beethoven accomplished for symphony may be quoted in this place : ' . . . . Beethoven's work raised the symphony to the highest pitch of earnest poetic feeling ; and the history of his development is chiefly the co-ordination of all the component elements ; the proportioning of the expression and style to the means ; the expansion of the form to the requirements of the expression ; the making of the orchestration perfectly free, but perfectly just in every detail of expression, and perfectly balanced in itself ; and the eradication of all traces of conventionalism both in the details and in the principal outlines, and also to a great extent in the treatment of the instruments.'*

THE STRING QUARTETS

I have devoted what may seem a disproportionate amount of space to a consideration of the symphonies because they seem to me to contain in them a key to practically all his music. They are, indeed, sonatas writ large, and as the greater includes the less, the understanding of them makes the comprehension of all Beethoven's concert music, his pianoforte sonatas, his string

* Grove's *Dictionary of Music and Musicians :* art. ' Symphony '.

G

quartets and other chamber music, comparatively easy.
Next in importance to the symphonies are the sixteen
string quartets, of which a brief account may be given.
The first six were published together in 1801, but the
exact dates of their composition are unknown, save that
Ries tells us the third, in D, was really the first in date,
and No. 1, in F, was the third. We may, however, take
it that they represent his first period, when he had
acquired a sound technique, and was just beginning to
develop a distinct individuality. Among the indications
of Haydn's influence we find the real Beethoven constantly peeping out ; more, indeed, than in the con-
temporaneous First Symphony, for in the more intimate
style of string quartet (as in that of the pianoforte sonata)
he was able to express himself more frankly and sincerely.

The famous set of three quartets by which Beethoven
preserved for all time the name of the Russian Am-
bassador in Vienna, Count Rasoumovsky, introduces us
to the full-fledged Beethoven of the second period in his
artistic development. They were composed in 1806 and
published in 1808, thus coming soon after the ' Eroica '
Symphony, which, as we have seen, marks a parting in
the ways. As a compliment to the Count, the composer
introduces two Russian folk-tunes, but has treated them,
as he treated the Scottish tunes commissioned by
Thomson, with very little appreciation of their racial
characteristics. One of them is the subject of the finale
to the first quartet, the other appears in the Allegretto
of the second. Though it is impossible to deal
with these quartets in detail, I must refer to the opening
subject of the first (in F), for it is among the noblest of
great melodies.

To the same period in Beethoven's career belongs the
next quartet, in E flat (Op. 74), written in 1809. The

introduction of many pizzicato passages have earned for it the nickname of the ' Harp ' Quartet, and the principal violin has a prominence unusual with Beethoven and more common with composers who, like Spohr, led their own quartets.   Dr. Ernest Walker calls attention to a curious and, of course, unconscious plagiarism of a phrase in the slow movement, which is found nearly note for note in the Adagio of Mendelssohn's Scotch Symphony.

The F minor Quartet (Op. 95), composed in 1810, furnishes a link between the second and third periods, and then we come to the last five quartets, which are grouped together as the ' Posthumous ' Quartets, though, as a matter of fact, the first was published in 1826, exactly a year (to the very day) before Beethoven's death. The order of the opus numbers is misleading, and chronologically they come in the following order : (1) Op. 127, in E flat (1824) ; (2) Op. 132, A minor (1825) ; (3) Op. 130, B flat (1825) ; (3A) The ' Great Fugue', intended as a finale to Op. 130, but supplanted and published separately as Op. 133 ; (4) Op. 131, C sharp minor (1826) ; and (5) Op. 135, F (1826).   These, Beethoven's last legacy to music, were so ' advanced ' that they were for many years dubbed the ' mad ' quartets.   While in their great freedom they are in advance of their time, they show occasionally a curious ' throwing back ' to an earlier period, as in the return to the fugal style, and, in Op. 132, to the division into a great number of short movements, reminding one of the Serenades and Divertimenti of Mozart's time.   The original finale to Op. 130 was the ' Great Fugue,' really a mixture of fugue and variations, which has been styled ' an exceedingly hard nut for even the most devoted Beethoven-lover to crack'.   In Op. 131, which is not always easy of comprehension, the composer's ideas seem almost too large for the medium of their expression, and altogether these quartets give one the sensation of a striving after an almost unattainable ideal. There are two interesting personal allusions in these quartets. In Op. 132 there is a section which goes back to the antique ' Lydian mode ' for its tonality, and is entitled ' Sacred Song of Thanksgiving to the Divinity by a Convalescent', referring to the composer's recent illness. The other is of a very different kind, and is in the last quartet (Op. 135), in which the finale is headed by a title, ' The difficult decision', under which are two short themes, with the words, ' Muss es sein ? ' (Must it be ?), and ' Es muss sein ! ' (It must be !). One would imagine that in such a connection these words had a very serious significance. But no ! Beethoven, who is said to have derived inspiration from the call of a bird, and the knocking at his door of a belated reveller, got this idea from a dispute with his housekeeper !

BEETHOVEN'S PIANOFORTE SONATAS

It is by no means a misfortune that in the home Beethoven should be best known by his pianoforte sonatas, for they are as representative of his individual genius as any of his works. In some respects one fancies they come to some extent in advance of his other compositions of corresponding date, and this may well be so, for no doubt the influence of his unfettered improvisations—of which that which so impressed Mozart is a famous example—is felt more intimately in the works which he designed for his own instrument. He wrote in all 38 sonatas, of which six are early and quite negligible, and are, in most editions, relegated to an appendix. The 32 which remain date from 1795 to 1822, and cover practically the whole of Beethoven's career as a composer, and display his genius in perhaps a more varied fashion than any of his other works. Here it is possible only to call attention to a few of the specially characteristic sonatas.

Of the first set of three comprised in Op. 2 (published

in 1796) the largo of the second, in A, is one of the
earliest of Beethoven's nobly conceived slow movements.
The E flat major Sonata (Op. 7), published a year later,
shows a distinct advance in sustained power, and Op. 10
(published 1798) consists of three sonatas, including one
in D which already reveals Beethoven's personality,
almost in its completeness, and to a degree far beyond
what one finds in the First and Second Symphonies, which
are of later date. Next comes the famous ' Pathetic '
Sonata (published 1799), which may owe some of its
popularity to its title (in this case authorised), but owes
more to its touch of dramatic force and passion, and to
its conciseness, in both of which qualities it is comparable with the Fifth Symphony—also in the key of
C minor. The two sonatas forming Op. 14, published
in the same year, are of much lighter calibre, but the
second, in G major, has a remarkable charm. So, too,
the Sonata in B flat (Op. 22, published 1802), is, though
not inferior, perhaps less generally interesting than the
well-known work in A flat (Op. 26, published 1802),
with its beautiful variations and its dignified funeral
march. The two Sonatas which were published in 1802
as Op. 27, are both described as ' quasi una fantasia,'
which explains the unconventional succession of the
movements, which are so contrived that they should be
played through continuously, thus pointing to a regard
for unity on which composers since Beethoven have been
more or less insistent. Both are most original and
beautiful works, but the second, the famous C sharp
minor Sonata, owes its much greater vogue in a large
measure to the fact that some one other than the composer chose to give it the name ' Moonlight ', which, as
is so often the case with nicknames, has stuck to it. The
next sonata, in D (Op. 28, published 1802), was also
invested with an unauthorised title, ' Pastoral', suggested
no doubt by the reiterated bass note in the first and last
movements, and by its generally genial mood. Opus 31

(published 1803) consists of three sonatas of very different calibre, of which the second, in D minor, surpasses its companions by its splendid dramatic force, which in the recitative passages of the opening movement becomes almost articulate. The two sonatas of Opus 49 (published 1802) are of trifling importance, and were originally announced as ' Deux sonates faciles ', but are followed by one of the greatest, the well-known ' Waldstein ' (Op. 53, in C, published 1805), which, owing to its opportunities for display, is still a favourite with virtuosi, though its claim to regard goes much deeper than this, and may be attributed to that sense of strong personal impulse that makes it resemble a perfectly organised extemporisation. Opus 54, in F (published 1806) is less distinctive, and consists of but two movements ; it is overshadowed by the so-called ' Appassionata ' (the title was invented by a publisher), which follows it. This magnificent sonata, in F minor (Op. 57, published 1807), vies with the ' Waldstein ' for popularity with soloists, and for sustained power and nobility takes a foremost place among Beethoven's works, of whatever class. The next sonata, in F sharp (Op. 78, published 1810), was a favourite with the composer, the next is a simple sonatina in G (Op. 79, published 1810). Then comes the sonata in E flat (Op. 81, composed 1809, published 1811), entitled by Beethoven himself, ' Les adieux, l'absence, et le retour ', referring to a journey contemplated by his friend and patron, the Archduke Rudolph. With it and its successor in E minor (Op. 70, published 1815) we come to the end of what has been designated Beethoven's ' middle Period ' style, and the last five represent his latest development. The first, in A (Op. 101, published 1817), is most original in structure, and a fugue in the finale indicates the interest Beethoven took in his later years in this form. The B flat Sonata (Op. 106, published 1819) is always known as the ' Hammerklavier Sonata', from its original title, due no doubt to a patriotic fit of the moment. It is of portentous length, probably double that of any other of the sonatas, and of prodigious difficulty. It is certainly among Beethoven's greatest works, and the tremendous fugue again attests to his interest in the form. The same note of elevation persists through the last three sonatas, in E (Op. 109, published 1821), with its beautiful variations ; in A flat (Op. 110, published 1822), in which the fugue steals in with such smooth, delicate effect, and in C minor (Op. 111, published 1823), which is in only two movements, but is so nobly serene in mood that it forms a fitting top-stone to the splendid series.

BIBLIOGRAPHY

The following books will be found useful for English readers :—

The chief authority on Beethoven is ' The Life of Ludwig van Beethoven ', by A. W. Thayer, edited by H. E. Krehbiel, and published in New York in 1921. (This was its first appearance in English.)

The article, ' Beethoven', by the late Sir George Grove, in his *Dictionary of Music and Musicians* (2nd edition, 1904) is largely based on Thayer, goes into great detail, and is thoroughly trustworthy as to facts.

The same writer's *Beethoven and his Nine Symphonies* (2nd edition, 1906) is also a useful book.

The Music of the Masters : *Beethoven* by Dr. Ernest Walker (1905) is an admirable review of Beethoven's works ; sympathetic, but critical and scholarly.

Beethoven's Letters, by Dr. A. C. Kalischer, translated by J. S. Shedlock (2 vols., 1909), is a virtually complete collection of 1,220 letters, and, though Beethoven was not to be classed with Mendelssohn or Schumann as a letter-writer, throws much light on his character.

The Oxford History of Music. Vol. V.: The Viennese Period, by W. H. Hadow (Oxford, 1904), has an illuminating chapter on Beethoven, and the opening chapter ' on the general condition of taste in the 18th century ' is of great value as an introduction to the subject.

On the Performance of Beethoven's Symphonies by Felix Weingartner, translated by Jessie Crosland, M.A. (1907), is a technical essay of great value, by one of the greatest of all Beethoven conductors.

Beethoven's Ninth Symphony : An Essay on Musical Analysis, by Donald Francis Tovey, Reid Professor of Music in the University of Edinburgh (Edinburgh, 1922), is a model of its kind.

ROBERT ALEXANDER SCHUMANN
(1810–1856)

By J. A. Fuller-Maitland

THE position of Schumann in the hierarchy of the great composers is even yet impossible to fix with any certainty. Like Mendelssohn's, it has altered more than once within the memory of elderly people ; obloquy has been succeeded by an admiration that was possibly excessive, and that again has given place to adverse criticism based on his undisputed shortcomings as a writer for the orchestra. But whatever the ultimate fate of his music—and it is difficult to imagine a time when his deeply felt songs, his piano music, in which the character-istics of the instrument are so adroitly provided for, and his masterpieces in chamber music, will not be loved and revered—it is beyond doubt that the influence of the man, his writings, and his compositions upon younger music-ians is of the greatest importance in musical history.

It is amusing to guess what would have happened to music if Schumann had not lived, or if he had succeeded in becoming a great pianist and nothing more. Take Schumann's name from the records, and we should probably find that German music had divided itself into two camps directly opposed to each other, the one dying out in a desert of conventionalities under the influence of Mendelssohn's followers, the other, led by Liszt and his friends, following one false ideal of progress after another. Wagner, indeed, seems to have been un-touched by any influence from Schumann, but without Schumann, Brahms must have developed on rather different lines, and the established forms which he used with such success would have expired at a much earlier date. The ' New Paths ' heralded by Schumann in one of his most remarkable writings, owed their existence to Schumann more than to anyone else. And even the liberty (or licence) enjoyed by the young composers of

to-day would hardly have been theirs if Schumann had
not lived. How far he directly influenced César Franck
it is not easy to say, but Franck's mental attitude, that
mysticism which appears more or less clearly in all his
work, is closely allied to the transcendentalism that
Schumann derived from Jean Paul. Schumann and
Franck seem always to prefer suggestion to definite statement, and in many other ways they have much in
common. Franck is mainly responsible for the breaking
down of so many of the old restrictions, and it is he who
has exercised the most weighty and lasting influence on
the modern writers of all countries. Whether he would
have struck out his new paths for himself, without the
conscious or unconscious influence of Schumann, it is
difficult to tell.

The youngest son of a bookseller at Zwickau, Robert
Schumann was born on June 8th, 1810, and for the first
twenty years of his life was half-heartedly studying for
the legal profession. His father had encouraged his
musical proclivities, and had even arranged for him to
go to Weber as a pupil ; but August Schumann's death
in 1825 put a stop to this, for the mother's determination
to make a lawyer of him now found no check, and so she
sent him off to Leipzig, where he matriculated as
studiosus juris. His uncongenial work could not
prevent his finding sympathetic friends among his
fellow-students, and sharing the enthusiasm they felt
for the writings of Jean Paul. It was these which led him
in the direction of that vagueness of musical speech which
is his most obvious characteristic. At Heidelberg, where
he went in 1829 ostensibly to complete his legal studies,
but with a firmer purpose than ever to become a musician
should fortune favour him, he came under the spell of
Thibaut, whom he reverenced not as a famous jurist,
but as the author of the treatise ' Ueber Reinheit der
Tonkunst', that book which, in after years, he recommended the young musician to read and re-read. It was

not until 1830 that his mother, at last convinced of his true vocation, gave a reluctant consent to his giving up the law and studying to become a pianist. Friedrich Wieck had already given him some instruction, but now he took up his abode in his master's house, and worked with him for two years. At the end of that time he secretly made experiments with some kind of mechanical device by which one finger was fastened in a strained position while the others were used on the keyboard. Fortunately for the world of music, he maimed his hand beyond recovery, and spoilt his chance of becoming a pianist. Heinrich Dorn undertook to teach him more thoroughly than had before been possible, and for thenext two years he devoted himself to composition, writing exclusively for the piano. As early as 1833 he began his career as a musical critic, with the wonderful article on Chopin's Op. 2, a composition which for ordinary people contains few of the characteristic beauties of Chopin's art, but in which Schumann descried the spark of genius.

The long and romantic attachment to Wieck's daughter Clara reached its culmination in marriage in 1840, after many difficulties, including a long lawsuit by which the father's consent was forced from him ; and from this time until, fourteen years afterwards, hopeless insanity declared itself, the union of the two kindred souls was ideally complete. The composer's life was not more eventful than that of the average musician of the time. We hear of his accompanying his wife to Hamburg, where the B flat Symphony was given ; of a tour in Bohemia ; and, later on, in Russia, where he and his wife made great friends with Adolph Henselt. Leipzig was his home from the time of his marriage until 1844, when he settled in Dresden. A long visit of several weeks to Vienna, and very successful concerts at Prague and Zwickau—where for once the town's most distinguished son was received with great honour—almost complete the record of his professional appearances. Application was made through friends for the post of conductor at the Leipzig Gewandhaus, and again at Dresden ; but neither was successful. In 1850 he was appointed ' Städtischer Musikdirector ' at Düsseldorf. By all accounts he was by no means an ideal conductor ; he never established that magnetic *rapport* with his players or singers which is the secret of great conducting, and stories of his constitutional reserve and even taciturnity abound in all the books. He conducted the famous ' Lower Rhine Music Festival ' in May, 1853, but after the first day relinquished the baton to Ferdinand Hiller. In the following winter the necessity for giving up this part of his work became more and more apparent, but it was not till February, 1854, that his frequent attacks of melancholy came to a climax in an attempt at suicide. After this he was an inmate of a private asylum at Endenich, near Bonn, where he died July 29th, 1856. Within a very short time of his ceasing to act as conductor at Düsseldorf, he had the great joy of recognising, in Johannes Brahms (who visited him with a letter of introduction from Joachim), the great man ' who was for to come', to quote Schumann's adaptation of the Baptist's words. In the last of his critical writings, called ' Neue Bahnen', he hails the advent of Brahms, as in the first of his essays he had hailed that of Chopin.

Down to the year of his marriage, his compositions, with the single exception of a lost symphony performed at Zwickau, were for the pianoforte, and they included such masterpieces as the ' Etudes Symphoniques', ' Carneval', and ' Kreisleriana'. The year 1840 was wholly given up to song-writing, and 1841 mainly to symphonic composition. In the same way, chamber music occupied him in 1842, and with ' Paradise and the Peri ' in 1843, he began the list of his choral works. His largest composition in this form, the ' Scenes from Goethe's *Faust*', was in process of completion from 1844 to 1850, and it is little wonder that it possesses not much unity of style or design. The final scenes, 'Part III' of the complete work, contain many of the composer's most beautiful passages, and this section bears revival better than any of Schumann's other choral compositions.

No one who knew the characteristics of his genius would have expected him to write an opera that would be likely to attract the general public even in tolerant Germany ; and in his single venture in that form Schumann was heavily handicapped by his libretto. After much deliberation he settled upon the story of Geneviève de Brabant, and wished to adapt a play by Hebbel, but the author would not modify his plot to meet the composer's wishes, and eventually, Schumann undertook the ' book ' himself, assimilating it to a dramatic poem by Tieck which he admired. In spite of many fine scenes, the impression the opera has always created when put on the stage is that it is not on the whole worthy of Schumann's name. Some of the situations are so hopelessly undramatic from every point of view that they are enough to condemn the work to perpetual banishment, except as a matter of historical interest for those who love the composer and every note he put on paper.

The soul of music is melody, and a creative musician's greatness depends in large measure upon the quality of his melodic invention. We can hardly tell if the process of this invention be entirely a matter of conscious volition ; to the composer's own mind, it often seems as if the germ of the thought had occurred to him from without, so that his art is only applied to the work of arranging its form and giving it symmetry. Very few of the great masters have been blest with such a wealth of fine melodic thoughts as Schumann, and every tune he wrote has the quality of real distinction. From the ' Papillons ' (Op. 2) down to that lovely melody which, in his last illness, he supposed to have been dictated to him by the spirit of Schubert, his melodic

ideas are new—so new, in fact, that it was many years
before his music took its firm hold upon the world at
large—and all are characteristic of him. To quote
examples of the choice melodies which abound in the
piano works of various dates, the multitude of his songs,
the chamber music, and the symphonies, would be a
vain task, for no two lovers of the master would agree
as to the favourites.

Perhaps the most prominent feature in Schumann's
music is his obvious liking for suggestion rather
than definite statement. The important themes in his
most characteristic works are often presented, even at
their first appearance, in a kind of haze, as though clear
definition were distasteful. Subtleties of various kinds
are employed to veil the melodic outline. For that
reason, his music is far from making an instant appeal,
excepting to more or less cultivated hearers. Now, as in
the song, ' Nussbaum', the accompaniment continues the
melody begun by the voice ; again, as in the ' Romance '
of the Fourth Symphony (in D minor), the delivery of
the theme by the first violins, is surrounded by passages
for the solo violin which weave so close a fabric that the
theme is made almost obscure :

in the ' Humoreske ' there are ornamental passages in
groups of semiquavers which produce the effect of two
parts in canon :

the usual signs for the employment of the sustaining

pedal are omitted in many of the piano pieces, as the composer preferred to leave the details of its use to the performer, being himself in favour of a very free employment of it. Once (again in the ' Humoreske ') he actually writes down an ' Innere Stimme ' which he directs not to be played, and in other places, as in the ' Davidsbündler', a theme already heard is brought in again ' as though from afar ' (' wie aus der Ferne '). At the same time, it is evident that in some of the best-known compositions, the themes are announced with as much clearness of definition as any of the other composers would have used. Sometimes, too, after a long stretch of music that seems to belong to a world of luminous mist, a theme of exquisite clarity will make its appearance, greatly enhanced in effect by the contrast. The unforgettable effect of the little quartet for boys' voices, as Faust's immortal part is carried up to heaven, is mainly due to this.

Schumann, like most of the post-Beethoven composers, was by no means satisfied with the conventional classical form, and, indeed, he nowhere displays much ingenuity in what is called the development of his themes, that part of the ' sonata form ' which is by far the most valuable and interesting. Even in the quintet and quartet for piano and strings, where he conforms most strictly and most happily to the prescribed pattern, the development section of his movements is not their most attractive feature. Among the early piano pieces, his few essays in sonata form are less individual and a good deal less inspired than the works in which he chose to express himself in a series of short sections, often on the *da capo* pattern. From Op. 2 (Papillons) to Op. 28 (Three Romances), there is a great preponderance of these slighter forms, whether the pieces are intended to be played continuously or not. The ' Carneval ', ' Davidsbündler ', ' Novelletten ', ' Kreisleriana ', are famous examples of this, and even the works which seem

more closely connected, such as the ' Humoreske', conform to this type rather than to the regular sonata-form.
The ' Humoreske ' has no doubt suffered in popularity
from its obvious want of continuity, for it really consists
of six or seven independent pieces, some of which contain ideas and treatment of the utmost beauty and charm.

Schumann would often take suggestions from some
arbitrary series of notes, as when, in his first published
composition, he makes a musical phrase

out of the letters of a young lady's name with whom he
fancied himself in love, or later, when the musical
letters in his own name turn out to be the same as the
letters in that of a town inhabited by a lady to whom he
was actually engaged for a brief space.   Allusions to well-
known tunes, often brought in with sly humour, are
frequent in his earlier works ; the lumbering ' Gross-
vatertanz', which appears at the end of ' Papillons', is
used with more effect in the finale of the ' Carneval ' ;
the last of the ' Etudes Symphoniques ' is built on a
phrase from an opera of Marschner's, introduced as a
veiled compliment to the country of the friend to whom
the work is dedicated, our own Sterndale Bennett.   The
proscription of the ' Marseillaise ' in Vienna led him to
introduce the tune in his ' Faschingsschwank aus Wien ',
and later on the same tune adds to the poignancy of the
' Two Grenadiers.'

But literary or other suggestions were not held of much
importance by Schumann ; we know that it was his
practice to write the piece first and afterwards to find an
appropriate name for it.   The three movements of his
great Fantasia in C, which was at first intended as a
musical monument to the memory of Beethoven, had at

first three titles without any very obvious reference to Beethoven, and when the work was published, their place was taken by a motto quite independent of the original purpose of the work. The third of the ' Kreisleriana ' was once inscribed with the words from *Macbeth*, ' When shall we three meet again ? ' but in this, as in so many other instances, the composer chose not to reveal to the world at large the literary or other sources of his inspirations.

Very few of the younger music-lovers in England have had the opportunity of hearing Schumann's orchestral works, for their production is of the utmost rarity. Nor is it at all surprising that it should be so, for the twentieth century is intolerant of music that appeals primarily to the intellect, and does not at once allure by rich orchestral colouring ; for the sake of this pleasure—a sensation mainly physical if we analyse it—we are ready to accept music of flimsy quality, empty of ideas and poor in treatment. While the present state of public taste remains, we must despair of hearing Schumann's symphonies or other orchestral works, for there is no disguising the fact that his scoring is very seldom interesting or beautiful in itself ; there are exceptions, such as the wonderful ecclesiastical passage in the ' Rhenish ' Symphony, but they are very few. Perhaps the Pianoforte Concerto contains some of Schumann's happiest writing for orchestra, but for the most part he does produce an impression of what is called ' muddiness ' by employing the strings too persistently, and seldom allowing the individual instruments to make their full effect. This may have been a conscious effort to transfer to the orchestra some of that allusiveness which succeeded so beautifully on the piano with its various pedal effects ; but whether conscious or not, the result is seldom successful from the point of view of the orchestral colourist. There are plenty of subtleties in modern scores, but they are not attained by shrouding the ideas

in a veil of string-tone. Wreaths of mist that add a
beauty to the atmosphere of pianoforte music are apt to
sink into the soil of the orchestra and there to reappear
as mud. Those who can appreciate design, expression,
and distinction in idea and development must always
love the orchestral works of Schumann, even though
they may have some time to wait until the general public
recovers the taste for what may be called drawing as
distinct from colour; and this taste is undoubtedly
necessary for the complete enjoyment of Schumann's
most individual creations.

With the two great masterpieces of his chamber music,
the Quintet and Quartet for piano and strings, it is very
different. These will never lose their hold upon hearers,
whether educated or not; their splendid unity of design,
their fine contrasts, the deft handling of the sound-
material, the real inspiration of their melodies, and the
skill with which these are worked out, must always make
for their appreciation, and they have, besides, that
strong feeling for colour which is so often missed in the
symphonies.

It is in some ways strange that Schumann should have
thus ignored the colour-effects of the orchestra, since
in his songs and piano pieces his feeling for characteristic colours is so plainly evident. The songs, or at
least those which are already most firmly established in
musicians' affections, have a fine unity of style, for all
their wide diversity of subject; his accentuation of
words is always right in the fullest sense, and it must be
felt by every hearer that the inflection and rhythm of the
words have suggested the musical themes. The stream
of melodic inspiration which wells out in such magical
profusion in Schubert's songs may not be quite such a
torrent in Schumann's; but even Schubert's actual
tunes are not more distinguished than Schumann's, and
in the younger man there is never a hint of the ' padding '
which occasionally disfigures the lyrics of the older.

Schubert rarely brings the pianoforte part to life as
Schumann so often does ; the epilogue to the ' Dichter-
liebe ' is an instance which will occur to every one.
As a cycle of exquisitely felt lyrics, the ' Frauenliebe-
und-Leben ' stands next to the ' Dichterliebe ' in that
intimate expression of emotion in which Schumann
delighted ; among the single songs, none are on a
higher plane of spiritual passion than ' Stirb, Lieb
und Freud' and ' Requiem', with their unobtrusive
suggestions of the organ in one and of harps in the
other. ' Waldesgespräch ' has not only the horns of
Elfland in it, but is full of weird suggestion, conveyed
not by the usual means of music that terrifies, but
throughout on a basis of exquisite melody, which yet
fills the hearer with dread of impending doom.   The
phrase to which the witch sings her spell, ominous
though it be, is absolutely simple, both melodically and
harmonically ; and scarcely less so is the climax of the
song,

If Schumann is seldom happy in his treatment of longer ballads—for even the best, ' Belsatzar', is not up to his highest standard—in lyrics with a change of mood in the middle, such as ' Schöne Wiege ' and ' Widmung,' he is perhaps at his best, and certain short songs, like ' Mondnacht ', ' Du bist wie eine Blume ', ' Die Lotosblume ', and ' Frühlingsnacht ', belong to the great songs of the world, since they convey the impression that they were conceived in one short burst of inspiration, and that melody and accompaniment must have taken shape at one supreme moment.

It remains to speak of a form of vocal music in which Schumann was in some sort a pioneer. His ' Spanisches Liederspiel', ' Spanische Liebeslieder', and ' Minnespiel', works in which single songs are interspersed with quartets and other concerted pieces, are characteristic and very effective, but their real importance is in the suggestion thay gave to Brahms for his two sets of ' Liebeslieder'.

As with many another composer, the outward circumstances of Schumann's life led him to write now in one form, now in another, according to the opportunities offered by his professional calling or personal experiences. It is not unusual for a young composer to begin by writing for the pianoforte, the most easily accessible medium of music all the world over, and it is no wonder that so large a number of Schumann's early works are for the instrument on which he had hoped to become a proficient. His love story, with its ' happy ending ' after the long and anxious period of doubt, naturally inspired those exquisite lyrics by which his name will always be preserved, and his appointment as conductor at Düsseldorf led to great activities in the direction of choral and orchestral writing. It is clear that the impulse from such accidental causes, as they may be called, is hardly likely to be as strong as that which inspired the songs of 1840, and it will not be wonderful if in the future

Schumann is remembered chiefly as a writer of immortal songs, even though his place in the great line of classical composers is assured by his pianoforte pieces and by the two noble masterpieces of chamber music.

SCHUMANN'S COMPOSITIONS

Pianoforte Solo :—Opp. 1, 2 (Papillons), 3-5, 6 (Davidsbündler), 7 (Toccata), 8, 9 (Carneval), 10, 11, 12 (Fantasiestücke), 13 (Etudes Symphoniques), 14, 15 (Kinderscenen), 16 (Kreisleriana), 17 (Fantasia in C), 18, 19, 20 (Humoreske), 21 (Novelletten), 22, 23, 26 (Faschingsschwank aus Wien), 28, 32, 56 and 58 (pedal piano), 60 (pedal piano or organ), 68 (Jugend-Album— 40 pieces for the young), 72, 76, 82, 99, 111, 118, 124, 126, 133 (Morning Songs).

Pianoforte, four hands :—Opp. 46 (Andante and Variations for two pianos), 66 (Bilder aus Osten), 85, 120.

Pianoforte with other instruments :—Opp. 44 (Quintet), 47 (Quartet), 63, 80, 88, 110, and 132 (Trios), 70 (pianoforte and horn), 73 (pianoforte and clarinet), 94 (pianoforte and oboe), 102 (pianoforte and violoncello), 105 and 121 (pianoforte and violin), 113 (pianoforte and viola).

String Quartets :—(3) Op. 41.

Orchestra :—Symphonies, Opp. 38, 61, 97, 120 ; Op. 52 (Overture, Scherzo, and Finale) ; Overtures, 100 (Braut von Messina), 123 (Festival), 128 (Julius Cæsar), 136 (Hermann und Dorothea).

Solo Instruments with Orchestra :—Opp. 54 (pianoforte concerto), 86 (Concertstück for four horns), 92 (Allegro Appassionato, pianoforte), 129 (Violoncello concerto), 131 (Violin fantasia), 134 (Concert-Allegro, pianoforte).

Songs :—Opp. 24, 25, 27, 30, 31, 35 (Liederreihe), 36, 37 (including three by Clara Schumann), 39 (Lieder-kreis), 40, 42 (Frauenliebe-und-Leben), 45, 48 (Dichter-liebe), 49, 51, 53, 57, 64, 77, 79, 83, 87, 89, 90, 95, 96, 98A (Wilhelm Meister), 104, 107, 117, 119, 125, 127, 135,

142, and three songs published in the Supplementary Volume of the complete edition.

Ballads for Declamation, with pianoforte accompaniment :—Opp. 106, 122.

Duets :—Opp. 34, 43, 78, 103, and a duet in the Supplementary Volume.

Concerted Music for Solo Voices :—Opp. 74 (Spanisches Liederspiel), 101 (Minnespiel), 138 (Spanische Liebeslieder).

Chorus, without Orchestra :—Female Voices : Opp. 29, 69, 91, 114. Male Voices : Opp. 33, 62, 65, 93 (motet with organ accompaniment), 137 (with accompaniment of four horns). Mixed Voices : Opp. 55, 59, 67, 75, 141, 145, 146, and ' Der Deutsche Rhein' (song with chorus).

Choral Works with Orchestra :—Opp. 50 (Paradise and the Peri), 71 (Adventlied), 84, 98B (Requiem for Mignon), 108, 112 (Pilgrimage of the Rose), 116, 139 (Sängers Fluch), 140, 143, 144 (New Year's Song), 147 (Mass), 148 (Requiem), Scenes from Goethe's *Faust* (without opus number).

Opera :—Genoveva, Op. 81.

Incidental Music to Byron's Manfred, Op. 115.

JOHANNES BRAHMS
(1833–1897)

By CECIL GRAY

IT may safely be said without fear of contradiction that in no art are criteria and standards of criticism so narrow and circumscribed, and at the same time so uncertain and confused in their application, as they are in music. This melancholy state of affairs can probably be ascribed in large part to the curious predilection which musicians have always exhibited at regularly recurring intervals of time for forming themselves into two hostile and irreconcilable camps, neither of which will admit the existence of any redeeming feature in the other, or of any defect in itself.

However pardonable and even inevitable such intolerance may be in a creative artist, whose attitude towards his art must naturally be determined to a great extent by the nature of his own particular talent and largely coloured by his personal sympathies and prejudices, it is an attitude which is neither justifiable nor forgivable on the part of the critic, who ought to be something more than a docile camp-follower in the train of one or other of the warring factions which periodically distract musical history. For it is not as if broadmindedness and universality of outlook lead in the practice of criticism, as they are apt to do in creation, to a somewhat colourless eclecticism and lack of conviction. Precisely the contrary, they are a source of strength, not of weakness ; and the unchallengeable superiority of literary criticism at the present time over that of all the other arts is primarily due to its breadth and catholicity, to its tacit recognition of the fact that it is possible for two artistic manifestations to be diametrically opposed to each other and mutually irreconcilable without the acceptance of the one necessarily implying the rejection of the other. We no longer consider that the highest tribute of admiration we can pay to the genius of Shakespeare is to abuse and ridicule Racine, or that a taste for Baudelaire and Verlaine automatically precludes us from appreciating the very different qualities of Milton and Wordsworth. But in music everything is still regarded from the standpoint of tendency ; if we admire Beethoven we must despise Rossini, and the ability to appreciate Bartók or Schönberg is considered wholly incompatible with a love for Bach and Mozart.

It is surely time that musical critics learnt a lesson from their literary colleagues and adopted the wholesome principle of religious toleration ; abandoning once and for all this Ormuzd and Ahriman conception of art, and recognising the truth that tendencies are in themselves nothing, that only works are good or bad, and that there are more roads than one which lead to Parnassus.

No composer has ever suffered more from the characteristic one-sidedness and narrow-mindedness of musical criticism than the subject of the present essay, and no better example could be found of the errors and misconceptions to which they inevitably give rise. On the one hand, he has been made the object of a cult, through which he has been raised to a position of equality with the greatest masters of all time, in stature comparable only to Bach and Beethoven (for by the formula of the three B's even Mozart is implicitly disqualified from competing with him) ; on the other hand, he has been made the object of a relentless and vindictive vendetta, first by the Wagnerians during his lifetime and by the representatives of modern tendencies since his death, according to which he is regarded as a symbol of everything that is most detestable and contemptible in musical art. There is this, however, to be said in partial extenuation of the latter point of view, that it has been almost entirely the result of the wholly disproportionate claims which have been put forward on his behalf. When one finds a critic writing airily, *en passant*, that ' *all* the

themes of Brahms have the *finest* melodic curves that
were *ever* devised in music ' (italics are ours), it is impossible not to experience a momentary irritation. Like
begets like, and an exclusive and esoteric cult such as
that of the Brahmsians could hardly fail to provoke an
equally violent reaction as a natural consequence.
Nevertheless, a cult has more to fear from the excesses
of its followers than from persecution, however violent,
and the experience of those who come eventually to
entertain a respect and admiration for Brahms resembles
that of the Jew in the tale of Boccaccio, who, on paying a
visit to Rome and seeing there the wickedness and
corruption of the priests, was forced to the conclusion
that the religion which could endure and flourish in spite
of such things must indeed be divine. And the fact that
neither the opposition of his adversaries nor the infinitely
more dangerous excesses of his adherents—not even the
terrible works which have been committed in his name
and under his influence—have succeeded in depriving
Brahms of his secure hold on the affections of the large
majority of intelligent musicians, or prevented him from
continually making fresh converts, is in itself sufficient
proof of the inherent vitality of his art.

The fact remains that this perpetual alternation
between two extremes has done Brahms an incalculable
amount of harm by creating a false perspective, the
effect of which has been to exaggerate his merits unduly
from the one point of view and his faults from the other,
and effectually to conceal his true nature from both alike.
In all the mass of literature which has grown up around
his work it is virtually impossible to find anything
approaching an impartial and discriminating estimate of
its significance. He has fossilised into a kind of historical concept, a highly conventionalised lay figure,
bearing little or no relation to actuality—a fate which is
all the more extraordinary because there is so little
justification for it. Brahms is not by any means either

the saint or sinner that he is commonly represented to be ; neither is he as simple a problem as he appears. Before we can hope to see him as he really is it will first be necessary to rid ourselves of any preconceived notions and historical prejudices which we may entertain concerning him.

For example, he has been so constantly painted by his admirers as a kind of musical Parsifal heroically resisting the insidious blandishments of Wagner-Klingsor and the seductions of Kundry-Liszt and the houris of Weimar, and restoring to its pristine purity the Holy Grail of the true musical tradition which had been sullied through the equivocal conduct of Schumann-Amfortas, that it is a distinct surprise to find that his early works reveal a quite marked sympathy with the lamentable tendencies which he is supposed to have been combating. Not only do they show manifest traces of the influence of the new school with respect to form, exemplified in his occasional adoption of the device of thematic transformation, *i.e.*, the employment of the same theme in slightly different guise as the subject of separate movements in a work (see, for instance, the First Sonata for piano, in which the theme of the *finale* is derived from that of the first *allegro*, and the second, where the same subject is employed in both *scherzo* and *andante*), but also definite indications of a leaning towards that most pernicious of all heresies in the eyes of the orthodox—namely, programmatic or poetic tendencies. The andante of the third piano sonata is prefixed by a quotation from a poem of Sternau, the fourth movement, entitled *Rückblick*, is similarly based upon another poem of the same writer, ' O wusstest du, wie bald, wie bald,' etc., and the first of the Ballads, Op. 10, is also headed by a quotation from Herder's translation of the old ballad 'Edward, Edward '. The last two examples are not merely programme music in the ordinary sense of the word, in which the general mood and atmosphere of the music is suggested by the poem, but the very rhythms are dictated by the rhythm of the verse. They are, in fact, quite literally *lieder ohne worte*, songs without words, instrumental transscriptions of poems.

In fact, the general impression induced by a study of these works is one of a composer who, so far from being in any way hostile to the new ideas which were then being disseminated, was rather in sympathy with them, even to the extent of seeming to be a promising recruit to the ranks of the revolutionaries. That he was so regarded by the leaders of the movement is certain. Liszt invited him to Weimar with open arms, and Berlioz, writing to Joachim from Leipzig, says : ' Brahms a eu beaucoup de succès ici. Il m'a vivement impressioné l'autre jour avec son *scherzo* et son *adagio*. Je vous remercie de m'avoir fait connaître ce jeune audacieux si timide qui s'avise de faire de la musique nouvelle. Il souffrira beaucoup.'*

On the occasion of the first performance of the first Piano Concerto in D minor (written about the same time as the works mentioned, although not published until some time later) no one had a good word to say for Brahms except the Weimar school, and it was the conservative section of musical opinion which was most uncompromisingly hostile, one representative organ going so far as to denounce it as a ' Dessert von schreienden Dissonanzen und mislautenden Klangen '.

Particular stress is here laid upon the romantic character of these early works, not merely because there has always been a tendency on the part of orthodox Brahmsians to ignore it as representing an aspect of their

---

*It is interesting to note that the only member of the Liszt party who regarded Brahms with suspicion and dislike was von Bülow, of all people. In a letter to Liszt he unburdened himself as follows ' Pour moi ce n'est pas de la musique—que m'importent les Br's ; Brahms, Brahmüller, Brambach, Bruch, Bragiel, Breinecke, Brietz'! strange words, surely, from the future promulgator of the famous formula ' I believe in Bach, Beethoven and Brahms '. It is evident that whatever changes took place in von Bülow's opinions, he was at least constant in his echolalian obsessions.

hero which it is difficult to reconcile with the particular
conception of him which they wish to see established
and accepted, but because it is a factor of the utmost
importance in helping us to understand the true nature
of his talent. Though these works may not be æsthetic-
ally as significant as many later ones, they are not by any
means derivative as are the early efforts of most artists,
or due to any extraneous influence. On the contrary,
they are the expression of a very much more definite
personality than many of the later works. Compare, for
example, the bold and ardent Scherzo in E flat minor,
in which Berlioz had found a spirit congenial to his own,
with the flaccid and nerveless Serenade in D major for
orchestra, Op. 11, which, as even an enthusiastic
Brahmsian like Mr. Colles is compelled to admit, ' bows
in turn to each classical predecessor, Haydn, Schubert,
and the early Beethoven, and accepts unhesitatingly each
convention of orchestration that they used'. There is no
question as to which is the more individual work of the
two. Indeed, it is difficult to realise that they were
both written by the same man. They seem to have
nothing in common, and to belong to entirely different
worlds. It is a difference which cannot be explained by
the mere interval of time which elapsed between them,
for it is not a logical development, but a sudden *volte
face*. Moreover, the change is not only sudden, unexpected, inexplicable ; it is also curiously incomplete
and not by any means permanent. It is like the intrusion
of a new personality, without the departure of the old,
which remains only momentarily in abeyance ; a case
of artistic possession in which two personalities strive
for mastery without either ever completely gaining the
upper hand. Brahms reminds one of the amusing satire
of Mr. Aldous Huxley, in which the hero, normally a
rather fastidious and intellectual young man, is at times
possessed by the personality of a popular lady novelist.
Similarly with Brahms, one is confronted alternately by

the romantic composer of the songs and piano pieces, and the stern, uncompromising classicist of the first and fourth symphonies. He is a dual personality ; with Faust he might say, ' Zwei Seelen wohnen, ach ! in meiner Brust'. This is the explanation of the extraordinarily diverse and conflicting impressions which his works arouse in different people. By some he is reproached for his austerity and intellectualism ; others find him too emotional and sentimental. He is alternately accused of a complete indifference to sensuous beauty and blamed for his luscious and cloying overripeness of sound. All these points of view are justified ; they are all true of different works—sometimes of the same work.

This curious duality is highly characteristic of the German race, particularly at the time in which Brahms lived. What ostensible connection is there between the Germany of, let us say, 1820, with its Brüderschaft clubs wherein young students, dressed in short black jackets and Byronic shirts and wearing top boots and long, flowing hair, holding a dagger in one hand and a quart tankard of beer in the other, drank to the radiant goddess of liberty, and the Germany of 1870, as exemplified in the arrogant militarist Prussian, with his pink, shaven head, high stiff collar, and aggressive bearing, who has become so painfully familiar to us of recent years ? What is there in common between the Germany of Tieck, Hoffmann, and Novalis, and that of Bismarck and von Moltke ; between the Rhineland with its ruined castles and vineyards and Loreley legends, and the monotonous, dreary plains of the Mark of Brandenburg ? Nothing, seemingly—except, perhaps, the beer, the undying symbol of the Teutonic spirit. Germany is the Jekyll and Hyde among the nations, and every German is to some extent a microcosm, reproducing in himself the duality characteristic of his race. The reason why it is more noticeable in Brahms than in any other composer—except, perhaps, Richard Strauss—lies in the fact that he is probably the most completely and exclusively Teutonic artist who has ever lived. Many much greater poets and musicians may have come out of Germany, but for the very reason that they are greater they are not so representative. Goethe and Beethoven transcend all national limitations ; Brahms, on the other hand, is the embodiment of the Teutonic spirit. Besides, it must be remembered that Brahms's life was spent at the very time of the change from the old Germany to the new. The turning-point or climacteric of the race came with the failure of the revolutionary movement of 1848 ; from that time onward the old Germany was dead to all appearances, although the old romantic spirit still continued to subsist beneath the surface.

It is interesting to observe that this psychological duality has its exact counterpart in the physical development of Brahms. One might well be pardoned for imagining that the drawing of him at the age of twenty which figures in most of his biographies was purely imaginary, or at least highly idealised, if its characteristic traits were not so fully confirmed and substantiated by the descriptions of those who were intimate with him at the time. In the words of a young lady of his acquaintance, he was ' shy and retiring, modest and timid, of delicate appearance, with blue eyes and fair hair, and a voice like a girl, still unbroken, and a face like a child which a young girl could kiss without blushing (!)' —how are we to reconcile this romantic youth, the exact description of a hero out of Jean Paul or Novalis, with the later Brahms of coarse and rough appearance, the *senex promissa barba* of our Latin grammars, with his harsh voice and rude behaviour, who was in the habit of eating a whole tin of sardines with his fingers and pouring the oil down his throat ? Fortunately, the change was not so complete and irrevocable in the spiritual as in the physical man, neither were its manifestations quite so disagreeable. Nevertheless, the

parallel is a very striking one ; for while, as we have
already said, the music of Brahms in both its aspects
typifies the German spirit, so in his physical personality
in both phases he is the living embodiment of the racial
type.*

Once this symbolical relation between Brahms and the
national temperament has been grasped we are in possession of the key to the proper understanding of his art.
It explains both its virtues and its defects. For while the
German mind is essentially lyrical, contemplative, and
philosophic, and fundamentally opposed to the heroic,
the epic, and the monumental, it is at the same time
adaptable and receptive to a quite remarkable degree,
and capable of performing feats which are wholly foreign
to its innermost nature ; and the obsession of the modern
German spirit by the ideal of the gigantic and the
colossal—perhaps the most remarkable phenomenon in
modern history—has its counterpart in the arts. One
sees the beginning of it in the music of Brahms as clearly
as one sees the end of it in the music of Strauss and
Mahler.

And so we find throughout almost all the work of
Brahms the sharp antithesis between his essentially
gentle and quiescent temperament with its predominant
mood of retrospective and wistful melancholy, and the
perpetual striving after the ideal of a grandiose, neo-
classic art which constantly impelled him to desert the
smaller lyrical forms in which he was an accomplished
master, in favour of the larger orchestral forms to which
his talents were not so much unequal as fundamentally
unsuited. For in the first place the symphony, or at
least its initial movement, is essentially a dramatic form.
Both in its derivation from the old dance forms and in its
consummation in Mozart and certain works of Beethoven,

---

*His biographer Max Kalbeck tells us that he was regarded by
ethnologists as a perfect example of the Teutonic type and that he
even figured as such in a technical work on the subject.

its characteristic feature is the contrast and opposition
of two dominant themes ; the first strong and masculine,
the second gentle and feminine—the Yin and Yang of
Chinese cosmology, the generative principles of the
universe. The whole development of the work is the
outcome of the interaction of these two strongly contrasted principles ; between them they beget the whole
course of the movement. The development section is,
so to speak, the child of the union of two musical sexes.

Now, Brahms could never write a great first movement in the classical style, along the lines of the conventional two-theme structure, because he was unable to
invent strong and vital first subjects ; in their place are
generally found thinly disguised variants of second subjects. They are either arid and sterile as in the First
Symphony, intermediary and hermaphroditic as in the
Third, or frankly feminine as in the Second ; and their
relations with the second themes are consequently un-
productive.

An explanation of this inability to conceive a strong
first subject is to be found in a remark which he once
made to his friend Dietrich, that whenever he wished to
compose he thought of some folk-song, and then a
melody presented itself. Hence the lyrical, *volkstümlich*
character of all his finest subjects ; hence their lack of
differentiation and variety. They all seem to conform
to a folk-song archetype, and Brahms nearly always fails
when he attempts the dramatic, classical, two-theme form
because the folk-song type of melody is fundamentally
unsuitable as its material basis. This is pretty generally
recognised to-day. On the other hand, it is equally
unsuited to the romantic symphonic poem form, which
is based upon the formal principle of a single subject
from which the whole organism evolves, as in the fugue
and in many of the works of Beethoven's last period.
The typical Brahmsian melody is as little susceptible of
spontaneous generation as of dual reproduction.

Consequently, one find that the form of Brahms's most successful first movements, such as those of the Violin Concerto, Violin Sonatas in A and G, and the Second Symphony, is neither that which we are accustomed to call classic nor romantic, neither symphonic nor fugal, based neither upon the principle of unity nor on that of duality, but of multiplicity ; in these works the form ceases to be dramatic and epic, without becoming a monologue or a soliloquy. For example, in the first movement of the Violin Concerto one could count some twenty or more thematic fragments of a very similar character ; they do not engender the course of the movement with each other, but are rather separate aspects of some archetypal melody ; free variations or improvisations on a theme withheld ; successions of lyrical episodes, like a sonnet sequence or a poem written in stanzas. Each part is a separate organic whole, but they are all so dexterously and cunningly welded together that it sometimes seems as if they did actually evolve from each other. Nevertheless, if one takes the trouble to examine such cases closely, one will generally find that some little figure or other has been surreptitiously smuggled into an episode out of that which is to succeed it, and artfully concealed until the moment for its appearance. In more homely terms, the rabbit is in the hat all the time. Not that it is necessarily any the worse for that ; my intention is only to show that Brahms is, formally speaking, neither the classic master or the *manqué* romantic of the Liszt school that he is alternately represented to be. He is at his best when he is neither one nor the other, but simply himself. He occupies a position apart from both schools, and it is only an historical accident that is responsible for the false conception of him which prevails to-day. In 1853, the year in which Robert Schumann's article appeared in the *Neue Zeitschrift für Musik*, proclaiming the advent of a new master in the person of Brahms, then a young man of

H

only twenty years of age, musicians were still accustomed to the idea of a kind of apostolic succession of great masters, stretching back in a long and unbroken line into the dim and distant past, whose authority, handed down from one to the other as from father to son, no one could venture to dispute or disobey without incurring the suspicion of heresy and the penalty of excommunication. But with the death of Beethoven the direct line appeared for the time being at least to have come to an abrupt conclusion, and the behaviour of the musical world was as pathetic and ridiculous as that of a faithful dog who has lost his master and is trying to find him again in a crowd of strangers. The most unlikely people were rapturously greeted by the poor animal—composers as far apart as Mendelssohn and Meyerbeer were hailed on their appearance as the long-lost heir to the classic tradition.

It all seems very absurd to us to-day. Actually, of course, no great master ever has a successor, but only imitators, for the very simple and obvious reason that his work is, humanly speaking, perfect, and consequently not susceptible of further development. The great master is an end in himself, a completion and a triumphant consummation ; only artists of the second rank, who suggest more possibilities than they are capable of realising and exhausting, ever have successors. Neither Bach nor Palestrina has any at all ; the real successor of Mozart is not Beethoven but Spohr, that of Wagner is not Strauss but Goldmark or Bungert. And Brahms has everything to gain and nothing to lose by the abandonment of the claims which have been put forward on his behalf to be regarded as the heir to the classic succession, for it only serves to concentrate attention on that aspect of his work which is least characteristic of him, in which he is at his worst, and causes his real gifts to pass unrecognised or insufficiently appreciated.

Unfortunately, there is little doubt that the Schumann

article and the subsequent von Bülow formula of the
three B's exercised a disastrous influence on Brahms
himself and gave him a quite wrong idea of the real
nature of his own talents, of the direction in which his
real strength lay. He was perpetually trying to live up
to a false ideal. He is like a man grappling with a task
beyond his powers. It is this more than anything else
which is responsible for the curious impression which so
many of his less successful works arouse in the listener—
an impression quite different from that produced by any
other music, and one which it is very difficult to express
in words. The First Symphony, for example, and particularly the introduction to the first movement, with
its atmosphere of gloomy apprehension and its sombre
and restless straining after something just out of reach,
recalls the sensations which we experience in that
familiar type of dream in which we are continually trying
to run away from something, but in spite of our desperate
efforts only get slower and slower until in the end we are
crawling on our knees. Brahms certainly felt that he
was a classicist, but at the same time was under no illusions as to the degree of success which had attended his
efforts. Speaking to a friend named Koessler shortly
before his death, he said : ' I know very well what place
I shall eventually take in musical history ; the same place
as that which Cherubini occupies—that is my fate, my
destiny.' But however true this may be of the one aspect
of his work, he certainly does himself less than justice
on another side, the side represented by the piano works
and the songs.

Actually it would be difficult to think of any composer
whose mentality was less akin to the classic spirit. He
had an entirely false idea of what it was, and how it was
to be attained. Classic art is not austere ; its spirit
is pre-eminently sensual and full of joy in the physical
aspect of things. Mozart, perhaps the only real classicist
in all music, is the very reverse of ascetic. No composer

is so preoccupied with sheer physical loveliness of sound for its own sake. But it is so in all great classical art. Many so-called admirers of the ' Greek spirit ' would be horrified if they could see the Parthenon as it really was, with its brightly painted statues, and its colossal chrys-elephantine figures, or were to find themselves on the Athenian Hampstead Heath during a Dionysian orgy. Yet one is perpetually hearing of the truly ' classical austerity ' and ' disdain of mere sensuous beauty ' in the symphonic music of Brahms. These qualities are certainly there, but they are the reverse of classical. As well call a desert anchorite an admirer of the Greek spirit as call the Brahms of the Fourth Symphony a classicist. Indeed, in his more austere and uncompromising mood Brahms reminds one strongly of Paphnuce, the monk in M. Anatole France's masterpiece, *Thaïs*, who imagined that when he was heroically struggling with the tempta-tions of the flesh he was struggling with the devil, whereas it was really God who had sent them in the hope of bringing him to a more reasonable frame of mind and a more natural mode of life. On the contrary, it was the devil who induced him to perform what he thought were pious acts, such as sitting on the top of a high pillar for many days and nights. And the spirit of sensuous beauty which Brahms was continually striving to overcome in himself, so far from being the devil, was the true classical spirit.

Fortunately for himself and us, his lapses from grace and righteousness were frequent and often prolonged. As a rule it will be found that his severe mood, like that of Flaubert, another Saint Anthony, is succeeded by a reaction in the opposite direction ; a spell of hair-shirts and matutinal scourgings is followed by a spell of self-indulgence. And so we find the period which culminated in the rigours and asperities of the First Symphony suc-ceeded by a long interlude in which were produced the Violin Concerto, the second Piano Concerto, the Sonata for Violin and Piano in G, and the Second Symphony, all of which are among the most popular and accessible of his larger works. Similarly, the grim and arid Fourth Symphony, at which even many of the faithful draw the line, was followed by the splendid Quintet for Strings in G, the lovely clarinet Quintet, and the last piano works. So, in miniature, the same tendency can be observed throughout his development; after the stern F minor Quintet for strings and piano come the bright and vigorous, almost un-Brahmsian Paganini Variations; the forbidding E minor 'Cello Sonata is succeeded by the Waltzes and the Horn Trio; and the Liebeslieder follow closely on the heels of the Requiem, and certainly, in this case at least, love proves stronger than death.

The Requiem has always been considered one of the landmarks in the music of Brahms, a view to which I have never been able to subscribe. Despite all its undoubted earnestness and sincerity, it fails to convince. The true religious spirit which redeems the frequent theatricality of the sacred works of Verdi and Liszt is lacking in it; it lacks faith, without which the eternal verities of life and death are apt to become tiresome platitudes. It does not need Herr Kalbeck to tell us that neither when Brahms wrote the Requiem nor even later in life did he believe in the immortality of the soul; one can see it clearly enough in every bar of the music. Piety without faith, reverence without belief, are not enough in a work of this kind. It is instructive to compare it with the Requiem of Delius; in the one the assertion of pious thoughts leaves one cold and unmoved; in the other the denial of the existence of a future life seems to receive a contradiction in the consoling and tender strains of the music. One might say of the Requiem, and, indeed, of many other works of Brahms, what Saint John the Divine said of the church of Ephesus : ' I know thy works and thy labour, and thy patience, and how

thou canst not bear them which are evil. Nevertheless I
have somewhat against thee, because thou hast left thy
first love. Remember therefore from whence thou art
fallen, and repent, and do the first works.' And in his
last years Brahms did so. *On revient toujours à son
premier amour*—how very true it is, in art as in life! How
often one finds an artist returning in his last works to
the spirit of his early ones! Berlioz returns in Les
Troyens to his first love, Gluck; the last picture
Gauguin painted in Tahiti was a Breton landscape,
recalling his earliest works; and so Brahms in the end,
particularly in the groups of piano pieces, Op. 116 to
119, seems to recapture something of the youthful
romantic mood, with an added mellowness and serenity.
In the collection of Volkslieder which he made in the
last years of his life the last number is a vocal arrangement of the melody in the andante of his first sonata,
his Op. 1, and possibly the first piece of music he ever
wrote; in his own words, ' The last of the Volkslieder
and the same in my Op. 1 constitute the snake with its
tail in its mouth, signifying symbolically that the story
is finished '—and symbolical it certainly is that both his
first and his last utterance should emphasise so strikingly
the most characteristic feature of all his best work,
namely, its lyrical, singing quality, its ultimate derivation
from song. For it is as a song-writer that he is perhaps
greatest. It is true that he may not attain quite to the
heights which Schubert does in a small handful of unex-
celled masterpieces, but with this one glorious exception
it is difficult to see whom one could place above him.
Schumann, for example, although he undoubtedly wrote
many fine songs, was, on the whole, of too introspective a
turn of mind to be able to enter completely into the poet's
conception. Too often the poem is for him merely the
starting point of a series of purely personal meditations.
Like the crystal or coloured disc which the clairvoyant or
mystic employs in order to hypnotise himself, the poem is

not an end in itself, but only the means to an excursion into the nebulous and misty depths of his inner consciousness.

Hugo Wolf represents precisely the opposite tendency. He possesses all the qualities which Schumann lacks. In the words of one of his most distinguished and consistent admirers, namely, Mr. Ernest Newman, ' He allowed the poet to prescribe for him whole colour and shape of a song, down even to the smallest detail. . . . He set his face sternly against the suspicion of mere music-making. . . . Wolf may not have had the exquisite disinterested loveliness of Schubert, or the same vision of the light that never was on sea or land, but he indubitably had a deeper comprehension of men and the world, a greater breadth of sympathy, a keener probe of psychology, and a more consummate flexibility of style '.

This puts the case both for and, unconsciously, against Hugo Wolf as well as it can be done. These are the reasons which induce Mr. Newman to put him ' at the head of the song-writers of the world '—above even Schubert ; they are the reasons which lead others, including myself, to relegate him with all due respect to a place in the second rank. Psychological probe, the understanding of the ways of this wicked world, and so forth, may be very estimable possessions, but they are not qualities which will enable a composer to become a good or even a tolerable song-writer, any more than they can make a good portrait painter. It is only too palpably true that the Hon. John Collier has admirably realised the type of the strong, silent man, and the type of the tender, clinging woman who have between them made the British Empire the peculiar thing that it is ; it is true that Mr. Sargent in the Wertheimer series has admirably depicted the types who are making it what it will probably be in a few years' time, and building Jerusalem in England's green and pleasant land ; but these worthy achievements do not, in my humble opinion, make either of them a great painter. It is the ability to handle a brush, not psychological insight, that makes Sargent, if not an artist of the front rank, at least one worthy of our attention ; it is Collier's inability to do so, not by any means his sentimentality—no one could be more sentimental than Raphael—that makes him unworthy of our attention.

Ultimately, a poem is a pretext for music in the same way that, as far as the purposes of art are concerned, a model is a pretext for a painting, and no amount of psychological or even physiological penetration can make up for bad painting or inferior music. And our complaint against Wolf is, that with all his veracity and ability to enter into the spirit of a poem he seldom succeeds in giving us just that one thing which we ask from a song, namely, good music—or, if Mr. Newman prefers it, ' mere music-making'.

The great song-writers understood this perfectly well ; for them 'the music's the thing '. A song of Brahms is not, as a rule, as a song of Wolf so often is, a mere turgid flow of notes without any intrinsic value apart from the poem, but a delicately organised and articulated structure with a logic of its own. As long as he has succeeded in preserving the correct accentuation and declamation, Wolf is generally satisfied ; his songs are often commonplace and deficient in musical interest and undistinguished in style and workmanship. Brahms, on the other hand, was never content until he had created a vocal line of intrinsic melodic beauty and an accompaniment as full of musical subtlety as he could make it.

Admittedly, the music must have some relation to the poem, as the portrait must to the model. A great portrait painter does not merely express his own feelings, any more than he confines himself to the accurate reproduction of his sitter's features. The picture is a kind of collaboration. Here and there a characteristic trait is slightly exaggerated, there another is omitted or left unemphasised, in order that the conception of the whole can be realised.   So in the music of the great song-writers one may occasionally find a faulty accentuation ; words may sometimes be repeated for some purely musical purpose whereby the poetic sense may perhaps suffer slightly, but these are only details which are sacrificed in order to contribute to the greater beauty of the whole. Wolf is almost always too preoccupied with the features in detail to see the face as a whole ; he often seems to work from line to line, from word to word, and fails to achieve formal unity and coherence.   Certainly there are limits to the liberties which one is permitted to take with a poem, a point at which the logical conclusion would be to make the work a purely instrumental piece, and it is precisely Schumann's inability to get outside himself, and his tendency to turn a song into a piano piece with vocal accompaniment that excludes him from the very first rank of song-writers.   He lacks objectivity of outlook, and resembles the portrait painter who is only successful with certain types with which he is in personal sympathy.

But to object, as many people do to-day, to a misplaced accent or faulty declamation as being a ' violation of the poem ', or a symptom of ' insensitiveness to poetic beauty ' is no whit less nonsensical than to complain that a painter who gives a lady a slightly longer nose in his picture than she actually possesses is guilty of a crime against humanity or thereby stands condemned as being insensitive to female beauty.   On the contrary, it is rather the photographic artist and the musician ' who allows the poet to prescribe for him the whole shape and colour of a song ' that give proof of their lack of appreciation of poetic and human beauty, by their naive assumption that they can supply to the original some quality that it lacks.   A good poem is a complete work of art, from which nothing can be taken and to which nothing can be added ; it is simply a piece of gratuitous impertinence for a musician to imagine that he is capable of improving it.   Respect for a poem would be more

truly shown by abstaining from setting it to music
at all, than by using it as a prescription for a musical
work ' down to the smallest details '—a procedure that
may be all very well in a dispensing chemist, but has
little to do with either music or poetry. A song is as
much a musical form as an opera ; it is not a poem set
to music any more than an opera is a drama set to music.
A good poem, like a good play, can only be spoilt by the
addition of music ; it cannot be improved upon. Song
and opera are as different from poetry and drama as
chalk is different from cheese ; the best poems for music,
like the best libretti, are those which afford the musician
the fullest scope and the least hindrance to his purely
musical purposes. To commend Wolf for only setting
the best poems to music is like praising a composer who
would only make operas out of the best plays. So far
from being a sign of good taste, this merely shows that
he had no understanding of the true nature of the art of
song-writing, and if we place Brahms far above Wolf and
Schumann it is largely on account of his thorough understanding of the form with which he is dealing, and
because of his remarkably sure instinct in choosing the
right poems.

It is not merely by virtue of a small handful of choice
favourites that Brahms takes his high position among
song-writers, but by the extraordinarily large mass of
fine numbers—in actual amount possibly less than in
the case of Schubert, but in an infinitely higher proportion to his output. It is perfectly true that other composers besides the latter may have equalled and even
excelled him on occasions ; a small handful of songs by
Mussorgsky, Borodin, Debussy, possibly even one or
two of Strauss, may be as good or even better than anything Brahms ever did, though this is very doubtful.
One can at least concede that they possess a quality of
imagination and sensitiveness to which Brahms cannot
lay claim. But what is certain is this : that if a musical

Palgrave were to set about making a Golden Treasury
of songs, excluding, of course, operatic arias and vocal
works of large dimensions, he would probably find that
he would have to include a greater number of examples
by Brahms than by any other composer with the exception of Schubert ; in precisely the same way, in fact,
that the actual Palgrave gave a larger proportion of space
to Wordsworth than to any other poet of his time. That
is not to say that Brahms is necessarily greater, or even
anything like as great as many of his contemporaries,
any more than it means that Wordsworth was greater
than Keats or Shelley, but simply that in such a test one
is judging him on his own ground, where he is at his
best and greatest, instead of on the wider ground of the
large orchestral forms, where he is at a disadvantage in
competing with such giants as Berlioz, Liszt, and Wagner.

There is no doubt that there are many striking analogies between Brahms and Wordsworth. After a youth
of ardent romantic enthusiasm they both cooled down
very suddenly into a premature middle age, and in the
bitter reproaches levelled at the former by the younger
generation of musicians during his lifetime one finds an
echo of the disillusionment of Wordsworth's former
admirers on account of what seemed to them his apostasy.
In the words of Browning,

He alone breaks from the van and the freemen,
He alone sinks to the rear and the slaves.

Again, both were made the object of an exaggerated
worship and adulation, and both have paid dearly for it,
by provoking the ridicule and obloquy of their antago-
nists. Both wrote a vast amount of second-rate and
uninspired work, particularly in the larger forms. Their
reputations will ultimately rest on their work in smaller
fields—Wordsworth's on the Lyrical Ballads rather than
on the Prelude or the Excursion, that of Brahms on his
songs and piano pieces rather than on his symphonies
or his Requiem. They are both lyrical, contemplative,

and philosophic in temperament, and fail when they attempt the epic, the dramatic, or the passionate. They are alike incapable of the *allegro con brio* or the *prestissimo* ; they lack *tempo*. Brahms is representative of everything that is most German, Wordsworth of everything that is most typically English. But there was in the latter a certain calm, mild grandeur, and ruggedness, as if something of his beloved lakes and mountains had entered into him. On the contrary, there is a distinct stuffiness and lack of fresh air in a great deal of Brahms's music. He preferred Vienna and the Prater to walking on the mountain-tops, and Baden-Baden where, as Kalbeck says, ' Die Natur stand wie ein wohlgeordneter Tisch für ihn gedeckt '—with its civilised forests ' Wo kein erstickendes Unterholz, kein abgefallenes durres Laub, geduldet wurde,' to the wilder grandeur of the Black Forest.

It is, of course, largely on account of his nationality and because he so completely typifies the German spirit that there is a widespread tendency at the present day to depreciate Brahms unduly ; but it also happens that there is also a purely artistic reaction against everything that he stands for. Our Zeitgeist is different, that is all ; and there is no reason to suppose that it will be permanent. But although we of to-day admittedly do not find in his music the expression of our innermost thoughts and aspirations, that is no reason why we should refuse to tolerate and even sympathise with different ideals and different qualities of mind. Criticism, after all, and appreciation for that matter, ought to be something more than a mere chasing of our own tails or a self-satisfied contemplation of our own features in a mirror, and those who take the trouble to look for them will find in Brahms many qualities without which music would be very much the poorer, and many works which are destined to endure long after the music of most of our contemporaries has lost the transitory interest it has for us at the present day.

MICHAIL IVANOVITCH GLINKA
AND THE RUSSIAN SCHOOL
(1804–1857)

By M. D. Calvocoressi

THERE are two essential facts in the evolution of musical art during the nineteenth century : one, what Wagner has called the fertilisation of music by poetry ; the other, its fertilisation by folk-music and other traditional elements. Both influences helped to restrict and to counteract the gradual encroachment of the conventions which were evolving formalism from the forms created by the classics, and rhetoric from their eloquence. They introduced a new spirit, and provided the means for its adequate artistic expression.

In both these progressive movements Russian composers played an all-important part. Russia possessed no musical culture, no tradition other than that provided by her church music and the folk music of the various nations constituting her empire or surrounding it. The story of the birth of the Russian school reads like a fairy tale. The country had played no part in musical art, and lacked the means of providing musical education. No public concerts took place before 1802, and the first school of music was opened half a century later. In Moscow, in Petrograd, a few foreign artists, enticed to Russia by various sovereigns, provided a certain quantity of Western music for the few. The people had their dance tunes, their choral and other songs of labour and play, their epic ballads—a treasure of surprising variety and richness, transmitted and increased throughout the ages.

The time when scraps of this native music began to gain admittance in what is called ' art music ' is remote. We hear of a play, *Baba Yaga* (The Witch), with national songs and dances, performed at Moscow in 1671 by the Boyars and ladies of the Court, of another in which were

incorporated 'songs from various provinces, Polish
dances, and musical games,' and of a third, *Russalka*
(The Mermaid), also with songs and dances, which was
written by the Empress Sofia Alexeevna in 1675.

During the eighteenth century, native composers like
Volkof, Matinsky and Fomin wrote operas in which
attempts are made at local colour, and perhaps a few
folk tunes introduced. Later Cavos, a naturalised Italian,
went further in the same direction. By their very
subjects, which later proved useful to other composers,
from Glinka to Stravinsky, his operas were prophetic;
and he resorted more freely to the folk-tunes which the
specialists Prach, Kirsha Danilof, and others, were
beginning to collect.

But it is especially after the time of Glinka that folk-
tunes were used extensively by Russian composers; so
extensively, and in a manner showing so profound a
degree of assimilation, that to detect them when they
appear is impossible without a thorough knowledge of
musical lore. Reading through the standard collections
of Russian folk tunes—Balakiref's, for instance, or
Rimsky-Korsakof's—one may be surprised to encounter
an enormous number of themes made familiar by modern
Russian opera, symphony, and chamber music; but even
more surprising are the ingenuity and sense of fitness
displayed, as a rule, in the adaptation to new ends. It is
an object lesson to see how in Glazunof's *Stenka Razin*
(one of the finest of Russian tone poems, and a model of
form and development) the whole material is provided
by the three phrases of a famous song of the Volga boat-
men, with the addition of one tune of Persian origin.
And it is hard to believe that all three themes utilised in
Balakiref's splendid piano Fantasia *Islamey* are textually
borrowed from folk music.

In the output of Russian composers, tone poems and
tone pictures, inspired by visions of natural scenery or
by poems and legends, occupy a conspicuous place.

Their fondness for seeking inspirations in concrete, definite data of this kind served the best Russian composers in good stead for more reasons than one.

The Russian mind, in one of its most characteristic aspects, inclines to reverie and objectless brooding, drifting towards or around vague generalities. It has a capacity for prompt, but not very profound, assimilation, and consequently may tend to revel in half-digested notions and conceits. It often falls an easy prey to sentimentality and abstraction. A sense of logic and proportion is not among the strongest points of Russian nature, although an acute sense of reality and keenness of vision often is. The lyric poetry of Russia, for instance, even at its best, has repeated examples that, however full of feeling and telling imagery, impress one as sketches, jottings, unfinished fragments, rather than finished products. The very language may be described as characteristic of the race, through its many shortcomings in definiteness and conciseness.

These indigenous tendencies might have proved especially harmful to composers in the absence of a strong tradition and discipline. Their dangers are strikingly illustrated in the looseness and complacency of Tchaikovsky and Scriabin, their entire lack of critical sense, their childish faith in commonplaces. But another danger lay in the temptation to appropriate wholesale the highly organised schemes and methods evolved and applied in other countries, which hereditary culture and experience alone enable composers to turn to genuine creative purposes. The Russians avoided this pitfall during the first period of their activities ; but later some of them proved less wise : and to-day there exists a considerable amount of music written by Russians which has all the characteristics of the by-products of musical academicism of other countries.

Of the great Russians of the nineteenth century, some went to the opposite extreme. Glinka, relating, in his

Memoirs, how he had found himself unable to carry
out his intention of taking lessons in counterpoint, says :
' All the better ; strict German counterpoint does not
always agree with the flight of free fancy ! '—thus
showing that the Russian musical mind was not yet ripe
for the assimilation of certain vital things in art. To the
present day, it remains in a similar respect unripe ;
for instance, one would vainly seek for signs showing
that Bach has exercised any real influence on musical
Russia. The only composer who showed a natural
understanding of polyphony was Borodin, who resorted
to it sparingly, but has given some ingenious, flowing,
and delightful instances of contrapuntal writing.

An unerring instinct, however, directed the best of ṭhe
Russian composers towards the forms that were most
suitable for their own purposes. Michail Glinka
(1804-1857), the founder of the modern school, was a
musician of surpassing originality and perspicacity,
whose example was to prove of the highest value to his
successors. Besides Glinka, the composers whose influence was most beneficial to the Russian school were
Berlioz, Schumann, and especially Liszt. Glinka did not
consciously aim at becoming the founder of a school.
His French biographer, Octave Fouque, rightly empha-
sised the fact that ' however great his influence, it would
have been greater, and have made itself felt during his
lifetime, not after his death only, if he had not lacked
will power as well as ambition. If he possessed the attri-
butes of a reformer and initiator, it was solely owing to
his unconscious intuition. He was unaware of the
function he was fulfilling, and incapable of waging war
against the prejudices and fashions of his time '.

But his most earnest desire was, as he once wrote to a
friend, ' to compose music which would make all his
beloved fellow-countrymen feel quite at home, and lead
no one to allege that he strutted about in borrowed
plumes '. He accomplished this purpose fully with his

first opera, *A Life for the Tsar* (1836), which at its first performance was acknowledged—as it still is in Russia—as the national opera *par excellence.*

It is very difficult for non-Russians to acknowledge in the music of this opera the profoundly national character which all Russians agree in emphasising : César Cui, for instance, declaring that ' every one of its tunes bears deeply stamped on it the imprint of the Russian character ', while others, voicing a protest which was often to be made by the more conventional factions of the public against the encroachments of the spirit and tone of folk music in contemporary art, dismissed the same tunes as ' mere cabmen's music.'

The difficulty does not lie in the fact that practically nothing in the score originates in or resembles native music. Such tests are fallacious. When Glinka utilises Spanish themes in his delightful *Jota Aragonese* and *Summer Night in Madrid,* he remains as characteristically Russian as Glazunof in his two fine overtures on Greek folk tunes. But there appears to be very little in the score of *A Life for the Tsar* which differs in any particular from the conventionalities of grand opera. Some of the music is fine in spirit as well as in workmanship, and a few passages are of epic grandeur. Yet it is in vain that one seeks in it evidence of the prophetic originality and highly imaginative beauty of Glinka's second opera, *Russlan and Liudmila.* What remains a subject for wonder is Glinka's consummate skill, the purity and ease that characterise his utterances. He was, as several of his successors—Borodin, Balakiref, and Rimsky-Korsakof—were to be, a born orchestrator ; but the extent of experience which *A Life for the Tsar,* the first attempt of a practically self-taught composer, reveals is marvellous.

Russlan and Liudmila, written six years after this opera, has one defect common to most Russian operas that are genuinely interesting to musicians (practically the sole exceptions are Rimsky-Korsakof's *Maid of Pskof* and Mussorgsky's *Boris Godunof*) : the libretto is unsubstantial and loosely put together. In this respect *A Life for the Tsar* is by far its superior. It also contains a certain amount of indifferent music, but a good deal more that is admirable and worthy of close study. The choral parts of the first act are of great beauty, and almost the whole of the fantastic scenes and fairy music in the second and fourth acts, as well as the Oriental dances in the fourth, are very lovely. It is by virtue of such pages that *Russlan and Liudmila* played no less a part in the evolution of Russian music than *Tristan and Isolde* in that of Western music. Balakiref, Borodin and Rimsky-Korsakof proceed directly from Glinka ; and also Tchaikovsky, though it is by the more facile and sentimental elements in Glinka's music that the last has been chiefly influenced.

Glinka also influenced Dargomyjsky (1813-1869) deeply. But Dargomyjsky's chief concern after he reached maturity was not purely musical invention, but accuracy in dramatic expression. In his early operas, and in most of his songs, he rested content with following Glinka's examples along the line of least resistance, occasionally, however, composing songs which, as humorous character sketches, are most interesting. Picturesque music interested him little ; yet he wrote a couple of orchestral Fantasias in which he displayed originality. His conception of dramatic recitative having matured, he eventually wrote the lyric drama *The Stone-Guest*, which shows that although his ideas were very similar to Mussorgsky's, his musical imagination was limited. *The Stone-Guest* remains more interesting in theory than in actual fact. It is perhaps in Mussorgsky's works that Dargomyjsky's ideas are most successfully carried out.

Balakiref (1837-1910) became at an early age the acknowledged leader of the Russian school. As a

teacher, as adviser, organiser, and propagandist he
worked with untiring zeal. He was Borodin's and
Mussorgsky's teacher, and later Rimsky-Korsakof's.
Tchaikovsky, who detested criticism, often courted his
advice and benefited by it, especially during the composition of his *Romeo and Juliet* and *Manfred*. Rimsky-
Korsakof's *Memoirs* bear ample testimony to the
influence Balakiref exercised all around him, even on
older men such as Dargomyjsky.

No description of Balakiref's admirable personality
would be complete without reference to this aspect of it.
The amount of energy he devoted to directing and helping other composers may help to account for the comparatively small number of his own compositions. It is
more difficult to understand how some of these, the
lesser ones especially, bear no trace of the genius which
inspired him to write the tone poem *Tamara*, the piano
Fantasia *Islamey*, some of the early songs (*A Song of
Georgia*, *The Song of the Golden Fish*, *Hebraic Song*), or
of the latest (*Prelude, A Vision, Vernal Night*), in which
his impassioned imagination and his profound originality are as fully expressed as they are in the tone poem
In Bohemia and in large parts of the two symphonies.

The joint influences of native music and Eastern
music co-operated in the formation of Balakiref's style
even more markedly than they had in the style of
Glinka's maturity. They co-operated to an equal extent
in the formation of Borodin's, of Rimsky-Korsakof's,
and of Glazunof's during the early part of his career.
All four composers, as regards style and technical equipment, owe much to Liszt. They utilised and extended
Liszt's discoveries in the domains of idiom and
method of treatment, and understood in its true
spirit the principle of ' poetic fertilisation ', writing
things such as *Tamara* and *Stenka Razin* and *Antar* and
many others which, although inspired by ' programmes,'
are as true and substantial examples of ' pure ' music as

may be wished for—such as are afforded, too, by Balakiref's and Borodin's symphonies, or the early symphonies of Glazunof (especially the second, third, and
fourth). Tchaikovsky (1840-1893) likewise proceeds
from Liszt, but alone assimilated more of Liszt's defects
than of his qualities. The many instances of theatrical,
turgid, or facilely sentimental music that occur in his
output recall the inferior Liszt, the Liszt who readily
succumbed to the doubtful lure of the *clichés* of Italian-
ism and romanticism.

It is in the quieter moods of his instrumental compositions (for instance, in the fourth symphony and in
the chamber music) that Tchaikovsky appears at his
best, if not always his most characteristic, showing grace
and skill as well as a sense of fitness and balance.

Borodin's (1834-1887) production of music is,
from the quantitative point of view, even smaller
than Balakiref's, but in artistic significance yields
to none. It was written of him (in the *Edinburgh
Review*, 1906): 'No musician has ever claimed
immortality with so slender an offering. Yet if
there be, indeed, immortalities in music, his claim
is incontestible'; and this is a judgement which music-
lovers will heartily endorse : for there is no work of
Borodin which does not tell of his genuineness of feeling,
vivid imagination, and sense of musical beauty. He is a
peerless melodist ; and there is always something in the
design of his melodies, as well as in their tone, that
belongs to him alone. Even his manner of using folk
tunes bears the imprint of his individuality, as in the
first movement of his Unfinished Symphony—which may
serve also as an instance of his direct simplicity of tone
and methods, and especially of the ingenuity and surety
of his harmony. He is essentially a lyric composer
as well in his one opera, *Prince Igor*, as in the few songs
which he has left, of which *The Discord*, *The Queen of
the Sea*, and *The Enchanted Garden* are perhaps the best.

Like *Russlan and Liudmila*, *Prince Igor* contains a proportion of indifferent music, but it is full of radiant gems
like the Dances (now made popular by concert and ballet
performances, but hardly ever heard as they were
written, that is, with the choral part that contributes
greatly to their intensity and variety of colour) and the
lovely arias and instrumental episodes.

In one of his letters Borodin narrates that Liszt once
told him : ' Do not let criticisms beguile you into
altering the form of your works. You have gone very
far, but not erred ; your path is the right path, and your
artistic instinct is a sure guide to you'. The two String
Quartets and the two Symphonies, which are his biggest
instrumental works, provide ample confirmation of this
verdict even when not conforming to the usual rules of
form as taught by theory, because they never fall short
of that logic which is the natural outcome of continuity
of interest, and is determined by the imagination, not
by rule of thumb.

That he had the makings of one of the truest and most
delightful musical humorists ever known is shown by his
whimsical contribution of a Funeral March and a
Requiem to the set of Paraphrases written by various
Russians to accompany the theme of the well-known
' Chopsticks ' Polka. These are by far the funniest and
most spontaneous things in the set.

To deal with Mussorgsky (1839-1881) within the
compass of a few paragraphs is extremely difficult,
and practically impossible if the æsthetic problems
arising in connection with his ideals and achievements are touched upon. From the mere musical
point of view, Mussorgsky may be defined as a
composer of rare intuitive genius, who held that
the usual technical equipment included much by
which spontaneous variety of utterance was impaired.
Whether this attitude of his was the outcome of a constitutional idiosyncrasy or of a deliberately matured

theory does not affect the issue. It should be noted, however, that he stood firm in his conception of an art that was to aim, in his own words, at ' point-blank truth.' His correspondence with Rimsky-Korsakof and others shows how eager he was to vindicate his views against all. Like Dargomyjsky, but with a far clearer outlook and far more pregnant imagination, he wished to achieve in dramatic music and in vocal music generally an ideal of artistic realism which, of course, was possible only in these two provinces of musical art.

After eliminating the cruder and looser definitions of realism in art, one is practically compelled to admit that artistic realism consists not in the choice of ' realistic ' subjects, nor even in a ' realistic ' vision of subjects (these are merely empty labels), but in particular methods of treatment whose characteristics are a minimum of elaboration and formal organisation. It is not enough that expression should be direct and definite—as it is in many instances of music that no stretch of terms would justify us in calling realistic. The spirit of realism is the very opposite of the spirit of instrumental music, which must always be one of high organisation even in its utmost simplicity. In music the true realist will attempt to translate his vision directly, without the adjunct of any comment or conscious expression of personal outlook or feeling.

Boris Godunof—Mussorgsky's masterpiece, and one of the great masterpieces of dramatic music—provides an elementary, but typical, illustration of this spirit in the bare fact that it is practically all dialogue. Only the brief preludes, the dances, and occasional briefer transitions (some of them lengthened by Rimsky-Korsakof in his deplorable revision of Mussorgsky's original score) are entrusted to the instruments alone. But this, naturally, is a detail.

There can be no question that in this work, as in the finest of his songs (the first three of the *Songs and Dances of Death*, the set *Sunless*, the *Nursery*, and the various Peasant Songs), Mussorgsky, besides achieving his ideals to the full, has given us some of the loveliest music in the world's repertory. The one act he wrote of his musical comedy, *The Marriage Broker*, is an unique instance of terseness and wit in musical characterisation.

On the merits of his other lyric drama, *Khovansht-china* (of which he left only a rough, so-called ' final ' draft, after working at it fitfully during the last nine years of his brief life) opinions are divided. Of the few Russians who really admired Mussorgsky during the first decades after his death, some held that *Khovansht-china* was even more significant than *Boris Godunof*. Others were of opinion that it is less substantial and less live—a view which nowadays appears to prevail, at least outside Russia.

Rimsky-Korsakof (1844-1908) produced an enormous variety of musical works, many of which bear the imprint of what has been defined by a French critic as the ' collec-tive individuality ' of the modern Russian school— something that undoubtedly exists, and whose presence is evinced by a comparative examination of Glinka's late works, Balakiref's, Borodin's, Rimsky-Korsakof's, Glazu-nof's, and Liadof's ; Mussorgsky's naturally standing quite apart, as they do in the whole history of music. Beyond it, however, it is easy to feel each of these artists' individuality. The collective individuality, so far as it goes, is characterised by a common taste for the pic-turesque and the concrete, for brilliancy of colour, for certain melodic patterns and harmonies and rhythms. But as unmistakable as the tenderness and intimate pathos of Borodin are Balakiref's tense earnestness and ele-mental passion, Rimsky-Korsakof's versatile ease and self-possession, his extreme virtuosity ; the stronger, at times heavier, touch of the early Glazunof, the greater intellectuality and thoroughness of his methods of working out, which gain an increasing ascendancy in his later symphonies ; and the quieter grace and more restricted focus of Liadof's works.

By his example and teaching Rimsky-Korsakof played as great a part as Balakiref in the formation of the spiritual and technical elements of this collective individuality. His pupils were countless (the list of them comprises Stravinsky as well as Liadof and Glazunof), and have all been deeply influenced by him.

It is in his early works that first-hand evidence of the originality and raciness should be sought ; especially in his programme-symphony *Antar*, the tone poems *Sadko* and *A Fairy Tale*, the *Easter Overture* and the Suite *Sheherazade*, the lyric drama *The Maid of Pskof*, and the opera-ballet *Mlada*. His fantastic *Snow Maiden* is held in particularly high esteem by Russians : others may feel that in it he displayed all the grace of his fancy, but not the vigour of which he gave convincing testimony elsewhere ; indeed, that the music might serve as an instance of the passionless and at times undetermined tone which prevails in many other works of his.

If there is less depth and glow in most of his later compositions, the truth remains that within his own province of festive elegance and picturesque, genial fancy, Rimsky-Korsakof achieved much that is of lasting artistic value. His evolution came as the result of a carefully weighed policy. Mussorgsky more than once pointed out to him that ' Western methods were not always suitable for the expression a Russian's individuality.' The truth of this utterance he elected to ignore. He set out to polish and purify his own methods in the light of current usage, as carefully and with as sincere a faith in the excellence of his purpose as when he undertook to polish and purify, in the same spirit, the music of Mussorgsky's *Boris Godunof*, regardless of Mussorgsky's clearly set forth desire, and not perceiving that in both cases he was sacrificing, without corresponding gain, much that possessed artistic significance

and not its mere semblance. He was prepared cheerfully to abide by the consequences of his determination;
but eager to seek renovation within the boundaries of his
creed, as is shown by the poetic mysticism of his last
lyric drama, *The Legend of Kitej and Fevronia the Maiden*
(curiously described by certain Russian critics as ' a
Russian *Parsifal* '), and the youthful alertness of his
Golden Cockerel.

Glazunof (6. 1865) is essentially a symphonist. From
the outset of his musical life he displayed exuberance
and a surprisingly precocious maturity of conception and
technique. His very first works were substantial and
forcible. The first symphony, which he composed at
seventeen, *Stenka Razin*, which he completed at twenty,
and the Overtures on Greek Folk-tunes, are the work of
a composer in full possession of his individuality and
means of expression. The *Oriental Rhapsody*, written a
little later, is one of his masterpieces, and the work
that shows him closest to Borodin in depth of poetry
and in essential characteristics of style. The Second
Symphony, a work of rare power and brilliancy, was
written a couple of years after *Stenka Razin.*

The later works evince a tendency towards the abstract
which, while winning many new admirers for the composer, has disappointed some of those whom his first
utterances had conquered. It has sometimes been said
that he was influenced by Brahms, which is true only
superficially, if at all. It would be more accurate to say
that his art, as exemplified in the sixth, seventh, and
eighth symphonies, and other works of the same period,
shows in certain broad respects affinities with that of the
German classical symphonists.

That he has since entered a new phase was lately shown
by his orchestral Preludes inscribed to the memory of
Rimsky-Korsakof and Stassof respectively, the only
recent works of his to have reached Western Europe at
the time of writing.

The Music of Liapunof (1859-1924) is in many respects akin to Balakiref's in spirit and in outward features. It adequately expresses the composer's thoughtful, genuinely lyrical nature, and its strain shows traces of both national and Eastern influences profoundly assimilated, not under the aspect of a surface glitter only. His piano music, and some of his songs, rank among the best produced in Russia. Although at times long drawn, his orchestral works (two symphonies, concertos and tone-poems) deserve greater attention than they have received so far.

In proportion as the contemporary period is entered, the task of describing and defining becomes increasingly hard. Ten years ago it seemed fairly easy to appraise Stravinsky (1882), who stood forth with the three beautiful ballets, *The Fire-Bird*, *Petrushka* and the *Rite of Spring*, and the one-act opera, *The Nightingale*. But nowadays any survey of his activities which would not include consideration of the baffling works which he wrote later would appear inadequate. The same applies, in a lesser degree, to Prokofief, another brilliantly gifted representative of the younger generation. Others have cropped up, such as Senilof, Miaskovsky, Feinberg, Gniessin, Alexandrof and Roslavets, whose principal works are not available for study ; and we hear of others who for the time being are but names.

Among the older and better-known composers it is easy to draw broad and correspondingly vague distinctions, pointing out that Rachmaninof (1873),Glière (1875), S. Taneief (1856-1915), and Metner (1879), are conservative and strongly under German influences, while others, after Liadof, but with less spontaneous charm of manner, represent in an equally conservative aspect the actual national tradition established by Glinka's school ; but assertions of this kind serve no useful purpose unless reasons for them are shown.

Among the names omitted here are those of Serof

(1820-1871), Rubinstein (1830-1894) and Arensky (1861-1906)—three second-rate composers, two of whom are already almost forgotten—and of a small number of minor poets such as Kallinikof, who are far from unworthy of attention, but could hardly have been included in so brief a survey. Cesar Cui (1835-1915), played a great part as propagandist of the Russian national school. His compositions, of secondary significance, are products of a cultured and sound mind, but not of creative imagination.

The omission of Scriabin (1871-1915) calls for a few words of explanation. There is so far no *juste milien* between those who consider him as a giant in art (most Russians do) and those who hold his music very cheap.

For a long time, as was once pointed out in a review of a book on Scriabin, ' the Scriabinists had it all their own way, owing to the indolence of those who happened to think otherwise.' This was quite true—so far at least as England is concerned—until the publication of Mr. Cecil Gray's *A Survey of Contemporary Music* (Oxford University Press, 1924), whose author displays the very reverse of indolence in his denunciation of ' the inherent falsity, artificiality, and blatant coarseness ' of Scriabin's music, excepting from his unfavourable verdict only a few of the short piano pieces of the later period of the composer's life. My own views are and have long been similar ; but I have no room to give my reasons here. What can be said against Scriabin generally is as obvious as what can be said in his favour. But it cannot be said usefully unless proof is given that the most searching possible tests have been applied to every step through which the conclusion was reached.

RICHARD WAGNER
(1813-1883)

By RICHARD CAPELL

MODERN European music is remarkably extended, compared with the music of other periods and peoples. It can grow to a huge size. The fugue and overture, sonata, symphony, and music-drama are comparable with the most elaborate and imposing literary forms. The finest musical art of the preceding period had resembled the lyrical inspirations of literature rather than the epic or the drama. Towards the end of the seventeenth century a new era—a new climate, as it were—set in. It favoured, to put it no higher, the development of bulk. The era of the Mass in B minor, the Choral Symphony, and *The Nibelung's Ring* is unique in musical history, and in retrospect may come to have the look as of an extraordinary geological era, which encouraged tropical beasts and an enormous vegetation to spring up in unaccustomed zones.

Some of the factors in this development may be indicated. The principal was the system of contrasts of tonality, which afforded a fund of new rhetorical resources, all favouring amplitude of expression. At the same time instrumental music was increasingly cultivated, and it ousted vocal music, within whose strict limits the leading composers of the earlier age had mainly worked, from the middle position in music. Instrumental music was capable, among other things, of an unflagging prolongation of exercise denied by nature to the human voice. The most eminent composers of extensive music belonged to the lands where musical instruments were particularly esteemed, and in their different ways they wrote on the largest scale, attracted by the sustained and, as it were, ' reasoned ' eloquence rendered possible by the organ, the pianoforte, and the orchestra. The most important of these architects were Bach, Beethoven, and Richard Wagner.

The works of these three have this much in common —a magnitude and a duration which represent the limits, as far as is known, of the musical public's faculty of attention. Of established works of music, Bach's is the longest setting of the Mass, the Choral Symphony is the longest symphony, and *The Mastersingers of Nuremberg* and *The Twilight of the Gods* are the longest operas. Looking a degree closer at the three masters, we find conspicuous differences in technique. The vast proportions of the music of Bach had their origin in the natural copiousness of an organist's improvisations, together with Bach's singular command over the polyphonic style, a style which spreads, so to speak, of itself. Beethoven's largeness had a different source, namely, a developed sense of key-relationship with its implications of dramatic contrasts and of striking adventures. Wagner's instrument was the modern orchestra, a world in itself, and he looked with a conqueror's eyes over the virgin territory. There (so we may be allowed fancifully to put it) his music was implicit. Only his hand was wanted to withdraw the veil. As when the new continent is discovered, the wonder is it was not discovered before. Wagner's music is not dramatic, like Beethoven's, but is a long flow of narrative—so long, because the numerous voices of his orchestra all seem to have their natural fresh tale to tell for the first time. This is a fancy from which, in considering Wagner, we shall not be able to escape, so incessantly does his music seem to speak of the wild life. Bach's compositions have frequently been held to suggest the piers and vaulting of the Gothic builders. Wagner's work rather calls to mind the more accidental vistas of forest and mountain scenery.

This ' wildness ' of his art was a character that resulted from his departure from the argumentative polyphony of Bach and from the design of Beethoven's tonalities, and it struck his contemporaries more than any other musical phenomenon of the time, conservative opinion declaring it to be a relapse into chaos, while the adventurous-minded were delighted by its promise of wandering and illimitable avenues. Wagner's music —of course, the music of his maturity is meant—was the principal counterpart of the romantic movement in literature.

' Jamais pays de plaine, quelque beau qu'il fût, ne parut tel à mes yeux,' Rousseau confessed, and for that age it was a startling paradox. ' I must have torrents and crags, the pine and its black forests, ways that are hard to climb and precipices that affright.' What began as a whim grew to possess all the authority of a fashion. It struck the fancy of Europe. For one age to have sought to make of nature a servant was enough reason for it to be the pleasure of the next to denounce comfort and equilibrium. The arts, in modern Europe so swift and violent in revolution, one by one took up Rousseau's hint. The superiority of rugged scenery and the more menacing aspects of nature began to obtain important sanctions early in the nineteenth century, Ruskin declaring that mountainous regions harboured exceptionally powerful spiritual forces. Within a century of Rousseau's death the movement with which we find it convenient here to father him culminated in the gloom and splendour of *The Nibelung's Ring* of Wagner. It was the century that witnessed the æsthetic discovery of the Alps, which since then have been well explored and are now mostly funicularised.

The French Revolution and the Napoleonic wars were some of the ' ways hard to climb, precipices that affright ' which Europe enjoyed. Wagner, whose works were to be so considerable an expression of the tendencies of the age, was born at Leipzig in the very year of the Battle of the Nations. Beethoven was the voice of the transitional period—of the transition from polite intercourse and persuasive oratory (portents of whose doom were the fall of the Bastille and the death of Mozart) to flushed prophecy. ' Dieu ', observed Hugo, ' changea la chaîne de l'Europe '. Beethoven was the first musician to snap his fingers at the protocol of palaces. Liberty and the individual sanction became words of magical attribution ; and less sanguine generations will always observe with curiosity the enterprising enthusiasm then current. Wagner belonged to the first generation that mountaineered for pleasure. There seems to have been an exhilaration in the air, depreciating perils and promising wondrous achievements. Napoleon's attempt to conquer the world looks preposterous enough to-day. And these Napoleonic composers, Beethoven with his symphonies, Wagner with his music-dramas, may be regarded—in contrast to the composers of perfect music, Mozart, Handel, and Bach—as having attempted something impossible to carry out to perfection. We are concerned at the moment to point to the current faith in large unexploited possibilities of life, a faith which incited young men of the lower middle classes like Wagner and Carlyle to stand up and harangue the world, each as his spirit moved him, in disregard of the old urbanity. The imagination cannot readily adjust them in a frame of the eighteenth century. How could they have conformed to a more settled society ? Would such arrogant individualism have been tameable ? They would certainly have had to define themselves more strictly. The eighteenth century, which had not much patience with ' mazed considerings ', would, more than Wagner's time, have wanted to know precisely what was meant by *The Nibelung's Ring* and *Parsifal*. What Rousseau, for all his aspirations after crags and torrents, did actually compose was *Le Devin du Village* (if, indeed, he did not steal it). But his whim was now a faith—a faith in the advantages of the uncurbed flight of the mind, instead of the cautious gait

previously considered desirable. Affability was no
longer artistic ; it had given place to the practice of
evoking wonders. Carlyle piled crags of minatory prose,
and out of Wagner poured a music that seemed to foam
about men's ears in something of the vague yet impressive way of nature's own demonstrations.

Even so early as *The Flying Dutchman* the drama of
Wagner was eminently enthusiastic ; and the previous
history of the art tells of nothing like the sort of sacred
tyranny which in the development of his life this
musician presumed to exert. *The Nibelung's Ring* has
already been mentioned in the same breath with the
Mass in B minor. The production of the Mass is a
mystery. Wherein lay Bach's satisfaction, as its author ?
What was the motive of the labour ? Was he content
that his music should be, but not be heard ? Did he
foresee its survival ? As for the King of Saxony, Bach
seems to have been contented, once his manuscript was
deposited in the royal library. Wagner demanded of the
princes of Germany that they should build him a theatre
and then come and hear his tetralogy in it. He was not
content that his big music should exist only as his dream.
The dream had to be materialised, or perhaps it should
be said that the world was to be made to share in the
dream.

A conservative and sceptical age would have ridiculed
Wagner's pretensions. But it was the age of the ' renas-
cence of wonder ', which welcomed surprise and counted
on expansion. This is certainly not to say that Wagner's
practical career was a path of primroses, and there is
available the fullest documentation of his political and
financial troubles, of his sufferings from erysipelas,
crossed loves, and musical criticism. But what is primarily interesting is that his century had plenty of room
for a man with a mission, even with so inordinate a
mission, and did actually allow of the complete fulfilment
of Wagner's well-nigh superhuman projects. During the

conception of *The Ring*, ' I shall not live to see it'*, he declared. Yet he did. The times favoured his power of communicating a kind of mystical experience to the sensitive spirits of Europe, and at its moment Wagnerianism distinctly had the character of a religion, not lacking its exaltations and its legends, its fanatics, pilgrimages, and exegetists. Such a movement does not come from art of a classic order, which, since its meaning must lie in a social application, canalises the exuberance of the artist. Wagner is the archetype of the romantic artist, whose object first and last is the rendering and exposition of his emotions. The classic at its most sublime retains a manner of reasonable intercourse. The other must fascinate, terrorise.

The work left to us by Wagner is less purely musical than that of the great composers before him. It is not so, however, because his musical ideas were often engendered by phenomena of the concrete world, or even because their ordering did not pursue a purely musical argument. Such an Act as the first of *Siegfried* is a symphony. But the execution of it comprises essential features which are not musical. From first to last Wagner counted only partially on music in the fulfilling of his ambition. This last was vast—not less than ' to bring myself, and Humanity at the same time, nearer to my perceived Goal for Humanity '†—and it is natural enough that, with such an enterprise in view, even a Wagner should be glad of all the available means.

Other good musicians had written operas. A peculiarity of Wagner was the genuine passion he felt for the extra-musical resources of opera, the verbal explanations and the various factors of scenic representation. Music, indeed, he declared to be ' die höchste, die erlösende Kunst', and music was assuredly his ' highest, redemptive ' gift. On the strength of his poetry and prose his fame would not have spread much outside Leipzig. Yet,

---

*Letters, 1852.   †Letters, 1854.

I

as is the work of no other musician of his rank, Wagner's music is hardly to be disentangled from matter addressed to the eye and to the verbal understanding. In the pride of his singular inspiration he made bold to override the consideration that the arts of words and of action had not been proved able to support the repetition which had always been the prerogative of music. The great mass of Wagner's music, then, is bound up with scenic business, a business assuredly, with him, of a very different skill and poetic import from ordinary operatic traffic, yet essentially of an order of interest that is exhausted before we have fairly begun to appraise the multitudinous attractions of the music.

To explain how he came to serve his art thus, there is, to start with, the circumstance that Wagner was born and bred among theatrical people, so that he grew up with the glamour of the theatre and the well-known attendant superstitions naturally woven in his mind. His career as a quite young man was in the theatre, and the opera-house dangled only just out of reach such plums of popularity and wealth as fell to Rossini and Meyerbeer. When ambition struck deeper roots an analogy suggested itself : ' As the portentousness of Beethoven's symphony was to the symphony of the eighteenth century, so . . . .' Wagner even as a schoolboy was steeped in Beethoven. At nineteen he threw off a symphony which rehearses glibly many of the turns of Beethoven's phraseology. To be the Beethoven of opera—that sounded well to a man of turbulent vitality, above all impatiently conscious of genius. A less masterful mind might have been more suspicious of traps in the enterprise. For the symphony was, before Beethoven, already some one thing—an absolute—music that lived in and for itself. But we may ask what there had ever been to indicate that opera could amount to more than a sociable convenience, a more or less amiable misalliance or workaday compromise between incompatibles. Music's whole life had, once upon a time, been humbly ancillary. Some 200 years or so ago it began to assert independent rights, and it has tended in modern times to be more and more of a masterful partner in association with any other form of expression. We know through Mozart of what a heavenly amiability it was momentarily capable in stooping to marry itself with a stage action. But in the new century amiability was not to be counted on.

To judge Wagner on the strength of a score (such as those of Sir Henry Wood's orchestral performances of long extracts) which suppresses the connection of the music with the stage, one would say that no music could be less theatrical. Here, one would say, is music of a rich and dreamy melodiousness, the tunes of which grow endlessly one from another, as intertwined as the plants of a tropical glade. Contrast and surprise, which stage music surely asks for, are hardly possible in such a modulatory style, in which one tonality never finds any difficulty in suavely melting into another. And (this imaginary critic might pursue) in a score in which the orchestra is so unremittingly eloquent, where is the room for the intimate whisper or the outbreak of *bravura* which shall concentrate all attention on the hero at a crisis in his destiny ? ' Better imagine the late quartets of Beethoven to be operatic music ! '

Wagner had got, of course, a notion of an ideal stage action that was to match and complete his music, and a version of it still holds the field. But in effect his actual music has been proved far to transcend all other con-currence. It was much too good if all he wanted was an equal partner for his human action. And of music so good one of our delights lies in repetition—precisely the bane of a verbal expression.

Opera before Wagner had not made all the pretensions, it had served as a mixed social entertainment. The action would at given moments stand aside and leave the field clear for the music. Music in return for this consideration offered no objection to an occasional plain declaration of the plot. Opera, before as since, has been the special beguilement of those for whom music is not exclusively absorbing, those who, instead of resenting, actually welcome a visible and verbal accompaniment to music. While the fatigued ear rests, occupation is afforded for the other senses. That opera house which enchained the affections of the young Wagner—excited his ambitions and at the same time infuriated his intelligence—combined for the contemporary public most of the attractions of our present-day theatres of variety, our grand miscellaneous concerts and our county-town pageants.

A measure of Wagner's vigour and pride of mind was his intention to raise all those factors to the power of matching his great musical eloquence. Plot and gesture, the stage decorations, the verse of the libretto, and the behaviour of the theatre's menagerie, all were to be of the loftiest poetic nature and to fuse with the music into one overwhelming phenomenon. From *Rienzi* to *Parsifal* he seems never to have doubted the validity of his cherished ' synthesis ' of music and drama. At first blush there was enough novelty in the Wagnerian spectacle and its strange earnestness and length, enough suggestion of a new wild world of poetry, to make the association plausible. Hence the doctrine that Wagner's music was merely one aspect of the almost unanalysable Bayreuth representations. Only in course of time the interest of the spectacle was found to languish first. The music may blaze bravely, none more so, but it fairly soon came to this, that while Wagner's camp fire roasts us on the one side we are aware often of being chilly on the other.

The world may come to regret it, especially since there is no means of fully disengaging Wagner's music. Most of us know mixed feelings at the prospect of a performance of *The Ring* : welcoming the music, which is, all said and done, one of the best things life has to offer, and rather dreading the all too well-known panorama. But there was no question for Wagner of an optional path. He went that way whole-heartedly, for he could hardly conceive of any other. It was rather more than a matter of environment and opportunity. It so happened that Wagner's musical imagination took fire from scenes of dramatic activity. The musical thought shaped itself in him as the equivalent of a situation in poetic drama, and when the right incitement came the music was formed with such rapidity and certainty as to strike us with awe at an inspiration so transcending normal experience. Deprived of the appropriate spark Wagner was nearly helpless. When commissioned to write a march for the opening of an American exhibition (1876), he found his invention sluggish. He laboured at the piece with irritation, almost with dismay, not in the end to make any very considerable job of it. But when in the course of his reading he met with the tale of Siegfried, ' I also spontaneously met with the truly perfect phraseology '. And when he was at work on *The Ring*, ' every thing springs as if wild from earth '.

In the Autobiography nothing is more impressive than the account of the conception of the prelude to *The Rhinegold*, at Spezia in 1853, after five years of abstention from composition. As he lay half asleep in the afternoon, ' a rushing sound in my brain formed itself into music, the chord of E flat . . . . I awoke in sudden terror from my doze, feeling as though waves were rushing above my head. I at once recognised that the instrumental introduction to *The Rhinegold*, which must long have lain latent within me, though unable to find definite form, had at last been revealed.'

Before the end of the following winter he had on paper the whole sketch of *Rhinegold*.

On the other hand, as an example of Wagner's occa-

sional music, there is the not very favourably characteristic march in *Tannhäuser*--originally composed to
celebrate the safe return of a Saxon prince home from
a visit to Windsor—not a precedent to encourage any
fanciful wish that Wagner had diverted, instead of
luxuriously indulging, his instinct. But that, of course,
is not seriously in question.

Given the best musical thought of a man, we can
afford not to care how he came by it. The agent that
unseals the thought in the musician's mind—poem,
opera libretto, or some casual sound in outside life, the
yellowhammer's chirp, the rhythm of a smith's blows on
his anvil—is a subsidiary and anecdotal interest, so
long as the world is given the thought fully composed,
fully transmuted into music. Some musicians have had
the gift of soaring quickly away from the first prompting.
Others have been so wrapped up in the circumstances of
the suggestion that they have not contemplated leaving
them behind.

Operas and symphonic poems may be regarded as an
exposure of a process of musical composition. A *Fidelio*
presents the view of the workshop whence a *Leonora*
overture and a couple of fine arias are the important products—not a musical drama. An operatic spectacle in
itself entertains only ingenuous minds. The real service
of opera is to act as a kind of diving board from which
music has often found it convenient to leap into independent activity. Wagner is peculiar in having so very
tenaciously carried with him into the new element all
the earthly paraphernalia.

We can think of Mozart writing his operas on utterly
different texts and of such operas being just as Mozartian.
Chopin can be fancied as a violinist composing for the
violin, and his work remaining essentially Chopin's.
Wagner's music is not so separable from its circumstances. The literature of his predilection materially
affected its character and form. There was no question

of choosing between methods. The method of Wagner's art was an irresistible fact of nature. And while, after *Tannhäuser* and *Lohengrin*, his musical genius became singularly fortified, so that all in all he rises above all the composers born since Beethoven, he did not any the more write with the intention of conveying the pure sensations of music. We, his audience, were to be made to feel as Wagner had felt—that was the heart of his pre-occupation. Nothing that had gone to stoking the furnace of his imagination was not worth commemorating ; nothing was held to be unimportant or foreign to the communicated emotional experience.

It was not a simple gift, for if we accept anything it has to be nothing less than all Wagner had and was—a tyrannical gift ! How has it been received ? The appreciation of his work is, more than with any other great composer, a personal matter. There is very little neutral ground between submission to Wagner's empire and rebellion. Incantation might have been a word invented for Wagner. Certainly no European music before him worked this quasi-hypnotic spell. It is a question of temperament and mood, how you yield to it or resist it. An overwhelming majority is only too pleased with the luxurious pleasure. A minority resents what seems positively a physical domination. You either like a measure of intoxication or you do not, and in the Wagnerian atmosphere there is a sort of intoxication, unknown in Bach or Beethoven. The entertainment in Wagner is not delicate. It is an orgy. Wagner monopolises the scene. For the time being, he ousts all other music, and any other thought for that matter, from the mind. The ascetic, then, detests Wagner. The temperate man leaves fair intervals between such pleasures. The willing subject, indulging unreservedly, obtains a sort of mystical reward. Although æsthetic fashions have changed a good deal, there remain in all countries great numbers of these ' perfect Wagnerites ' who religiously adore many things in Wagner which in detachment could only be considered as incoherent, tautologous, morally reprehensible, or even dull. Wagner's work is, in consequence, still performed very frequently everywhere, more or less in the manner he designed. It is sometimes said that his music will find its eventual home in the concert room, in the form of extensive extracts, without singing or scenery. But Wagner's future is not a pressing problem, since up to the present his music has in practice been strong enough to support all its encumbrances.

These are an uncommon load. Take, for example, the extra-musical machinery of *The Nibelung's Ring.* (We will forego a recapitulation of it, for fear the reader should quail.) The radical falsity of the libretto is this, that the simple barbarians of the old saga are endowed by Wagner with a new consciousness and a manner of expressing themselves which are by no means simple—and all the while they retain their antique savagery of action. Wotan's cunning and Siegfried's brutal prowess were all very well before these persons took to heroising themselves, but then they become unpardonable. As unmistakably as the milder race of Tennyson's Arthurians, they are figments of the 1850's, and we can never allow ourselves to forget it. And so at each of the bold, barbaric deeds we feel they ought to have known better. Look at the scene in the first act of *The Twilight of the Gods,* where Siegfried with violence robs Brynnhilde of the portentous ring. It was the sort of thing that was no doubt commonly done on the banks of the Rhine in the Stone Age, and even later. But this youth is not there to give us a naturalistic picture of family life in the good old days. He is a symbol and an ideal, a demi-god, a saviour. He is Siegfried, Wagner's ' ordained man of the future '—and he is nothing but an ordinary looting *soudard.* Similarly Wotan, ' the substance of the Intelligence of the Present ', turns out to be the substance of the intelligence of a fraudulent army contractor.

Two other works of Wagner's prime are *Tristan and Isolde* and *The Mastersingers of Nuremberg*. The dramatic business of *The Mastersingers* is a slight, sentimental comedy, remarkable in Wagner's work as containing the one unmistakable human being—Hans Sachs —among the throng of his symbolic figures and abstractions. For the pint pot of this comedy Wagner poured out music in quarts and gallons. The little tale is told in five hours. In *Tristan and Isolde* the movement of the wonderful, yearning music is accompanied on the stage by rather more than life-size gestures of actors who, no matter how gifted, never can avoid bringing to mind the Siegesallee statuary. To choose in Wagner the best matching of music with operatic action we look outside his musical maturity, to *Tannhäuser*. The story is interesting. Wagner handles it with spirit, and it is not too far outstripped by the music. The latter, indeed, might in places have served the story better, and in the second act is to be found the singular example in Wagner of stage action coming to the support of weakish music. The glowing ballet was written sixteen years later. In general, the music of *Tannhäuser* is crude enough. Yet in association with the action it undoubtedly meets the case, and the spectator finds his interest in the various factors gratified and exhausted more or less simultaneously.

After *Tannhäuser* and *Lohengrin*, during Wagner's exile after the Dresden insurrection, he became more and more exalted, and the composing of operas wore the aspect of a prophetic mission. ' I was thirty-six before I divined the exact substance of my artistic impulse—till then Art had counted for me as the aim and Life as the means.'* The prophet cried Reform. What in the farther ranges of his thought he particularly desired—what special improvement in the behaviour or aspirations of men—is merely adumbrated in his play

*Letters, 1854.

with the ideas of Power and Renunciation. In the fore-
ground there shaped itself the concept of a reformed
theatre. ' Les théâtres sont les mauvais lieux de la
musique,' according to Berlioz. Wagner had not so
much an objection in principle to the sort of alliances
contracted there as a desire for a greater solemnity in the
rites. The Wagnerian theatre, cool, dark, and favourable
to *recueillement*, was to be more austere than many
cathedrals. All the circumstances were to prepare the
spectator for portents and the awful spell which were to
take the place of the ordinary sociable operatic amuse-
ment. The audience, until then not the least attractive
fraction of the spectacle—self-important, and in the
Latin lands often actively intervening—was to become a
dark and huddled anonymous throng assisting almost
clandestinely at the enacted mysteries. The same strong
will further determined to subdue the singers ; and to
such effect that down to to-day his intentions have
proved almost insurmountable and Wagnerian singers
are least of any the ' spoilt darlings ' of our opera
houses. Their mouths are full of ' the large utterance of
the early gods ', and the nature of the music imposes on
them a slow, prehistoric gait verging on the inhuman.
This was the new convention which Wagner substituted
for more frivolous inverisimilitudes. The singers' music,
too, was as never before subjugated to the voice of the
whole—to Wagner's voice. They were caught up and
used as threads like any other in the general fabric.
The individual Wagnerian singer might serve well
or badly, but it should be impossible that he could
dominate, so awful was to be the landscape, like an
Alpine pass that belittles the agony of a whole heroic
army.

Wagner the reformer had this extraordinary success,
that all his reforms were duly carried out under his own
eyes—at Bayreuth in 1876. On the whole, Wagner's
reforms have had rather too much importance attached

to them, like most reforms. Perhaps the best of Bayreuth
is that it allows of the hearing of good music on a
summer holiday in the country. After all, the Three
Choirs had been doing that for generations. The
machinery of Wagner's playhouse and the creatures of
his stage are rejected by our essential idea, our mental
representation of his art. This idea represents his music.
His brood of uncouth heroes, their excessively substantial womenfolk, and their loquacious deities, all so
addicted to superlatives—these are only a background.
The lively image we all posses is of the music—of one
man's almost superhuman eloquence, ' music made of
change and conquest', wondrously rich—cajoling or
stormy—infinitely apt and copious, and always the outpouring of one unmistakable voice, Wagner's. Wagner
in the summer morning of *The Mastersingers*, the languorous twilight of *Tristan*, in the tempestuous spring-
tides of *The Ring*, or yellowing autumn of *Parsifal*—in
all hours and seasons the twelve notes of the octave and
the hundred timbres of the orchestra were always faithfully celebrating him, the omnipotent master.

The eloquence of Wagner's music belongs to the order
of wonders rather than of surprises. We can never cease
to admire the majestic resources with which the act-long
symphonic discourse is sustained. Wagner had to
struggle to find and shape suitable stories for his operas,
but the minute he came to write the music he was—so
the music is all the while telling us—a simple giant at
play. No situation was impossible, or even difficult.
No boulder could stand in the way of this stream when
it came pouring down. We are not aware anywhere in
Wagner's music of intellectual stress. (Think of the
grimness of it in Beethoven.) In the adequacy of his
technique to his imagination he is comparable to Mozart.
The sounds in his thought were just as tractable.

The giant is perfectly self-confident. Nothing can
make him hurry himself. The world must take him at

his own time. He is too sure of himself ever to feel the
need of springing on us anything odd or precipitate.
There is no music more deliberate or more consistent.
It visibly assembles its force for an exceptional effort.
Take the blow of the D flat against the pedal C in
Hagen's summoning of the clan. The blow has been
foreseen half-a-dozen bars away It is none the less
grand when it falls, though it falls without, as it were,
doing damage. This music does not come to smite, but
to bear us and everything away and along with it.
Nothing insuperable is met with in its course. It may
seem to be making for a splintering crash. But over and
over again after the most tremendous gathering and
swelling, it disperses swimmingly, without catastrophe,
as it turns out. It is an adventure in a dream. The
music rumbles and billows, and all the while there is no
peril.

The idea of fluidity always presents itself when we
think of Wagner's music. One thing melts into another,
tune into tune, key into key, mood into mood. The
movement, with all its variations (there never was
another tide of music which could, moving, seem so
nearly asleep, and where else are there such mighty
storms as those of the piling of the Nibelung gold in
Rhinegold, and of Isolde's ship heaving in sight of
Kareol ?), is always a flowing movement. Nothing stands
out as of a different element from the broad flood. The
countless recurrences of the tunes, and the transformations that are nearly recurrences, help to make the effect
of one consistent outpouring. In each of the dramas a
majority of the principal tunes is closely related. Those
of *The Ring*, for instance, might for the most part be the
fanfares of a huntsman's horn—one of the first and most
' natural ' sorts of instrumental music. And throughout
the *Ring* dramas some kind of woodland call is nearly
always haunting us, reverberating vigorously, or plain-
tively, or solemnly, from the heights or the depths.

These tunes have in their recurrences a part to play, according to Wagner's theory, in elucidating the stage action. The important interest in such a theory is how it works musically. The associations of a tune used for illustrative purpose may at times heighten the poetic effect of a scene. At other times the device may become fidgetty—for instance, Siegfried cannot be allowed to cut Brynnhilde loose from her armour without the fanfare of the sword turning up faithfully. In bare places things are kept going by old material being served out again rather mechanically—for example, the ' Unmuth ' which over and over again solemnly punctuates Wotan's speech-making in the second act of *The Valkyrie*. But that is incidental.

The main thing is that Wagner was launched, by his association of certain musical figures with the various personages and features of his dramas, on the writing of music good enough to justify this or any system. His system has in other hands been proved to have no fixed inherent virtue. But it gave to the inner genius of Wagner's music what it wanted—primarily an incitement and a spacious field of operations and, after that, a motive for exerting on a grand scale the fascinating powers of repetition in music.

The return of the themes in Wagner plays on the same feelings which are affected by the re-entries of the subject in fugue and the disguises and rehabilitation of the material of a symphony. There is no process in literature possessing the peculiar properties of repetition in music. The refrains of old ballads, of the rondeau and villanelle, give the barest hint of them. Repetition in music makes for symmetry and for emotional seductiveness. Perhaps it is because we feel the language of music so ready to be elusive, hovering beautifully but precariously near the boundaries of the comprehension, that a second execution of the same manœuvre appears improbable and hence agreeable to recognise. There are

the different pleasures of wandering abroad and of
homecoming, and Wagner handsomely indulges us in
both. In lulling alternation the flood bears us out-
wards and then rolls us shorewards again. Similar emotional effect was, in the classic sonata movement, incidental to the formal design. In Wagner the design is
much submerged. He seems to be playing directly for
the emotional reaction. He brings his characteristic
tunes back again and again. He is superbly assured of
the interest they have aroused from the first, and in this
he is usually right.

The melodiousness of Wagner is incessant. This melodiousness consists mainly of short musical figures linked
with their fellows by countless varieties of interrupted
cadences, or else sequentially prolonged, rather than of
true symmetrical melodies. One of Wagner's greatest
gifts lay in the invention of these striking figures of his
to which tuneful and rhythmical elements unite to give
life. We indeed come to think of them as vivid and individual objects of the concrete world—one might say,
as one's living acquaintances. They have been considered as melodies in the germ, apparently a false
consideration, since they regularly refuse to expand into
full melodic form. Such a nobly tuneful theme as
' Valhalla ' or the great fanfare of ' The Volsungs ' does
not from first to last take on a form that can be called
strictly a melody. They are not germs, but are of a
different order.

Wagner's fanfares are related to such elements in
Beethoven as the motto of the Fifth Symphony, and their
nature is open to comparison with that of the fugue subjects of Bach. In the profusion of them variations are
natural. While some strike on the ear with the
value of a phrase of Dante or Shakespeare, there are
others which are simple commonplaces of the century,
disguised by splendid trappings. Such tunes as Isolde's
Death-song, and the languorous D flat tune at the end

of *The Twilight of the Gods*,* looked at in isolation, may indeed seem to have little character, but even so, that is to judge them as they are not heard, namely apart from their skilful placing and from the enveloping beauties of Wagner's orchestral polyphony.

Wagner's fully structural melodies are comparatively few, and are hardly a powerful part of his art. Such a formality was not ordinarily needed by his style of endlessly flowing writing, and at such moments as the climax of Siegfried's Funeral March, Wagner is content to reiterate a well-known fanfare, confident in the affecting associations of that figure and in the splendours with which he can attend it.

His forms are, at his discretion, outvied by the colouring, and in any case they do not fight out their destinies so frankly as the themes of the earlier music. They lead a life of a certain romantic mysteriousness. They swim into our ken and out of it before, as a rule, we have grown too familiar with them, and one of Wagner's principal arts lies in his resourcefulness in investing their re-introduction with new allurements. He will often disclose only the least glimpse of a favourite shape, and he is hardly ever at a loss for a transfiguring light and colour.

The force with which Wagner felt the influence of his dramatic subjects is to be recognised not only by the high characterisation of the motto-themes he invented for them, but also by the different aura of each subject, so that though there is much love-music in *The Ring* none of it is like that of *Tristan*, with its peculiar expression of sick longing. It is indeed hard to imagine any interchange of material between different works, and it is always a distasteful moment when the *Tristan* quotation occurs in the third act of *The Mastersingers*—it is so obviously in the wrong company, like an ice pudding

---

*'Nothing better than a tune which is hardly good enough for a third-rate German beer garden.' R. Vaughan Williams.

on the breakfast table. *Parsifal*, again, with its more extreme chromaticism, breathes an air of its own. But there is an essential Wagnerianism common to all the four masterpieces, and at the bottom of it is the impression of a romantic phantasmagoria, an impression inherent not less in *The Mastersingers* than in the others, for all its purely diatonic stretches and the exceptionally square and song-like vocal writing.

All this music forms the middle of that period of dreaming, or at any rate of dreamily brooding, music which may be said to have had its beginnings in Schubert and to have been continued into our own days in different ways, by Elgar and Delius among others. This prevailing character could be simply ascribed to the composer's own nature, if Wagner had been Schumann. It is not so easy ; for Wagner personally was a brilliant man, and in his young days there seemed nothing against his vying with the composers of vivacious, brilliant music, Rossini, Berlioz, Verdi, his great contemporaries. Of the two early operas, one, *Die Feen*, rather leaned towards German pensiveness, but the other, the *Liebesverbot*, towards animation. Wagner's choice was made between the composition of *Rienzi* and of *The Flying Dutchman*. ' Choice', one says, without at all understanding how much deliberate volition there was in it—or is in human decisions generally. It is pretty certain, at least, that Wagner's art would not have taken the same road if he had been flattered instead of wounded on his first visit to Paris. After that, however, he decided to be a whole-hearted German composer—which at that date meant the exploitation of certain technical elements, a melting chromaticism notably, which make for the effect of dreaminess in music. He would naturally write at length—Germany was already the land of a long-winded music. It was the land of the symphonists, and we have seen that the emotional effect of the recurrences of themes in the symphony was seized on by him for an

enormously developed use. It was the land of instrumental music—there, more than elsewhere, the orchestral
instruments were listened to for their own sake, and were
being encouraged more and more to indulge each in its
natural expressiveness.

Expressiveness became by this means (and by various
other means, too) a great absorption for the German
musicians. I am suggesting that men do not always
forge tools in order to make a desired object, but may
amuse themselves by making that which is feasible by
the tools at hand. Expressiveness is not compatible with
quick movement, which is self-forgetting. We have
said that Wagner did not hurry. Since he had chosen to
be expressive, it should be with all the passion of his
genius—since he was to have the time, time should stand
still while he communed with his eternal soul and
timeless nature.

Here, then, were lengthiness, artful repetition, slow
rhythms, and emotional luxury, factors of daydream
music. After all, Wagner took to them too well for his
choice to have been simply voluntary. The departure
from Paris in 1842 we should on the whole guess to have
been predestinate.

Wagner's music, so far from insisting on our being on
the alert, freely allows the attention of the listener to
slacken, and, indeed, orders its slackness and tautness
with a sort of rhythmic purpose, so that however uninteresting, comparatively, such or such a page may be·
picked out in cold blood, the abbreviating of Wagner is
dangerous. The fine deep colour of the ' purple passages ' is likely to be damaged by a shortening of the
approach designed by the author. There are, after all,
few places in Wagner like those in the second act of *The
Valkyrie* (which, if the second act is always, in Wagner,
the least strong, is of all the second acts of his maturity
the weakest), where the music is obviously waiting
on the libretto ; and the hands that attempt to cut

Wagner down to elegant extracts risk letting him slip
away entirely through their fingers. In this music the
wide prospect and the general surge are nearly everything. Take the first act of *The Valkyrie*. Its one possible extract, the Lenzlied, though charming in its
Schubertian way, makes the effect of an anachronism, but
otherwise it is an hour of peculiarly touching music.
Its delicacy and tenderness are not to be matched elsewhere, but you either know it all or know it not at all.
Wagner seems to be not susceptible to ' improvement '
by scissors and paste. The only way would have been a
different beginning in 1813. If we acquiesce in the usual
clumsy cutting-down of Wagner and admit a relief in
thus escaping spells of some rather dull weather, it is an
admission that we are not really in love with the wild
country, much as if someone said, ' Nowhere would
delight me like Cumberland if only one could count
there on always getting the hard, bright light of
Monte Carlo'.   The grand ominous growling makes
up much of the value, when it comes, of the radiant
gleam.

The favourite extracts from Wagner, the Lenzlied and
the Ride of the Valkyries, for example, might be the
music of a composer of less than the first order. Only by
long stretches of it is the typical drowsy delight induced,
with that sense of the illimitable, in which it seems as
though we might go on blissfully drifting and dreaming
for ever. One reason for that sense is Wagner's abandonment of the architecture of tonalities of the symphonists.
Another is the absence of patterned figurations. Patterns
virtually disappeared after *Lohengrin*, or when there
were any, as now and then in *Valkyrie II.* and *III.*, in
which more than in all the rest of the mature Wagner
fragments of the *Tannhäuser* period are cast up,* they

---

*See Fricka's Song of Entreaty with accompanying triplets, and the
curious eight bars of *stretto* in G minor at the end of the Valkyries'
chorus, just before Wotan concludes his curse on Brynnhilde.

were a momentary jolting disturbance of the gliding dream. To the first entranced Wagnerians this dream appeared like an escape from a circumscribed earthly life into an angelic cloudland.

What, then, takes the place, with Wagner, of the patterns which made up the body of the music which had just preceded him ? The fabric of Wagner is essentially, like the music of a much earlier time, an assembly of vocal parts.

How all things in Wagner sing ! Not, perhaps, most easily and spontaneously the human voices ; but the instruments at his command seem always to be eagerly pressing forward into songfulness, and the fancy often strikes us that his act of composition was simply a release of their natures—one of those pleasing feats of the fairy-tales that can set all the mute population of the forest talking. Even in the dark hollows and undergrowths everything here is alive and harmoniously vocal. The instruments have learnt their tune from man, but have far outranged man's uncertain voice, and their musical assurance is beautiful in the way of the thoughtlessly graceful movement of the brute creation. This Pan cannot be hard on his faithful beasts, for their will is gladly one with his. Hear the prelude of *Tristan and Isolde*—how soon after the first soft call of the violoncelli some of the affectionate woodwind are anxious to sigh with it—how when it reiterates the call the rest of that tuneful family are awake and chiming in, until before long the whole host is contributing to the blended clamour.

He strengthened the population of the orchestra in a number of well-known ways, multiplying the horns and calling into existence the bass trumpet and a new family of tubas. His division of the strings, as, for instance, in the last scene of *Tristan* (16 parts), was unheard of at that time, and he drew upon previously unreached sentiments in nearly every instrument's nature. None was

too fierce or too earthy-deep to yield to him a tender
wail. The clarinet first under him grew to maturity.
Wagner was at home in the orchestra. In his most
impressionable days music was for him the sounds of
the orchestra, as for Chopin it was the pianoforte. He
conveyed his thought through the orchestra without the
intermediary of an ' abstract ' music. There had been
long before Wagner an instrumental writing more impressed by the author's own intellectual processes. Other
composers have set the orchestra dancing with a different
brilliancy. No one until Wagner had treated the
instruments with such general sympathy for their
expressiveness.

In this characteristic singing utterance of his orchestra
there is a line of approach to the harmony of Wagner,
which cannot be looked upon as having been conceived
in abstract parts and afterwards allotted to this and that
voice. Wagner's polyphonic texture was the outcome
of the multitudinous contributions of sympathetic word,
sigh, or concurrent song from the enthralled tribe who
played Valkyrie to his Wotan—' To my own will I speak,
speaking to thee'. It was polyphony of a species not before
exploited, its source being expressiveness and not formal
design.

There is a clue, too, here to the origin of Wagner's
themes in themselves, the best of which are, we
have noted, not of the order of symmetrical melodies
whose laws of being are determined by the original association of melodiousness with human singing and consequently with the logic of poetical metres. Wagner's
best things included hardly any actual songs : hence
the complaint of opera-goers in his time that he lacked
tunefulness, for their ears were expecting the extended
and balanced phrases of vocal melody, the form of which
is affected by the organised structures of words which it
is natural for the human voice to sing. Some of the rare
songs which Wagner put into the mouths of singers do

not allow us to forget his predilection for instruments,
and Tannhäusers can do their best with the song to
Venus without ever making it sound natural.   It is an
instrumental theme (a bandmaster's theme even, we may
say), as the overture has shown.   In all *The Ring* there
are perhaps four songs, and not more than six themes
in all which have their origin in human singing.

By contrast, Wagner's sympathy with his instruments,
with the simple pastoral woodwind, the melancholy
horn, and the urgent trumpet, elicited any number of
new characteristic phrases into which the wild beings of
the world seem to have put their feelings.   The unem-
barrassed simultaneous play of these utterances constitutes the Wagnerian polyphony.   There is no line to be
drawn between harmony and polyphony, but in Wagner
the impulse is very generally away from harmonic
writing—music of which a part serves, so to speak, as a
backcloth in front of which the principals dance—
towards a polyphonic style in which the various parts
may have not so very much less interesting a time
individually than in the ancient vocal polyphony.   The
characteristic richness of his sound comes from the
generous share all his voices are allowed in giving
expression, by imitation or counter subject, or simply
by some sympathetic ejaculation, to the passion of the
moment.

The history of music has often been written in the
terms of the biographies of the great musicians.   One
can imagine an interesting social history of music, and
also a history of its development since about 1500 considered as influenced by instrumental inventions.   Valve
horns and trumpets* were the great innovations of
Wagner's young days, and he grasped at their possibilities.   These instruments were gaining possession of
their new flexibility between the time of *The Flying
Dutchman* and *The Mastersingers*, and as this time went

*First composed for by Halévy in 1835.

on Wagner more and more called on them as chromatic-
ally complete melodic instruments. His use of them is a
most interesting example of the interplay between an
artist's disposition and the nature of his medium. If
Wagner had written for Beethoven's brass he would have
found an obstacle in the way of the liquefying of his harmony. The rigidity of the ' natural ' instruments was
turned into a value by the composers who knew no
others. There is no question of progress in art ; but the
valve instruments represented a mechanical progress,
and there is great interest in the response of the artist
to the means at his disposal. The orchestra for which
Wagner could write in the middle of the nineteenth
century served him as tractably and responsively as
the pianoforte served Chopin. The instruments of
both composers could lend themselves to the rich,
chromatic, and enharmonic progressions which their
generation was invited to explore. Hence it is that
Chopin seems in many ways a nearer relation to Wagner
than any of the classical German musicians. Both found
a fascination in gliding or slipping from key to key, or
alternatively in inventing rich new decoration to screen
an ordinary bass. As men, the two could hardly have
differed more.   As composers, the current of music
brought Pole and Saxon into kinship, and the Prelude
to *Tristan*, reduced for the pianoforte, might have been
brought out (thereby no doubt winning a better recep-
tion in Paris in 1861) as a posthumous Fifth Ballade.
We often hear in the mature Wagner sensuous and pathetically vehement things which take us back to the Chopin
of twenty years before. Take the episode which begins
in G flat after Brangäne's Song of Warning in *Tristan*,
II. Can we not imagine Chopin improvising very much
to this effect on the subject of his Prelude in D flat ?
Above all, the common ground is the relaxing of formal
frames of address for the sake of the wild, impulsive,
personal cry.

On paper Wagner may appear to make use occasionally
of the concatenations of Bach. The ' Frohn ' chords of
The Twilight of the Gods :—

are met in Bach,* but the motives of the two musics are
as different as can be. Bach assuredly did not dream of
playing for this direct effect of cries and sobs, or anything
like the insistent personal appeal uppermost in Wagner's
music. Bach was music at its most masculine, and the
sob and the cry, as they appear in him, are in intellec-
tualised forms.   In Chopin and Wagner music was
feminised. An old reticent social manner was relaxed,
and the feelings of impulse were allowed more importance than anything. Wagner's music in particular is a
tyrannical siren.

The austere line had gone. The compensation was a
rich, shadowy colour. Wagner's orchestra is comparable to the painting in oils of the Renaissance, the
voluptuous superseder of severe tempera-painting. The
most telling of the original things in Wagner, such as the
play with the sinister ' Tarnhelm ' chords which throw
a mysterious menace over the first act of *The Twilight of
the Gods*, are like reflections in water, and it is hard to
say what it is that beguiles us, whether the actual
shape or the luminous, liquid medium. The sighing
ejaculation of the above-quoted ' Frohn ', the ' Tarnhelm ', and other characteristic Wagnerian figures is some-

*Chromatic Phantasy.

thing hardly to be detected in music before Schubert, in whom are many of the elements of Wagner. Compare the soft exhalation of wind and wave at the beginning of ' Am Meer ' :—

Yet there is a connexion between Wagner's chiar- oscuro and Bach's draughtsmanship. For we associate with Bach's name the establishment of the system of tuning by equal temperament, and in the implications of this system there lay the enharmonic style of the nine- teenth century composers. Bach's ' well-tempered key- board ' bequeathed to Chopin a scale the ambiguities of which afforded a diversion at every turn on every way. The implications of it had to wait some time before being realised ; that is, before any casual chro- matic ornament was accorded its right to divert the tonality of the whole stream. Beethoven's characteristic way, in the free fantasias of his sonata movements, was to modulate boldly with an air of profound decisive- ness. The risks have been faced, he tells us ; the deed, the irrevocable deed, shall be made as conspicuous as it is important. Wagner's habit is to ramble without giving the sense of incurring so much responsibility, but the principle of tonality is just as much retained. The clouds cf chromatic alterations of *Tristan* and *Parsifal* deeply colour the scene, but by one means or another Wagner avoids the obscurity which comes from aboli- tion of tonality. Some of Wagner's earliest listeners

certainly seem to have been bewildered, and even
Berlioz declared that he could see no sense in the
prelude to *Tristan*. The explanation is that the style,
particularly in operatic music, was unexpected, and ears
that are confidently prepared for the expected let
the unexpected escape them. Only the ears pre-
disposed towards an accustomed manner of address
found a difficulty. For in Wagner, after all, we are
always hearing tune, and although, tonally, there is much
diversity in the possible paths it may take, there is never
a sense of the path being lost. Wagner all along has been
eminently a successful popular composer.

Listening to Wagner has always seemed to some almost
too easy a pleasure, and hence a notorious business of
introducing intellectual complications—what the whole
thing is ' about ',* what the orchestral voices ' mean ' at
any given moment, and what the singers mean to say as
they sing. Wagner countenanced this business. For we
come back to it that this great magician of music was not
content that his magic was a good and rare enough thing
in itself. He himself insisted on argument. The human
voice is not used in these dramas simply for its musical
sake. Indeed, Wagner, who never denied himself any
other sort of beauty, habitually kept his voice parts going
singly, nearly always denying himself the delicious possibilities of voices in consort. The voice, in Wagner, is
persistently summoned to act as a go-between, in order
to keep us informed of the trend of the music. It is an
indefatigable guide, but is frequently behindhand with
its labours. It frequently has the air of toiling to interpret what has already been signalled to us over its head.

If Wagner had foreseen our willingness and pleasure
in following without explanation the call and course of
his instrumental music, would he (it may be fancifully
asked) still have given the vocal parts of his dramas quite

---

*Mr. G. Bernard Shaw once found thus in Wagner a gratifying
substantiation of Karl Marx's economic theories.

such a hard-working function, pressed and pushed ?
Well, it was Wagner's way to insist that we should enjoy
the beauties of his music as he saw fit and not otherwise.
Even if he composed a piece of wordless music he made
out for it an elaborate literary commentary—for instance,
for the prelude to *Lohengrin*, music that tells its own tale
if ever music did. Wagner elucidated it for the listener
with a description of a vision of the Holy Grail—which
he seems to have assumed to be a more simply intelligible
phenomenon. In this preoccupation of Wagner—who
never, if he could, would leave the future of his work to
chance—lies the reason why he composed so little independent music. The voice was a feeble vehicle for his
musical ideas, and generally he did not compose for it
for its musical sake. Even a dramatic use of words is a
comparative rarity. Wotan's exclamation about ' Sieg-
mund's and Sieglinde's bond ! ' and Isolde's desperate
cry, ' Greet thou my father and mother ! ' stand out,
amid their singing of mere protracted explanations. But
if Wagner had not the warmest of feelings towards
singing, it nevertheless was, simply because of its power
of verbal articulation, a necessity. It alone was able to
be, as it were, his architect, since the great imagination
had not devised a purely musical form to sustain the
vastness with which he felt he had it in him to impress us.

It is not a question of going back to the old complaint
that Wagner could not write for the voice. No single
page of the dramas but is written in a way that can or
should be sung. It was formerly considered that their
demands on the musicianship of singers were exor-
bitant, but these are now ordinarily fulfilled. Yet the
impression remains that, in the whole, the vocal writing
is mostly no match for the abounding free life of the
rest of the music. Strain—the strain of all that vehement
declamation, and the strain, even in the most ravishing
melodious writing, of rivalry with those choirs of wordless voices which spring to melody with superhuman joy

and triumph—is an unescapable characteristic of Wagnerian singing.   No one hearing an orchestra flag and
fail in Wagner could think of an excuse, for surely, you
say, all it has to do is to live its natural life a thought
more intensely.   But Tristan in his third act and Brynnhilde in the last evening of the tetralogy, however admirable the performers, cannot help afflicting one with a
certain discomfort by the excessive feats they have to do.
This was no new thing in German music.   There are
tenor arias in Bach which might have been meant as
illustrations of humanity's frailty in its attempts to emu-
late the unearthly exemplar which is suggested by the
obbligato of violin or oboe.   The ruthlessness in the
choral writing of Beethoven's Mass in D tends to blunt
the effectiveness of the sound of that great composition,
unmistakable though the sublimity of its intentions may
be.   Possibly there is a moral lesson to be found in the
spectacle of Wagner's singers—always persevering however outrivalled, always pushing on doggedly, imper-
vious to snubs, even when, like Sir Walter's in *The
Mastersingers*, their Preislied is nearly as much a struggle
as a song.   It was left to the Wagnerian epigoni to engage
the free spirits of the orchestra in similar toils.

Singers in Wagner are Nibelungs under the lash.
Their cries frequently bring into his music a sense of
harshness and constraint which his orchestra was too
delightfully easy to express. ' Chromatic tunes most like
my passions sound,' they might say.   Hear Amfortas :—

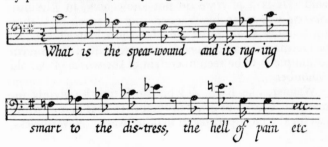

What is the spear-wound   and its rag-ing

smart to   the dis-tress,   the hell of pain etc

His personages were frequently pressed along such
jagged lines for the sake of a more and poignant expression, and in the course of it any number of admirable
finds were made—possibly, indeed, too many, for often
a typical bit of violent Wagnerian declamation, when
looked at in isolation, will strike us as more telling
than we remembered it in a long course of excited
utterance.

This romantic violence of the Wagnerian manner was,
like anything else that was imitable in the great
man's work, industriously exploited by the succeeding
composers of tetralogies and the like, who somewhat
saddened the latter years of the nineteenth century.
Roughly speaking, it may be said that it was not found
hard to keep on writing Wagner, all but the tunes. In
Germany this practice was pursued with a particular
zest, but few lands altogether escaped. Except in remote
parts, it has now gone the way of the forgotten crops of
pseudo-Mendelssohn and pseudo-Haydn.

Another matter altogether is the growth of Wagnerian
seeds in musicians of true personal gifts. In the case
of the affecting song-writer, Hugo Wolf, there were
achieved with Wagnerian technique the miniature forms
which Wagner himself seldom attempted and never
succeeded with. Various processes of Wagner were
turned to a happy account and, so to speak, domesticated,
by Humperdinck in *Hänsel und Gretel*. A good deal of
Richard Strauss and of the later Scriabin is Wagner run
wild. It is a pity we do not know how, in Elysium,
Salomé was taken by Wagner—not to speak of Weber,
the founder, in a simpler age, of the once blameless school
of German romantic opera. The twilight of Wagnerian
technique is to be seen in certain of the works of Arnold
Schönberg.

Wagner, like Bach, did his work too thoroughly for
many successors to glean profitably in that field. Music
has for the most part taken to other ways. Nevertheless,

his influence, broadly considered, is immense. For he represents the triumph of earnestly sensuous music. His example may well remain an inspiration for those composers disinclined for a career either of ascetism or frivolity. It is a licence for the serious expression of the tender passions. In France the victory of Wagner established the right of a musician to be aloof and reflective, whereas, until then, the ' verdict ' of a casual mob in a French theatre or concert room had always had importance attached to it. The pupils of Franck were naturally the pupils, too, of Wagner. In England, Wagner's music was an encouragement to such men as Elgar and Delius to indulge to the top of their bent in introspection and the revelation of their admirable sensibilities.

The Wagnerian chapter, strictly speaking, is no doubt closed. The world, as it turns out, is still as full as ever of a number of things, even though at Bayreuth in 1876 it seemed compact of that one only—so vast and overwhelming was its look in the days of its newness, a creation that superseded everything, while itself beyond supersession. It seemed so to many there, but not to the wise Liszt. Liszt was the Merlin of the Wagnerian epic. But for him, what, a quarter of a century before Bayreuth, would have become of the whole of Wagnerianism ? It is extremely curious that no sooner had Liszt brought *Lohengrin* to light at Weimar than he put his services at the disposal of Anti-Wagner—of Berlioz,* who never cared a fig for the luxury of introspection or Alpine solitudes ; whose vivacious art fed on city life and showy French talk. Later on, just after Bayreuth, we see Liszt opening his arms to Borodin. What an uncanny old seer ! He was as wise as the rest of Europe put together. His incomparable wits can be fancied darting into the future and delighting, before the event, in certain of our contemporaries whose song, if song is

---

Benvenuto Cellini was, after various difficulties, at last performed at Weimar in 1852. (*Lohengrin*, 1850).

still the word, goes out to a nonplussed world. The genial encounter with Borodin spoke for so much. At the moment when Wagner's high-water mark was touched it spoke up for a world which, like Liszt himself, would not want to be always steeped in Wagner. It spoke up for patterns, for primary colours, for the excitement of the dance, and all the other things which in 1877 might have been thought banished for ever from music by the fashions of Valhalla.

We just now admitted the fancy that Liszt foresaw the course of music from his own day to ours. Well, if he could have done so he would have been comfortably reassured that he had after all lived at the right time. For to Wagner the encouragement of his friendship had been crucial. And there does not appear to have been another so good a case for that sovereign beneficence anywhere between that horizon and this.

1923.

From CÉSAR FRANCK (1822–1890) to MAURICE RAVEL (1875)

By M. D. Calvocoressi

OF all topics current in writings on music, none has become more hackneyed and more thoroughly spoilt by empty talk than that of musical nationality and national characteristics in music. Yet there is a measure of reality in the distinctions to which nationality leads, if they are properly understood: and to ignore them in criticism would be as fatal as it is to overrate them.

It is nearly eighty years since Schumann wrote : ' It seems as though the nations around Germany were trying to shake off the yoke of German music and to speak their own musical language. Thus Chopin represents his country, and Bennett England. Verhulst bids fair to stand worthily for Holland. National tendencies are asserting themselves in Hungary and in Scandinavia.' Long before, he had called attention to the national significance of Glinka in Russia and Berlioz in France. Schumann was, in fact, the first to notice (one might almost say, considering the time of his writing, to foretell) the movement which essentially characterises the evolution of music during the nineteenth century, leading to a revival of musical nationality in France, Britain and Spain, and elsewhere to the birth of the Russian, the Bohemian, the Scandinavian and the Hungarian national schools. But Schumann added : ' All these composers consider Germany as their first and most beloved teacher ', and thereby showed his failure to see that the movement was not a novel phenomenon, but a reversal to the normal conditions of musical art—a failure natural enough in the state of historical knowledge at the time.

Musical nationality is as old as music. At times, it is true, the features which constitute it become less noticeable, or even seem to have disappeared, temporary eclipses of this kind generally coinciding with a decrease in creative activity, and being due to a variety of reasons which need not now concern us. What is of interest here is the fact that when France, in the course of the nineteenth century, became the field of a truly wonderful musical Renaissance, and a Renaissance emphatically national in character, it was not through her music's having liberated itself from bondage to the German or any other school ; nor was French music asserting national idiosyncrasies for the first time.

The French school of music is one of the oldest in Western Europe, and during the Middle Ages was in more respects than one the most advanced. In its output, practically everything that went to the making of musical art can be traced back to its founthead ; and throughout the course of ages French music shows as specific and unmistakable signs of nationality as any music in the world.

It is temptingly easy to seek the signs of nationality in local colour, such as is often provided by the use of folk-tunes or of processes derived from the study of folk-tunes. But this will be found to lead nowhere. If a true conception of nationality is found to be, in Cecil Sharp's words, ' an abstraction, a deduction, the greatest common measure of a large number of more or less dissimilar units ', we may say roughly that the nearest possible definition of French national character is pro-vided by adducing the French taste for measure and common sense, for rationality rather than for imaginative-ness. In art, they cannot do without something positive on which to rest the mind. Gregorian plain song, founded on the normal intonations of the speaking voice, and abounding with recurrent patterns, to many of which a fixed symbolic meaning is attached, is grave, subdued, and ordered ; it makes no allowance for irregularity and surprise. Likewise, early examples of ' art ' music, as

opposed to traditional music like Trouvère and Trouba-
dour songs and thirteenth century motets, show French
composers, as Pierre Aubry tells us, ' encircled in a network of compulsory rules by which the field of imagination is greatly restricted.' Abstractness and strictly
dialectic methods, which imply much absolute brain
work, prevail in the achievements of medieval contra-
puntists. At the times of the Renaissance, topical expression and accurate, matter of fact description were
aimed at.

These tendencies towards clarity, order, and logic were
helpful during the primitive periods. But they were
restricted in scope, and eventually prevented French
composers from playing in the further elaboration of the
highly organised types of instrumental music a part
similar to that which they played in the progress of
poetic music. The Couperins, Rameau, and others are
the true ancestors of Debussy and Ravel in the latter
respect. But the Fugue, the Sonata, and the Symphony
flourished in other countries while France (in the late
seventeenth and in the eighteenth century) evinced a
growing inclination to protest, in the name of her
outraged common sense, against the complications of
pure abstract music.

The ultimate stage was reached during the second
half of the eighteenth century, when Rameau was
abused as a ' distiller of extravagant chords,' and a writer
of chaotic or merely mechanical music, and when
Diderot, Fontenelle, Rousseau, and their disciples
preached the gospel of the crudest and most puerile
types of music, of music which ' imitates nature ' and
owes nothing to technique.

The consequences of this reaction were far-reaching.
They made themselves felt throughout the nineteenth
century—not exactly delaying progress, but creating an
atmosphere of incomprehension and hostility around the
composers who were to make French music great. It is

K

reported by the French critic Gaston Carraud that
Ambroise Thomas, the head of the Paris Conservatoire
from 1871 to his death in 1896, when pressed to include
the study of instrumental forms in the curriculum,
replied that ' no composer would consent to lower himself by reaching symphony.' It is necessary to emphasise these points in order to show the extent of the ground
that had to be covered before France could reappear in
the front rank of musical nations, and to show what she
and the world at large owe to the few composers whose
steadfast efforts won the battle against such odds.

The same forces which produced the decadence were
at work during the period of the modern Renaissance.
They retarded progress, and rendered the task of its
pioneers very hard indeed. The true spirit of instrumental music was revealed to France chiefly under the
influence of the overwhelming impression created by
Beethoven's works in Paris. The new ideals made rapid
headway while Berlioz (1803–1869), carrying to their
utmost consequences the conceptions of his master
Lesueur, gave a new and wonderful impulse to poetic
music, which was to be carried to its greatest height by
Liszt and by later composers of the French school and
others.

After Beethoven's, the chief influence that proved
beneficial to the French school was Wagner's. The
revelation of his music not only kindled enthusiasm,
but introduced an altogether new spirit of earnestness
and thoroughness.

It was to be expected—for it was altogether in accordance with the leading idiosyncrasies of the French mind
—that France, reawakening to music, should concern
herself with types whose inspiration is derived from
definite poetic, picturesque, or dramatic sources. But
the miracle is that she should have re-entered the field of
pure music suddenly, with firm deliberation and
broadened outlook, sacrificing nothing of her own par-

ticular sense of fitness and measure, of her thirst for clear, firm, all-embracing logic, of her dislike for anything that smacked of looseness or vagueness, but benefitting by these idiosyncrasies in her progress towards the highest artistic aims.

Henceforth, France possessed a school of composers of pure music besides the ever-increasing school of composers whose chief or sole concern was with the lyric stage, from Gounod and Auber and Adolphe Adam to Bizet, Delibes, Ambroise Thomas, Bruneau, Charpentier, and countless others. And naturally enough, it is —with a few signal exceptions such as Gounod and Bruneau, and among the minor poets Bizet and Delibes —from those composers of pure music, who had a broader conception of their art and a greater culture, that France's most significant—although not necessarily the most popular—contributions in the domain of opera and the lyric drama came.

The pioneers of the musical revival were, after Berlioz, Gounod (1818–1893), César Franck (1822–1890), Lalo (1823–1892), Saint-Saëns (1835–1922), and Fauré (1845-1924). To their names should be added Liszt's, who, let it be remembered, worked mainly in France during the 'thirties and 'forties, learning from Berlioz and Chopin and the romantic writers and thinkers. His influence was to assert itself throughout musical Europe ; but nowhere did it bear earlier and richer fruit than in France. The principle of thematic unity established by him made for greater logic and coherence in form and substance, opened new ranges to both poetic and pure music, and enabled composers to seek, as Debussy was to put it, ' discipline in freedom and not in formulæ'. It was bound to appeal forthwith to the French mind, and to be considerably extended by French composers. Liszt's influence is especially marked on Saint-Saëns, who in his turn played an important part in the evolution of French music.

Liszt's influence is discernible, too, in César Franck's music. Franck's commanding individuality, however, was chiefly formed at the school of Bach and Beethoven. He is at his best when, concentrating on instrumental music, he extends the principles of Sonata form and Variation form, or revitalises the Fugue. His chief disciple, Vincent d'Indy (b. 1851), avers that he is the direct heir of Beethoven, and was the first to understand and to apply the teachings contained in Beethoven's last quartets. And Jean Chantavoine summed up all that can be said of him in the following terms : ' His part in the evolution of French music was to bring it back to the inner life. Franck is the poet of self-contained, independent thought, whose inner power suffices to create its form of expression. His music proceeds straight from the soul ; and he proved to be for his pupils and disciples, and subsequently for the musical public of France, a great awakener of souls.'

A study of Franck's music will reveal the ingenuity, originality, and firmness of his form—at times slightly marred, as in his Symphony, by diffuseness and heaviness. Circumstances compelled him to follow the profession of organist : organ playing, and especially extemporising at the organ, may have influenced his methods of working out, as it has obviously influenced his methods of scoring. A story told by his pupil Gabriel Pierné of church services held up while Franck, after having been carried away by his inspiration, methodically reverted to his main key, shows that his occasional tendency towards prolixity originated in an excess of scruple and thoroughness.

He never wrote, like Saint-Saëns, for instance, without having something vital to express. Hence his music always rings true ; it is remarkable, and in many respects unique, for its artlessly persuasive and convincing accents, for the genuineness and depth of its emotional qualities. Nothing could be more characteristic of Franck than the wistful, dreamy, yet glowing tenderness of the first movement and larghetto of his String Quartet. With this and his other big instrumental works—the Quintet, the Violin Sonata, his one Symphony, the *Variations Symphoniques* for orchestra and pianoforte, the tone-poem *Les Eolides*, the organ chorales, and the *Prélude, Choral, et Fugue* and *Prélude, Aria, et Finale* for pianoforte—Franck carries French music to a level which it had never reached before.

Gounod's were less lofty ideals. His musical gifts included a faculty of original invention and a sense of poesy which impart an unmistakable individuality to his music. He shares with Bizet the distinction of having composed one of the most popular operas in the world, his *Faust*—which, unlike many popular operas, contains much that will always appeal also to the educated musical taste. Its music represents Gounod at his best, although it shows in parts his tendency towards the shallow, the facile, and the sentimental. It is by virtue of his charming melodic invention that Gounod exercised a widespread influence, not altogether restricted to French music.

Lalo, a highly cultured and original composer, was essentially a classic in his tendencies, but owes a good deal to the influence of the musical romanticism of Weber and Berlioz. His imagination and skill are brilliant, and in his orchestral works much of the poetry and picturesqueness of the Russians is foreshadowed. Typical instances are his superb *Rapsodie Norvégienne*, his *Symphonie Espagnole*, and the Ballet *Namouna*, which contains some of his finest music. His various concertos and his chamber music are equally characteristic of the clear and expressive quality of his inspiration. All these works are far less known, in France and elsewhere, than they deserve to be.

So much has been written upon Saint-Saëns, and estimates of his work and place in the French school vary so greatly, that the time seems hardly ripe to sum these up and to decide between conflicting currents of opinion. On the surpassing excellence of his technique all are agreed ; but many people hold that his works owe more to this technique than to any particular gift of imagination. During his extraordinarily long and active career he left no branch of music untouched ; but it is in symphonic music and in opera that he achieved the most. His third Symphony, for orchestra, pianoforte, and organ, is generally acknowledged as one of his masterpieces ; and some of his chamber music works, as well as some of his works for the stage, are favourably known. But it is chiefly to the four tone-poems, *La Danse Macabre*, *Le Rouet d'Omphale*, *Phaéton*, and *La Jeunesse d'Hercule*, that the student of Saint-Saëns should turn his attention. They exemplify the composer's best qualities, the mastery of his skill, which is admirable in itself, the ease and fluency of his discourse, and its perfectly balanced proportions ; and, above all things, perhaps, his delightful, beautifully finished scoring.

This, and a good deal besides, he owed to the study of Liszt's works. He was the first to realise the artistic significance and fertility of Liszt's innovations, which he never tired of proclaiming. In many other respects he exercised an equally beneficial influence. He did not become, like César Franck, the actual head of a school comprising many direct, eager disciples. At one time an acknowledged leader of progress in music (he was, in 1870, one of the founders of the Société Nationale, created for the purpose of introducing new works), he later became emphatically conservative, and uttered loud protests against modern tendencies. In a speech of 1921, for instance, he declared that music could progress no further without relapsing into primitive barbarity. But the policy of moderation which he maintained had its uses, especially at the time when Wagner's influence, while doing a great deal of good to French music, was threatening to sweep many young French composers (and, what was more serious, a large part of the public) off their feet. And it was a pupil of his—practically his only pupil—Gabriel Fauré, who was to become the chosen teacher of a large majority of the composers who now rank foremost in the French school.

The history of the latest generations begins with Fauré and Vincent d'Indy (b. 1851). Both are in the front rank as composers, and also played an all-important part as educators, with the difference that d'Indy was a born leader, and, acknowledged as Franck's successor by common consent, of set purpose started to devote a large part of his energies to maintaining and extending his master's precepts and influence ; whereas it was without premeditation or special exertion that Fauré, by his teaching, profoundly stamped his mark upon a small but fine group of younger composers while fostering the development of their own artistic individualities.

But it is necessary to deal first with a few points of the intermediate period.

Practically a contemporary of Franck and Lalo, Emmanuel Chabrier (1841–1894) was one of the most originally gifted musicians ever born in France. Despite his exuberant fancy and a rare sense of colour and humour, he was long prevented by circumstances from devoting himself to composition, and paid the penalty by never producing a work embodying to the full the genius with which the greater part of his music is instinct. He was further unfortunate in never being able to get hold of a good libretto, dramatic or comic. But even with the poorest material to work on he achieved such fine things, musically, as the lyric drama *Gwendoline*, or the comic opera *Le Roi Malgré Lui*. His songs, his *Habanera*, his *Bourrée Fantasque*, his *Pièces Pittoresques* for pianoforte, his *España* for orchestra, his lyric scenes *La Sulamite* and his *Ode à la Musique*, are his other most characteristic works.

Chabrier's music has exercised considerable influence on Debussy's and Ravel's. The same historical interest, as well as the artistic interest of originality attaches (though in a slighter degree) to the early works of Erik Satie (b. 1865), most of them mere sketches, but full of a delightful musical fancy, especially the *Sarabandes* and *Gymnopédies* for pianoforte, the Preludes to *Le Fils des Etoiles*, and the *Sonneries de la Rose-Croix*.

But one of the principal influences that affected modern developments in French music was that of such Russian composers as Borodin, Mussorgsky, Balakiref and Rimsky-Korsakof, whose works were known and loved among French musical circles long before they started making headway elsewhere.

The point, important as it is, can hardly be pressed here, but will serve to introduce a French composer and educator whose claims to recognition are often over-looked : Louis-Albert Bourgault-Ducoudray (1843–1910), one of the chief pioneers of progress among his con-temporaries and juniors, the first to study and to make known not only Russian music, but also the folk tunes of Greece and Brittany, to point out to the possibilities in modern composition of ancient and exotic modalities. His course of musical history at the Paris Conservatoire (from 1878 to 1909) served to introduce his views to many students ; and his compositions, the *Rapsodie Cambodgienne*, the *Carnaval d'Athènes* for orchestra, the opera *Thamara*, and others—all far less known than they deserve—show that he was capable of applying them to good purpose. Although most people who know his music think highly of it, no work of his enjoyed any considerable success. His main achievement, the lyric drama *Myrdhin*, remains unpublished.

Towards the end of the nineteenth century the school of César Franck, under Vincent d'Indy's leadership, made considerable headway. Its main representatives were Charles Bordes (1863–1909), Henri Duparc

(b. 1848), Alexis de Castillon (1838-1873), Ernest Chausson (1855-1899), Pierre de Bréville (b. 1861), and Guy Ropartz (b. 1864). The creation by Bordes, Guilmant, and d'Indy (in 1900) of a School of Music under the auspices of the *Schola Cantorum*, founded six years before as a school for religious music, marks a new stage in its evolution. The principal of d'Indy's pupils during the later period are Albéric Magnard (1865-1914), Albert Roussel (b. 1869), Déodat de Sévérac (1873-1921), and G. M. Witkowski (b. 1878).

D'Indy's music leaves no one indifferent. It has won whole-hearted admiration and been made the object of fierce onslaughts. Coming from an impassioned, but controlled mind, it has been described as showing a predominance of the intellect over the imagination and emotions. It certainly bears the imprint of an individuality which Romain Rolland defines as mediæval in its fundamental traits ; but it is, no less certainly, music of power and not music of knowledge only. Besides the intellectual appeal of strongly logical structure and texture, there is much in his music of flame that shines and glows, especially in his magnificent *Symphonie sur un Chant Montagnard Français*, in his lyric dramas *Fervaal* and *l'Etranger*, in the racy symphonic triptych *Wallenstein*, in the later tone-poems, and in the Fourth Symphony. Some of these works contain magnificent evocations of the atmosphere of landscapes. French folk-music has played a part in d'Indy's artistic formation as well as Franck, Wagner, and Weber have ; and Gregorian music an even greater part. Some of the finest pages in his third lyric drama, *La Légende de Saint Christophe*, are those whose musical idiom is deliberately evolved from the elements of plain-song.

Among his pupils, Magnard occupies a peculiar position. His tragic death attracted greater notice than any work of his had attracted, except among small circles. Even nowadays he is little known in his native

country and unknown elsewhere. His works (the chief
of which are four symphonies, the lyric dramas *Guer-
cœur* and *Bérenice*, and a few examples of chamber music)
are characterised by deep earnestness, stern resolution,
gravity, and concentration. They ought to appeal to far
greater a number of music-lovers than they have
hitherto reached.

Next to him should be mentioned Paul Dukas (b. 1865),
who, although not properly belonging to the school of
César Franck and d'Indy, has shown many spiritual
affinities with its members. His aspirations are as high
as Magnard's. He is first and last a symphonist ; his
characteristic moods are equally abstract and grave,
although his music shows no trace of the strife and
doubts and bitterness which characterise Magnard's.
His equipoise is perfect, and some of his works, the
Pianoforte Sonata, for instance, the *Variations sur un
Thème de Rameau*, have a tendency towards discursive-
ness. He is at his best in his Symphony, his well-known
Apprenti Sorcier, and especially the choregraphic poem
La Péri, the most imaginative and convincing music he
ever wrote. His lyric score *Ariane et Barbe-Bleue* illustrates both his merits and shortcomings ; it is dignified
and sincere, beautiful from the point of view of structure
and technique, yet somewhat cold and formal.

Gabriel Fauré's music is precisely of a kind that might
be expected to appeal most strongly to music-lovers,
irrespective of race or tendencies. His output comprises
a number of slight and even indifferent things, but his
best works—many of his songs, and the greater part of
his chamber music—are firm and pure enough in form
and texture, and substantial and original enough, to
delight both the most exacting purists and the most
eager seekers of untrodden paths. His music is alert
and subtle, but beneath its easy grace and persuasive
charm the steadfast purpose is always present and never
lost sight of.

It is perhaps by this supreme charm and ease, by the extraordinary simplicity of even his boldest and most forcible utterances, that certain critics are led to overlook the pregnancy of his inspiration. It may be for this or for other reasons, not easily discernible, that, for the time being, the claims made on his behalf by his many admirers find little endorsement outside France.

Fortunately, it is no longer needful to take up the cudgels in defence of Debussy's genius. This composer (1862–1918), whose very name, at the beginning of the century, was anathema when it was not altogether ignored, is now acknowledged as one of the greatest and most lovable artists of his times ; and at least the *Nocturnes*, the *Prélude à l'Après-Midi d'un Faune*, *Pelléas et Mélisande*, and the Quartet, as well as a number of his songs and pianoforte pieces, are well-known to all.

Most striking is the fundamental novelty and surpassing boldness of Debussy's musical idiom, which exploits relationships between notes and chords far subtler and more varied (and, all told, far simpler) than anything allowed for, or foretold, by current theory. Hence he commanded a range of tone-colour and expression which covered many unexplored regions, and was able to translate into music the impressions created and fancies awakened by visions of sunshine and clouds and waters, as well as the manifold undercurrents of Maeterlinck's dramatic masterpiece.

The question of idiom, however, is of interest mainly to the theorist. Debussy's idiom is a marvellous medium, almost entirely evolved (and without question entirely organised) by him alone, for his own purposes ; but it is his pregnancy of purpose, his deep sensitiveness and keen imagination, his sense of poesy and subtle pathos, that make him in many respects a unique figure in the history of music.

Originality of idiom is not an unusual feature among

modern French musicians. It is, indeed, a marked
feature of most of the greatest—Fauré, Franck and
d'Indy, as well as Debussy and Ravel (b. 1875). This
fact may be interpreted as the natural outcome of the
elemental idiosyncrasies of the French mind, which were
discussed at the beginning of this essay. The desire for
close, inner logic rather than outer, and chiefly formal,
logic gave birth both to the ' cyclic ' form of Franck and
d'Indy on one hand, and on the other to the undefinable,
yet perfectly proportioned and homogeneous form which
is the essential quality of the musical substance in
Debussy's works, a form ' evolved from within.' The
desire for definiteness, calling for the utmost refinement
in shades of expression and for the elimination of a vast
number of generally accepted commonplaces, led composers to extend and enrich their idiom in proportion
as they expurgated it.

In Debussy's works, and Ravel's as well, we notice a
return to simplicity which constitutes a reaction against
the structural elaborateness often inseparable from
' cyclic ' form proper, and against the tendency to dis-
cursiveness noticeable in certain products of the German
school. Complex in the light of theoretical analysis, the
idiom of Debussy and that of Ravel is, in point of fact,
entirely free from complexity. In Debussy's, the
articulation is so simple that believers in the intrinsic
virtue of an elaborate apparatus of cogwheels, belts and
hinges have described it as inarticulate.

In Ravel's music there is the same fundamental simplicity of means, which is made to serve a purpose even
more delicate, and unquestionably more rigorous. There
was much of the dreamer in Debussy, and his music is
often the expression of elusive moods and fleeting
fancies ; at times, as is often repeated, of atmosphere.
Ravel has little use for the elusive, and is not content
with atmosphere. In his poetic or picturesque music
(of which the *Miroirs* and *Gaspard de la Nuit* for piano-

forte and the orchestral *Rapsodie Espagnole* are the best instances) he goes straight for character in addition to atmosphere, sharpening contours where Debussy might have blurred them, and defining where Debussy would have merely suggested. A comparison between Debussy's *Chansons de Bilitis* and Ravel's songs *Shé-hérazade* or *Sainte* (not to mention the *Histoires Natu-relles*, his masterpiece, with the *Alborada* of *Miroirs*, in the domain of musical humour) will illustrate the differences. Ravel has produced more pure music than Debussy. To this category belong some of his most significant works. From the Quartet of 1904 to the *Tombeau de Couperin* (in which a *Forlane* is a remarkably poetic and telling achievement) and the late Sonata for violin and 'cello, he evinces an unfailing capacity for renovation, coupled with an ever-increasing sense of simplicity and economy. Their form is, not more definite, but more easily definable than that of Debussy's works, and remains closer to tradition. Other illustrations of his sense of pure music are provided by the scores of his musical farce, *l'Heure Espagnole* and of his beautiful ballet, *Daphnis et Chloë*. In the former there is a wealth of purely musical fancy, which lends grace to the clever, but at times crude humour of the text. The latter teems with music of a kind too rarely met with in works written for the pur-poses of dancing, music that is as forcible and poetic as it is picturesque.

Ravel, in whose formation Fauré played an all-important part, owes, like Debussy, much to Chabrier and to various Russians. The brilliancy and delicacy of his scoring bears some testimony to the joint influences of Liszt and of Rimsky-Korsakof, as well, perhaps, as to that of Saint-Saëns.

The other principal pupils of Fauré are Charles Koechlin (b. 1855), Florent Schmitt (b. 1870), Louis Aubert (b. 1877), Paul Ladmirault (b. 1877), and Roger-

Ducasse (b. 1875). The least known of the five, Charles Koechlin, is one of the most earnest and inspired composers of the present day, whose chamber music and pianoforte pieces, long unpublished but now available, are as worthy of consideration as his numerous orchestral works, all still in manuscript. Ladmirault has written most original and attractive music, which is comparatively little known outside a small circle. Déodat de Sévérac occupies a special place among d'Indy's pupils. Whether he died before having given his full measure, or whether his fine pianoforte sets, *Le Chant de la Terre, en Languedoc, Cerdana* and other works, attractive though less significant, represent him to the full, is difficult to decide. His genuineness and originality are beyond question, but he gave few signs of versatility. What he actually achieved, however, is enough to remember him by.

Roussel, who asserted from the outset a broad outlook and a keen, versatile musical intelligence, is another gifted pupil of d'Indy. Like Florent Schmitt, he baffles classification, and even all attempts at plain definition. Like him, again, he is one of the livest, most genuine and most industrious among his contemporaries, and he displays a similar fondness for vast forms broadly treated. The parallel ends there: for Schmitt has undergone a variety of influences, and his vigorous, though uneven, imagination is more inclined to abruptness and less disciplined.

André Caplet (1879-1925) is another composer whose output deserves close attention. It is especially in his religious music, his septet for female voices and bowed instruments, and his songs, that his outstanding originality is revealed. Indeed, he may be said to stand quite apart as a composer of vocal music. But his instrumental output comprises fine things such as the *Légende* for harp and the *Epiphanie* for 'cello and orchestra.

Nothing but a full description—which cannot be attempted here—of the manifold activities of French composers could show the amplitude of the Renaissance that starting with Berlioz, Franck, and their contemporaries has entered a new phase to-day.   Even a rough survey should include names and tributes which I have had to omit.   No mention has been made of the weaknesses or errors which are no less plentiful and glaring in France than elsewhere.   Nor does the present sketch include any reference to more recent tendencies, as exemplified, for instance, in the works of Darius Milhaud, Arthur Honegger, and others.   Many reasons might be given for the exclusion ; one is that not only the title but the character of this essay made it necessary to break off, if not at Ravel, at least at his actual contemporaries, about whose works there is more certainty and less debateable opinion.